D1112404

SWEDEN AND THE PRICE OF PROGRESS

Sweden and the Price of Progress

by David Jenkins

Coward-McCann, Inc. New York

PRINTED IN THE UNITED STATES OF AMERICA

Contents

Preface

The difficulties of studying countries other than one's own have often been recognized. The hazards were aptly summed up by the Athenian historian Herodotus (who, not being a native Athenian himself, must have been especially conscious of the dangers): "If anyone, no matter who, were given the opportunity of choosing from amongst all the nations in the world the set of beliefs which he thought best, he would inevitably, after careful consideration of their relative merits, choose that of his own country."

In my efforts to understand the customs and habits of the Swedes, I have at least been aware to these dangers (even if I cannot hope to have been immune to them), and I trust that this awareness may have provided some minimal protection. Moreover, I have tried to guard against the deleterious effects of my biases by balancing my impressions against the opinions of the several hundred Swedes—as well as a number of foreign residents of Sweden—I talked with in gathering material for this book. (This is by no means to say that I expect Swedes in general to agree with my conclusions about them or their country.)

At occasional points in the book, I draw comparisons between Sweden and the United States and other countries, but only in order to give the non-Swedish reader what appears to me to be a useful point of reference. My purpose is not to demonstrate that Sweden is better or worse than any other country, a point on which readers are cordially invited to make up their own minds if they feel it is important. (My reactions to different aspects of Sweden are, I believe, sufficiently varied to provide support for a number of viewpoints about Sweden, and I thereby

7

hope that the book can prove equally satisfying to those who find this country appalling as to those who find it appealing.)

My work on this book was made possible by an organization called Meet Modern Sweden, an information program financed partly by the Swedish government and partly by private Swedish business interests. This program brought a number of writers of various kinds—including me—to Sweden, where they were then left alone and permitted to write whatever they pleased or nothing at all if they saw fit. This organization supplied financial resources that enabled me to go to Sweden and assisted me during the first two years of my stay. Despite this great generosity, for which I am truly grateful, those in charge of the organization have never attempted to influence my writing about Sweden and have not asked to see, nor have they been shown, the manuscript. Whether they will be pleased or outraged with the final product is a matter of conjecture. In any case, I should like to express my deep appreciation to those connected with that program, principally Tell Dahllöf and Sture Bråsjö.

The main bulk of the raw material in this book was supplied to me by the hundreds of people who generously allowed me to interview them. Some of them are mentioned by name in the text, but all of them are due my thanks. In addition, I should be ungracious were I not to acknowledge the very valuable assistance given me by numerous Swedish and American friends and acquaintances in Stockholm (with whom I have discussed Sweden often and at almost unendurable length and from whom I have freely borrowed ideas): Ann-Mari Anttila, Philip Benson, Cam Cyrus, Fred Fleisher, Barbro and Bengt Hellermark, Steve Hopkins, Yngve Lindung, Nancy and Ed Maze, Hannes Oljelund, Karl Sjunneson, and Leonard Silk. Many of these good people disagree vigorously with my opinions, and it is to be noted that my conclusions, for better or worse, are my own. A special merit award of some type should go to Siv Wilén and Aina Johansen, who typed successive versions of my manuscript.

Stockholm　　　　　　　　　　　　　　　　　　D. J.
January, 1968

SWEDEN AND THE PRICE OF PROGRESS

I

Is Sweden Really a Paradise?

One of Sweden's outstanding, though not particularly useful, achievements has been an ability to stimulate a highly varied panorama of reactions. This has doubtless been at least in part attributable to the claims that have been made by, or on behalf of (and modestly accepted by), the Swedes in respect to their country's accomplishments. It is true that the Swedes have more than a slight tendency to smugness and generally regard any flattering remark about their country as accurate, but even they do not commonly refer to it as a paradise. Yet foreign reporters have often announced to the world with stop-press breathlessness the discovery that Sweden is not a paradise. *Trouble in Paradise,* warned an American TV documentary a few years back. "Sweden: Paradise with Problems," the *Saturday Evening Post* ominously intoned. There are "worried men in paradise," a researcher from the London *People* revealed. "The Boring Paradise," succinctly reported the *Rheinischer Merkur.*

A brief examination of some of the criticisms of Sweden can be instructive. Many of them are attempts to show that the country's wide-ranging program of welfare benefits—Sweden's answer to the problems of poverty, ignorance, misfortune, and sickness—is harmful and even dangerous. Actually, this category of comments shows a fair amount of variety—sometimes bewilderingly much. In 1955 the London *Daily Sketch,* in documenting the claim that Sweden was crassly materialistic and had "everything but a soul," found to its horror that the Swedish female was "Europe's best-dressed woman." The condemnation was unequivocal: "I have never seen a badly dressed Swede." What more conclusive evidence of soullessness? Yet the following year Taylor Caldwell visited Sweden in a similar investigation (her article, in fact, was called "Have the Swedes Sold Their Soul?") for the Fall River (Massachusetts) *Herald News,* and she was able to reply in the affirmative, thanks in part to her finding that "all women's clothes were nearly exactly alike . . . and totally without style."

Miss Caldwell discovered that through the "Marxist welfare state" which she found to be in force, the Swedes were "well-paid and well-fed" and that there was "no poverty, no slums, free medical care," but that otherwise the country was hardly bearable: "Everything shines in Sweden like polished chromium. And Sweden is a chromium nightmare, sterile and empty and faceless. But people cannot be held in shackles forever, no matter how beautiful the chains are. . . . Perhaps the Swedes will one fine day take up the word against their well-meaning but stupid bureaucrats."

The mid-fifties were good years for lady American journalists to sound the alarm over the shocking state of affairs in Sweden. In 1955 Dorothy Thompson informed the readers of the Washington (D.C.) *Star* of the "degenerate symptoms" she had detected in a country where social reform was so complete that "there is little" for the reformers "to look forward to." Crime was only one of these problems: "Relations between the sexes are extremely free and . . . there is a remarkable amount of homosexuality . . . they are not at all religious. . . . The divorce rate is very high. . . . There is an indisposition to be burdened with children, or the home is neglected. . . . Except for Denmark the suicide rate is the highest in Scandinavia." Miss

Thompson concluded: "Economic stability is not accompanied by psychological and emotional stability. God knows why. Maybe the Swedes are just bored with too much of a good thing. I could not say."

In a similar, though even harsher, vein a magazine called *The Freeman* claimed in 1954 that "Sweden today is a country without a future.... As a place to live in it is a failure—for anyone interested, that is, in anything more than beehive security. It is a country without incentive, without hope, and without initiative.... Sweden is simply uninspiring. It is politically and intellectually passive, economically inactive." A correspondent for the Flint (Michigan) *Journal* in 1956 warned that "the so-called liberals" who wanted to "abolish free enterprise without setting up Communist concentration camps" were taking the Swedish "middle way" as a model. After pointing out, somewhat paradoxically, that "the Socialist welfare state" was possible only because privately owned business produced "93 percent of Sweden's industrial wealth," the writer concluded: "With the private initiative of the citizens stifled, the much-publicized 'middle way' of the Socialist welfare state, as we find it in Sweden, leads merely to planned inefficiency and dull regimentation...."

In 1962 the German paper *Die Welt* noted that the Swede was "materially spoiled," that his home was a prison, and that he lived in a "spiritual vacuum." The reasoning was simple: "The better everything is organized at the top, the less the individual's personal responsibility for work and welfare is, the more difficult it is for the Swede to find his way in his expanded conditions of leisure." At about the same time *La Voix du Nord* (Lille, France), in a detailed survey of Swedish conditions, announced: "The government has taken care of everything—except the disease of happiness." An interest in sports, for example, was only a refuge from "the boredom that an overly organized society causes, a too-efficient administration, a thoroughgoing materialism—enemy of the spiritual life." In discussing the "disturbing increase in suicide," a Swede ("a cultivated man who loves his country with all his heart") was quoted: "The endless perfection of production has turned the Swede away from higher values. We live in a country where, for every citizen, everything is amply and wisely taken care of, from birth to death." In 1965 *Look,* through what was called a "paraphrase" of the opinions of Lars Gustafsson, a well-known young poet and editor (who later complained he was wildly misquoted), was able to affirm: "The welfare state has given Sweden social but not emotional security.... Materially secure, they [the Swedes] turn to comics and bad movies...." Also in 1965, the *Wall Street Journal* remarked that "any society deliberately fashioned in the framework of governmental gratuities for everything from planting wheat to painting water colors is bound to grow mediocre or worse. That is practically an immutable law, whether the people concerned are New Zealanders, Swedes, Russians, Britons or Americans...." *U.S. News & World Report* wrote in 1966: "If you wonder about the rewards of a 'Great Society' in which poverty and social troubles are absent, Sweden can help provide an understanding.... Sweden is faced with a rising wave of crime and juvenile delinquency, as well as alcoholism, drug addiction, suicides and moral recklessness among teenagers."

Swedish sex habits—or a visionary caricature of them—have furnished considerable material for foreign journals anxious to express moral righteousness on circulation-building topics. One of the most famous appeared in 1955 in *Time,* which rushed to inform the world that "birth control, abortion and promiscuity —particularly among the young—are recognized as inalienable rights...." This article apparently revealed a rich but hitherto neglected vein to be mined, for the theme was quickly taken up by others. A magazine called *Inside Story* reported on "Sweden: Land of Free Love," which it further characterized as a "Nordic love nest in comparison with which the 'romantic' tropics are a puritan's paradise." A French weekly called *Ici-Paris* sent a journalist to investigate the situation, but he had difficulty facing up to the task: "I went for a month, but only stayed a week in Sweden: the eighth day, I was gripped by an inexplicable nausea.... I had a panic fear of being forever dis-

gusted with love." However, he managed to hang on long
enough to discover that the Swedes were "obsessed with sexual
problems." Along similar lines, *France-Dimanche* described in a
detailed three-part series the "MORAL DECADENCE" in "the land
of boredom and disillusionment." A South African paper, *Die
Transvaaler*, in describing Swedish immorality, claimed that
"young demonstrators are demanding that nuns wear shorter
skirts."

A good deal of the criticisms of Sweden is contained in political discussions, where Sweden itself is not the central point
of interest, but is used merely as a whipping boy in a local
political argument. The practice is for conservative parties to
point to the miseries of the Swedes as proof of the dangers of
nonconservative policies. In this way, Sweden has been knocked
around during election campaigns in Britain, Germany, and
the United States. Without doubt the most famous incident of
this type occurred during the 1960 Republican convention,
when President Eisenhower (who reportedly had been reading
an article in the *Saturday Evening Post*) referred to an unnamed
"fairly friendly country"—*i.e.,* Sweden—which follows a "socialist philosophy and whose rate of suicide has gone up almost
unbelievably and I think they were almost the lowest nation in
the world for that. . . . Drunkenness has gone up. Lack of ambition is discernible on all sides."

Sweden not only has been attacked by those eager to point up
the dangers of Socialism, but has also been regularly trounced
by commentators from Iron Curtain countries, with much the
same sort of comments. In 1962 *Izvestia* reported in detail on
the Swedes' "spiritual poverty." A book on Sweden published
in East Germany in 1965 described the country as "the air-
conditioned hell," scarred by crime, discomfort, lack of freedom, and a retarded cultural standard. For such critics, however,
the causes for the situation are just reversed: the damage is
clearly traceable to too much capitalism. As *Izvestia* said, none
of the social reforms carried through in Sweden have succeeded
in shaking the "power of capital." Another article in the same

paper squarely pinpointed the blame for the country's deplorable condition: "American big business...."

It should be quickly pointed out that a great deal of accurate and even admirable reporting on Sweden has been published in other countries. In fact, I have read several hundred books and articles on Sweden published from 1586 to the present (mostly in Britain, France, Germany, and the United States), and the overwhelming majority of all these writings has been clearly favorable, very often excessively so. But the amount of absurdity written about Sweden is sufficient to be noticeable—especially within Sweden—and anyone who identifies himself to Swedes as a foreign journalist is apt to get some surprising reactions. "Why do you write such terrible things about us?" one lady demanded of me. Lars Gustafsson writes bitterly of the "avidity for sensationalism, the vulgarity and the thoroughly tendentious character" of some of the reporting about Sweden (amusingly enough, Gustafsson writes for *Expressen,* Sweden's largest-circulation and most exuberantly vulgar newspaper).

Taking Sweden apart has become such a popular sport that some observers are sated. After a particularly obnoxious British TV show in 1962, in which most of the reliable workhorses (suicide, the pointlessness of life, sexual promiscuity, etc.) had been trotted out for yet another exercise, one critic suggested: "Time somebody founded a Hands Off Sweden society." Another English critic, reviewing Kathleen Knott's book *A Clean, Well-Lighted Place,* a smoothly urbane attack on Sweden published in 1961, lamented: "Does any country bring out the worst in a writer as readily as Sweden?"

This is not to say that these critical writings about Sweden do not contain grains of truth; they often do, and often quite large grains. Moreover, there is nothing particularly objectionable—at least I do not object—in the clear-cut dislike for Sweden that many of the writers possess. A great many people dislike Sweden, and there is no more reason that everybody should like Sweden than that everybody should like toasted marshmallows. But a notable characteristic of much of this writing is the way in which casual observations, personal preferences, facts (or near facts or misstatements of facts), and emotional reactions all are hashed up together in a semblance of causal relationships. A case in point is the suicide rate, which is frequently said to be nearly the world's highest and is often blamed on too much social welfare. An article in so respectable a journal as *Encounter* has stated that the suicide rate is the highest in Europe. The fact is that the rate runs around 18 per 100,000 population and has shown little change over the past several decades. Higher rates are usually reported in such countries as Hungary, Finland, Japan, Switzerland, Denmark, and West Germany. The rate in the United States is around 10 per 100,000. Sweden's record gives no reason for jubilation, to be sure, but if a suicide rate almost double that of the United States reflects deep social sicknesses, then the murder rate in the United States (five times that of Sweden) should be even more indicative of moral failings. Similar carelessness is frequently shown in reporting on the deleterious effects of Sweden's welfare benefits in stimulating drinking and illegitimacy. The Swede's consumption of alcohol today is about half that of a century ago, and the illegitimacy rate has been high for several hundred years. About 100 years ago, more than 40 percent of all children born in Stockholm were borne by unwed mothers.

Nevertheless, despite the silliness that permeates some of the Swedological writing, there is often a real interest in the Swedish way of constructing a society and possibly a serious concern about the wisdom of doing it in the peculiarly Swedish way. Even if the Swedish system does not promote drinking and illegitimacy, it could conceivably have other effects which would be even more disastrous—and less fun. In my opinion, there is no question that the Swedish way of life is highly unusual and probably unique, but attempts to present the essentials of what makes it so have not been common. I believe it is worth the effort, even though I cannot pretend to have made a thoroughly scientific survey of the subject and am not prepared to offer technical details on how to plan a city or design a prison (two fields in which the Swedes have achieved distinction). This is especially the case if, as is sometimes said, it is true or even partly true that Sweden represents the wave of the future and that advances made in Sweden today will pop up in the rest of the world tomorrow. This is the rest of the world's problem— or will be—but I trust that the inner tickings of Sweden today may be of interest in themselves.

II

The Practical Swede

It is ironic that Sweden should arouse so many emotionally loaded responses, since the Swedes' foremost characteristic is a pronounced devotion to unemotional practicality—a
sure talent for organization, combined with a deep-rooted conviction that all problems can be solved calmly and satisfactorily
through the proper application of reason. If there is passion, it
is a passion for progress, in an unquestioning—but with none
of your blubbery, starry-eyed optimism—acceptance of the de-
sirability and attainability of endless steps of progress.

Such characteristics might not be particularly remarkable in
themselves (after all, a great many people believe in progress),
but the Swedes have shown an unusual thoroughness in trans-
lating their character traits into social reality. They have thus
built up a singular, but sensible, way of life: a calm, well-
ordered mode of existence, part welfare, part technological advance, part economic innovation, part common sense, a rational,
hyperefficient society—in short, what might be loosely desig-
nated as the Swedish system.

Although the prosperity which has made it possible for the
country to be rebuilt along functional lines is a relatively new

19

phenomenon, the Swede has long been known for his no-nonsense practical bent. An Englishman named Joseph Marshall, who traveled through Sweden in 1769, reported that one might search among the Swedes "in vain for a painter, a poet, a statuary or a musician," but allowed that "they are unrivalled" in the natural sciences. Likewise, a traveler named J. T. James, complained in 1819 that Swedish architecture resembled more "the outlines of a drawing than 'a finished design,' " yet pointed out: "On the whole, with regard to science, there is no country in Europe which, in proportion to her numbers, has contributed so largely to its advancement as Sweden, and none where it is still so steadily and successfully pursued."

The Swedes thus early displayed their talent for orderly classification and systematization. The country is a mecca for researchers into economic history and similar arcane matters, because of the extreme diligence with which precise statistics have been recorded and preserved over the past several hundred years. The world's first systematic registration of population statistics was begun in Sweden in 1749—a practice which, in the opinion of William Coxe, an awed British traveler of the period, "could not fail of being highly advantageous to every country." The image of the Swede interested chiefly in technical matters and the like has become a stereotype, but is no less firmly rooted in reality for that. The most prestigious occupation in Sweden has long been that of the engineer, and the Swedes usually consider themselves—and are sometimes considered by others—to be most gifted in this field. "In general, Swedes are not given to intensive mental work—except when it concerns mechanical or other natural studies," wrote Gustav Sundbärg, a prominent Swedish statistician in 1912. Sundbärg further observed that "we Swedes love and are interested in nature, not people."

This preoccupation with solid reality no doubt stems in large part from many centuries of battle against the hostile elements in a vast, cold, damp, and sparsely settled country. It is hardly surprising that primary attention should have been fastened on nature (and on organizing methods to combat, harness, or control it) rather than on human beings, since the former was so overwhelmingly more conspicuous than the latter. A deep mark on the Swedish temper was made by this unending fight to master the natural forces (it is peculiarly appropriate that some of the most notable Swedish advances have been in the field of hydroelectric power), and it is entirely understandable that the Swedish genius should express itself primarily in the mechanical arts.

This interest in the mechanical has had a gigantic impact on life in general: the goal in organizing society has tended to be the same as that in constructing a machine—*i.e.*, to get it into proper working order. In order to reach the goal, every development that promises to make the social machinery work better is taken advantage of, if at all possible. Therefore, the Swedes are constantly on the lookout for new twists, and though they basically lean to conservatism, once they become persuaded of the virtues of a new approach, they willingly and unhesitatingly embrace it—whatever the cost in discarding the old. By a wide margin, Sweden has Europe's highest per capita population of self-service stores, supermarkets, computers, numerically controlled machine tools, scientific market researchers, management consultants, and other such signs of the up-to-date society. Kai Stub, a Danish-born consulting engineer who lives in Stockholm and who has worked in England, France, and other countries, once remarked to me that the Swedes were without doubt the most eager of any people in Europe to adopt the newest twists in automation processes. Erik Bil-Nielsen, also Danish-born and experienced in a number of countries (including the United States) and head of Sweden's largest management-consulting firm, remarked to me: "Change doesn't frighten anybody in Sweden. You can sell a Swedish executive on the value of a change much more easily than an American or an Englishman." Swedish labor unions, far from obstructing the introduction of automation and other job-eliminating moves, joyfully welcome such steps as the obvious road to more prosperity for all—a seemingly elementary lesson that labor groups in some other countries find hard to learn. William Hemp, former head of the Swedish subsidiary of the Minnesota Mining & Manufacturing Company, told me shortly after the firm had purchased a going Swedish company that the willingness of the Swedish employees—who were included in the deal—to adapt to new ideas was remarkable: "It is sometimes very hard to convince people that the old way of doing things can be improved on, but not here. Within a few years I'm sure this will be the most 'American' of all our foreign companies, because they will have put all our ideas into practice."

Signs of the Swedes' devotion to mechanization and efficiency are not difficult to find. Automatic vending machines are everywhere—not only for ordinary items such as cigarettes, chocolates, and soda pop, but also for wide varieties of other merchandise: groceries, fruit, contraceptives, stockings, toys, and flowers. A number of the advances in automatic vending have been thought up by the Swedes. In 1964 a Swedish-designed hot-dog machine—which delivers a red-hot frankfurter complete with roll, mustard, and catsup in a few seconds—was launched. In 1966, Esso began testing a Swedish method of selling gasoline through a self-service credit-card-activated pump. In 1967 a Swedish savings bank installed a "moneymat" whereby depositors could make withdrawals after hours. Restaurant mechanization, including such gadgets as electronic ovens, advanced potato mashers, and automatic push-button serving systems, have long been old hat. Even the Stockholm Stock Exchange—though hardly the beehive of activity that might complicate a desire to mechanize—is automated to a degree: As the list of stocks is called off, the members register their bids and offers through a system of push-buttons which control flashing lights on a large board; when bid and offer meet, the sale is noted by a ringing bell.

Even the casual visitor to Sweden must be struck by the country's incessant urge to progress. Immense city planning projects are at every turn, particularly noticeable in Stockholm, where the centuries-old "city between the bridges" has been ringed with superhighways, its majestic harbor crisscrossed with bridges, and the center of town systematicaly plowed under and replaced with (so far) five skyscrapers, endless strings of shiny new banks, department stores, and radiant-heated sidewalks. Such operations inevitably, of course, include the massacre of old landmarks but do not for that reason arouse strong objections. In 1965, I happened to visit Örebro, a sparklingly modern town in central Sweden, and I could have easily gathered that the entire city had been built the previous week if numerous signs did not proclaim it was in the midst of celebrating its seven hundredth anniversary. When I asked the city architect if a great many buildings hadn't had to be pulled down to make room for the new ones and whether the citizens had not objected, he replied that, yes, indeed there had been protests. In the process of rebuilding, a selection of representative older structures had been set aside and reassembled in a specially designed park as a sentimental reminder of the past, and angry voices were raised against spending money on outdated buildings that could just as well be junked—until it was discovered that the park proved a first-class tourist attraction. Stockholm had an even more depressing experience in this department. In 1967 it suddenly became known that the lumber from disassembled old houses—earmarked for preservation and eventual reconstruction—had been lying neglected around the city exposed to the weather and that nobody had bothered to keep track of exactly where the disassembled houses were or even how many there were.

In Sweden practicality is king, and when there is a conflict between practicality and other values, the other values give way. Important elements of national policy are most assuredly influenced by this fact. Staunchly neutral Sweden (her last war ended in 1814) might be said to forgo war largely because it isn't practical—as was discovered during the heroic but costly escapades of Charles XII and Gustav III in the eighteenth century. The present Swedish government, though claiming to be unswervingly Socialist in theory, doesn't nationalize industry because it simply doesn't believe such behavior is rational, and being rational is obviously superior to being doctrinaire.

One of the great advantages of this cool, unemotional approach to problems is that it saves a lot of arguments. When intelligent people get together to make decisions with their minds firmly on the objective, there is no particular reason to disagree. An American journalist, writing for a U.S. trade magazine an article on Swedish practices in establishing technical standards, received a request from his editor to get some quotes from people who criticized the prevailing practices. The journalist was, of course, unable to find any such people, but the editor repeatedly urged him to find them anyway and gave up only when the article finally had to be printed. It was hard for him to understand that arguments over such questions do not often occur in Sweden. As Patrick O'Donovan once wrote: "It sometimes seems that the whole of Sweden is one great committee of hard-headed, clear-eyed, like-minded men."

The Swedish interest in practicality turns up in the most unexpected places. In 1964, Lars Ullerstam, a young student of psychiatry, published a book called *The Erotic Minorities,* an attack on the social injustices to which sex deviants are subjected. The book proposed, among other things, a state-operated exchange to arrange contacts between perverts of matching tastes; a corps of "sexual samaritans" to visit and minister to the needs of the bedridden, crippled, and otherwise handicapped; and various other forms of assistance to the sexually deprived. The book shocked a great many Swedes, but in a sense the solutions offered were peculiarly Swedish. If satisfying the tastes of sexual deviants is a problem, then it is only practical to organize assistance in more or less the same calm, rational way that one approaches any other problem.

It is important to note that the Swedes' enthusiasm for finding rational solutions to problems does not mean they are reluctant to borrow the ideas of others when necessary. Quite the contrary. I have been astonished at the frequency with which they openly and gratefully express their debt to other countries. The technology gap between the United States and other countries is a well-known and much-discussed phenomenon, and I therefore became accustomed to encountering strong American influences in such areas as manufacturing, science, and business methods and to having it pointed out to me by people I interviewed that their main inspiration came from America. But occasionally the news was totally unexpected. Sweden is justly famous for its economic policy measures, and I was therefore surprised when a prominent economist remarked to me in the course of an interview: "Of course, your economists are far more advanced than ours—the methods of Simon Kuznets and econometric models and that sort of thing —though we are more involved in practical problems." The last straw came when a city planner—and surely the Swedes are world-famous for their city planning—suddenly interrupted an explanation of his theories with this statement: "Of course, you know that all our best ideas come from America."

The difference, of course, is that in America brilliant ideas often remain only brilliant ideas—put into practice (if at all) spasmodically, partially, and unsatisfactorily—whereas in Sweden good ideas are eagerly rushed into application as soon and on as broad a scale as is practicable. But whether the Swedes work out their new ideas themselves or borrow them from others is only a detail; the point is to put them into practice.

So zealous are the Swedes in attacking problems as soon as they appear or threaten to appear that they have by now solved all the major clearly identifiable problems (or have solutions in the works), so that lately they not only have been importing solutions to problems, but have also been importing the problems themselves. An outstanding example is the "private affluence and public squalor" syndrome analyzed in John Kenneth Galbraith's *Affluent Society*. It would be difficult (for anyone with any familiarity with the U.S. conditions Galbraith was actually discussing) to find anything in Sweden approaching "public squalor." Yet this book has had an enormous influence in Sweden, spurring the Swedes on to bigger and better public spending programs in their attack on squalor. Similarly, the concern in the United States over pollution has been followed by a similar uproar in Sweden—partly as a result of the translation of Rachel Carson's *Silent Spring* into Swedish. While there is a certain amount of water pollution in Sweden because of the pulp and paper mills (though both the mills and the pollution are primarily in remote areas), the fresh air is one of the country's truly great delights, not least in Stockholm. Yet public discussion of pollution problems is endless. At the time this is being written, the Swedish auto manufacturer Volvo is attempting to calm the storms of protest which arose when it turned out that its very efficient auto exhaust gas cleaner, developed specifically to meet the official standards set by California authorities, was not available in Sweden. It would be difficult to imagine a greater contrast between the fresh, clean air of Stockholm and whatever it is that the people in Los Angeles breathe, but the Swedish newspapers have insisted that the gas-cleaning device be made available forthwith to combat the lethally dangerous air pollution in the capital. Perhaps the most absurd example of problem importation was the concern regarding invasions of privacy following the Swedish publication of Vance Packard's book *The Naked Society*. I can hardly believe that electronic eavesdropping and other such horrors are of any significance in Sweden, but at this moment a government investigation commission is solemnly pondering the question.

Needless to say, even though this great concern for even minor problems has its ludicrous aspects, it helps prevent the problems from arising or at least from becoming so gigantic before being recognized that it is nearly impossible to solve them, as happens too often in the United States.

The habit of approaching all aspects of life as problems to be solved as quickly and efficiently as possible—in the same way that one expects a machine to function as smoothly and efficiently as possible—has its obvious advantages; it also has its drawbacks. One of the latter is a tendency to overlook the human element in all this intense concentration on getting the wheels and cogs to work properly.

I can almost hear a certain snicker already developing among people familiar with Sweden when they stumble across my comparison of Sweden with a machine that runs "smoothly and efficiently." The fact is that almost nothing works in Sweden.

There is even an expression for it: *krångel-Sverige,* which roughly means red-tape Sweden and carries the idea of a terrifying assortment of complications, circumlocutions, regulations, time-consuming formalities, senseless rules of procedure, channels of authority, and other Gothic machinery all built into the system at various key points. But all this does not indicate, as some observers seem to think, that the system has broken down. The inconvenience caused to those who are caught up in the system is no more telling evidence of its breakdown than a machine's being nailed to the floor means it cannot function properly. The main function of the system is to operate; if it should also give pleasure, or alleviate irritation, or spawn some other by-product, this might be of some conceivable advantage to someone, but it is irrelevant to the principal goal of the system. It may be regrettable that the human element is so often ground out in the gears, but in assessing the seriousness of this defect, one should stop to consider that if the Swedes did not find it so easy to think in these mechanistic terms, their accomplishments, which are truly considerable, would never have been possible.

In any case, the fact is that all the webs of regulations, entanglements, and complexities often become closed systems serving only the needs of the systems. I recall a conversation with a young lady who had worked on those pleasant baby-blue Stockholm tramways (now unfortunately abolished in favor of greater efficiency) in which she stoutly defended the practice of passing up would-be passengers when the tram was behind schedule, since the function of a tramway was obviously to meet the established timetable; serving the public was only secondary. More logically, but somewhat similarly, the function of Sweden's medical care system is to provide medical care. When I was looking into this system, which I regard as admirable in most respects, I asked some of the authorities about the problem of waiting in line, since it is a well-known fact that almost any contact with the medical system (except for clear-cut emergencies) means waiting in line. The Swedes' eagerness to set upon any problems that turned up was already obvious to me, and I thought there might be efforts under way to develop better scheduling procedures. But this was when my understanding of the system was as yet at an underdeveloped stage; I could not even find anyone who considered this a problem, and I soon gave up. The answer is that the purpose of providing medical care is to provide medical care. And since waiting doesn't seriously interfere with the provision of medical care (it is unlikely that anyone will ever die from waiting in line), it therefore is hardly worth talking about.

All this is, more or less, a question of service, and the reason why my claims for Sweden's great efficiency will be quickly laughed down by most people who have ever lived in Sweden is that these intricate and beautifully designed systems are ill-adapted to the concept of service. They have little flexibility; sometimes the system that solves one problem only creates another, and sometimes two systems set up in adjoining fields get tangled up in each other. In any case, it is service functions that are most apparent to the casual observer, not automated assembly lines, computer-controlled paper mills, and scientifically planned work-measurement techniques. The people who plan restaurants in Sweden—who I assume are roughly the same people who design assembly lines—naturally work toward the objective of getting the food into the customer. But arranging this function quickly and efficiently, while adapting to the varying preferences of the diners, providing courteous service along with the food, transforming the process into a pleasurable activity, or, for that matter, making the food taste good—such additional achievements are outside the realm of competence of the Swedish system makers, who would be as dumbfounded (if they should happen to think of it) by the great individual variations among human preferences (or that humans even have preferences) as they would be if one of the engine blocks in Volvo's automated engine-block factory should suddenly decide to come down the assembly line upside down or wearing a straw hat.

In many ways, the Swedish Pavilion at the 1964–1965 New York World's Fair was a perfect Sweden in miniature. Smartly designed, neat, clean, sparkling, and a trifle boring, it contained some industrial exhibits of obscure nature and a store that reportedly did very well. It also contained a small bar and some extremely attractive tables (with ceramic tops, as I recall) and chairs just outside the bar. Having invited the footsore young lady I was with to join me in a refreshment and having waited twenty minutes at the table with no sign of a waiter, I concluded there was no table service and went inside to fetch some thirst quenchers. I ordered "Two beers," which the bartender handed over and which I paid for. I waited another minute and then reminded him that he had forgotten to give me glasses. "No," he said, "if you want glasses, you have to pay a fifty-cent deposit on each." I paid. Someone less system-minded might have figured that the loss of an occasional glass (they were cheap glasses) could be absorbed as part of the cost of doing business, but the possibility of irritating a visitor to the pavilion (which was not supposed to make money, but to build goodwill) as the price of keeping track of all the glasses would not be likely to occur to a Swede.

The difficulty is that it is always the form, not the human consideration, that gets attention. This fact can explain, among other things, some apparent contradictions. One is the frequency with which one encounters great efforts to please in the midst of huge quantities of terrible service. To take a trivial, but agonizingly universal, example: a familiar sight in the Swedish landscape is the kiosk—a newsstand that also sells cigarettes, candy, soda pop, fruit, books, magazines, canned food, toys, simple hygienic supplies, and what seems to be an interminable variety of other merchandise. Since these establishments are in most areas the only retail outlets functioning in the evening and on weekends, lines of customers waiting to be served are often the rule. But no matter how long the line and no matter how carefully a customer deliberates over the proper candy bar (sometimes asking that several be served up so that he can squeeze them as part of the selection process), the most inviting book (he frequently feels obliged to leaf through several potential choices and asks if other specimens can be hauled out of the back room), or the most appetizing apple (or should it be an orange instead, or perhaps a banana?), never does the saleslady display the slightest desire to move to the next customer—who may want only a box of matches and be in a hurry to catch his nearly departing bus—while the first one ponders his decision. The saleslady is not deliberately attempting to give one customer good service at everyone else's expense. It is simply that being Swedish, she properly considers it her job to show the customer as much of the merchandise as he wants (since that is her job), not to become irritated (since that is not rational), and to wait on one customer at a time (since that is the logical way to do things).

A similar apparent contradiction exists between the Swede's reputation for coldness and unfriendliness with the astonishingly elaborate courtesy that visitors often receive. I first visited Sweden as a tourist in 1961. Before leaving New York, I had telephoned Curt Bloch, the foreign editor of *Barron's,* a financial magazine (I specialize to some extent in writing on financial and economic subjects), to ask if he would be interested in articles written from Europe, in case I should happen on a likely subject in any of the countries I visited, which would probably include Sweden. He told me he would be happy to consider any articles I might care to write but pointed out that the Swedes were a stiff and remote bunch and that merely getting to see the right people would be so exhausting and time-consuming that if writing articles were a primary goal, I would probably be better off to try a different country.

I went to Sweden anyway, and I happened to run into some people in the financial field who were extremely generous with their help, and I did write a few articles, one of them for *Barron's.* When I went back to New York, I hastened to inform the editor that he had the Swedes all wrong. I had interviewed bankers, brokers, economists, a Cabinet minister, and top executives of some of Sweden's largest companies, and I was invariably greeted with the utmost cordiality. I remember one occasion when the public relations director and the treasurer of a large company not only asked me to lunch but even insisted on eating in the American style (that is, switching the fork back and forth between the left hand and the right) in deference to my nationality.

When I later came to live in Sweden, I was therefore full of enthusiasm for the friendly Swedes, but after three years of living in the country I have concluded that however pleasant and however widespread the form of extending a cordial welcome to visitors, it is only a form. It is something like the *skål* and, like the *skål,* has no particular feeling behind it but is carried out only because that is the way to do things. For those who may not know, the rules of the *skål* can be easily learned. One must first realize that when one is a guest, one does not drink until the host proposes a *skål.* This does not apply to beer, which may be drunk at will. One does not simply throw out a *skål* and toss off the drink with a smile, however. It is not proper to smile at all, in fact. Before drinking, one gazes deep into the eyes of the host—if there are several people present, into several sets of eyes—and after one drinks, one lowers the glass to approximately the level of the left lung, still gazing and slightly bowing. During a meal the host will *skål* everybody in turn, going from left to right (or is it right to left?). A gentleman is expected to *skål* the lady to his immediate left (or is it the right?). After the initial *skåls,* anyone may *skål* anyone else. Technically, a lady is not supposed to drink at all unless she is the subject of a *skål.* This does not, however, apply to the hostess; no one is supposed to *skål* her—unless there are fewer than eight guests present. And so on. The ritual is so elaborate and so time-consuming and makes so much noise that one can easily get the illusion of genuine conviviality, but the actual emotional content of the thing is approximately on the level of, say, a military drill.

Nevertheless, when one gets past the initial courtesies... well, it is hard to say what happens, because in the several hundred very cordial welcomes I have received in Sweden, I have almost never got past the initial courtesies. Swedes have countless times suggested that we must one day have a cup of coffee, a dinner, a drink or, in one case, that we should "discuss these ideas over a bottle of wine some evening." I have always been careful to declare my practically unlimited availability for all these occasions, but I believe it is only the suggestion of a future invitation that is included in the form, not the invitation itself, because in not one of these cases has the promise of a future invitation been followed by the invitation. (I should say that in one case I was proffered, not the promise of an invitation to dinner, but the actual invitation, which, of course, I accepted with alacrity.) One extremely amiable and gregarious American resident of Stockholm who, because of his work, has met probably several thousand Swedes from every class of society said to me: "You know, I have two friends who are Swedish and I think that's pretty good—I've only lived here nine years." As Mary Wollstonecraft Godwin remarked in 1796: "The politeness of the north seems to partake of the coldness of the climate and the rigidity of its iron-sinewed rocks."

In my work in Sweden, I have often been struck by the extreme willingness of many important and busy people to be interviewed by me, combined with an odd abruptness and bluntness. It is almost never possible to warm up with a little talk about the weather, and at first I was somewhat taken aback when the person I was interviewing started out by asking questions like "What is it that you want here?" Well, he wants to know, and the best way to find out is to ask. Similarly, my interviewees often break off the interview suddenly and unceremoniously with the announcement that it is terminated. After all, when it is time to stop, the best way to do it is to stop.

The Swedish bluntness—the insistence on getting everything set forth clearly and properly and with no misunderstandings —sometimes appears in the most surprising contexts. Perhaps the most striking experience I have had in Sweden occurred at an evening of informal discussion arranged by a group of young people who had studied in America and who met every so often, preferably with invited guests present, to discuss various aspects of America and Sweden and in a way to promote Swedish-American friendship and understanding. On this particular evening the subject was the press; four or five American journalists had been invited to join in, and a large newspaper agreed to act as host, furnishing a meeting hall, sandwiches, and a lecture on journalism careers delivered by the paper's managing editor. The program consisted for the most part of a rambling and unorganized discussion—largely in English—of differences between the press in the two countries, but the defects of the discussion didn't matter terribly, since the purpose of the meeting was in principle more social than educational. One feature was a short talk in English by an American journalist on the subject of the American press. The talk was not in truth of the highest quality, but that didn't matter either in the very casual mood that was supposed to be prevailing. At one point the speaker compared the press in America with the ombudsman in Sweden. Possibly an interesting thought, or possibly not, but the chairman of the meeting suddenly jumped up, brusquely interrupted the speaker, and told the audience that what was meant was the "JU-STI-TIE-OM-BUDS-MAN-NEN," explaining that the American journalist's pronunciation of the Swedish word was so ghastly that the audience had probably missed it. This was debatable, since the chairman had got it and he didn't appear noticeably more intelligent than the rest of the audience, but even if it was true, it was difficult to see that it was of any real importance. Considerably shaken, the journalist continued his talk and was beginning to elaborate his idea further when the newspaper's managing editor also jumped up and loudly announced to the audience that the journalist had misunderstood the whole function of the ombudsman and volunteered to explain the facts. Before he could begin, he was also interrupted—by one of the other American journalists, who angrily told him *he* (the editor) hadn't understood what the journalist was saying and clearly implied this was because of his faulty comprehension of English. The managing editor reluctantly sat down, and the speaker, by this time reduced nearly to complete incoherence, somehow managed to limp through the rest of his talk.

The Swede is not generally given to dropping his concern for getting everything laid out in an orderly and straightforward fashion, even when the occasion would hardly appear to demand rigorous insistence on the facts to the exclusion of all else. In selling, the Swede is apt to lean heavily on technical descriptions of his products and the well-known Swedish reputation for quality. A market survey among businessmen in the Netherlands on their opinion of Swedish businessmen turned up this typical response: "Swedish exporters are quite conceited, and it is impossible to negotiate with them. It is rare one can arrive at a compromise. A business discussion usually takes the form of a purely technical, not a commercial, discussion. . . ." The Swedes themselves frequently bemoan their inferiority to the Danes as salesmen—an opinion in which the Danes heartily concur. As one Danish marketing expert remarked to me, "A Swede will buy you a drink only after you've agreed to buy."

With his interest riveted on the mechanical, the Swede is thing-oriented, rather than people-oriented, and even tends to attain his own identification through attaching solid suggestions of tangibility to himself. Every Swede must have a title, and the title is far more important than the name; telephone subscribers with the same last name are classified alphabetically according to title, not first name; if you do not know the person's title, you literally do not know him at all. No matter how low a person's station in life, he cannot be said to exist without a title; newspaper marriage announcements solemnly identify the young couple as "plumber's helper Sven Svenson" and "assistant office clerk Birgitta Andersson." Similarly, a Swede strives to attain identity through the things he owns. It is almost impossible to talk to a Swede for a few minutes without being informed that he owns an automobile, and if you are invited to his house, you may be sure he will show it to you in great detail. A Swedish tradition is the "fine room"—that is to say, the living room—but it is never, never used except in the presence of guests (a particularly inconvenient custom when apartments larger than two rooms were rare). But all these trappings—this heavy emphasis on "things"—are not mere status symbols; they are, for the Swede, the person himself.

It is not surprising that the Swede's mechanistic view of the world should be accompanied by a certain lack of human contact. The problem of contact is often discussed in the press, and great parts of Swedish literature and Swedish films (many of Ingmar Bergman's productions, for example) are devoted to the difficulties of communication. One Swedish acquaintance explained to me that this had had a larger impact on the development of society than one might suspect: "That's why we have to have so much security provided by the state; we have so little security in our relationships with each other."

In discussing these questions, the Swedes often invoke their shyness. A Swedish lady said to me: "I've been told that Americans are very friendly, that they are very ready to invite you to their homes for dinner and so on—is that true?—but that it is very difficult to become really good friends with them." I conceded that there might indeed be some truth to this, but that the superficial friendship you get from Americans may in some ways be better than what you get from most Swedes, which is nothing. She smiled, as though in pity for my lack of understanding, and said: "Oh, but we're shy, didn't you know?" The Swedes often speak of their shyness and even boast of it as if it were a kind of national asset, like the iron ore deposits in the north. But it is not easy to find evidences of it. On the contrary, much of the really antagonistic deportment of the Swede would seem to reflect considerable boldness—the salesclerk who icily stares you down as you browse in a store, the waiter in a luxury restaurant who responds to your complaint about the food with a shrug and a "Don't tell me; I didn't cook it," the pointed reminder (which a foreigner hears surprisingly often) that one can't expect friendship with a Swede to develop quickly. I think the truth is that such seemingly strange behavior is neither shyness nor hostility—it is indifference. The Swede is simply not accustomed to thinking in terms of other individuals. Moreover, it is not certain that he would care to change his habits in this respect. The dream of almost every Swede—and the reality for a great many—is to own a vacation cottage where he can be alone. Moreover, the most popular participation sports are those that can be best pursued alone: skiing, hiking in the mountains, and that peculiar Nordic sport known as orientering—wherein the participant is set down in a remote, unfamiliar spot and challenged to find his way with the help of only a map and a compass. An American sociologist of my acquaintance who had lived and worked in Sweden for some years pointed out to me that almost all offices were tiny cubicles for one or two persons, with numerous doors (double doors are for some reason very common); even though the Swedes eagerly import virtually every American business method they can find, they are apparently able to do without the huge hundred-desk offices. In other words, individual isolation does not appear to be a handicap that the Swedes are struggling to get away from, but an accepted and welcome condition.

Further evidence that it would be a mistake to stamp the Swede as actively hostile to others may be seen in what I believe is true compassion for the misfortunes human beings are prey to. The efforts of the government to cater to the needs of the underprivileged and the handicapped enjoy, so far as I am able to judge, enormous support among the people at large. Although the Swede may be blissfully able to ignore people as individuals, he is quite capable of caring about them in large masses, when the care can be properly formalized, proceduralized, organized, and systematized, as any part of life should be.

III

The Road to Welfare Socialism

The neat, well-organized Sweden of today—and the affluence that made it possible—is a relatively recent phenomenon. The system's very newness, in fact, may explain why its incidental drawbacks can seem minor irritations compared with the large advantages—to those who have become enmeshed in the system, at any rate.

Throughout much of her history Sweden was regarded as little better than an impoverished wasteland. As recently as the early nineteenth century the country lay morally, physically, and financially exhausted—hampered by her lack of natural resources and drained by the military adventures of the previous century, conducted by the heroic Charles XII, the eccentric Gustav III, and the inept Gustav IV. The Industrial Revolution, already coursing at full gallop elsewhere, loomed but distantly in Sweden's future. An English tourist of the time named Robert Porter remarked on the signs of "poverty of this little kingdom . . . and most forcibly do they strike strangers coming from Russia or England. . . ." Of Stockholm, he wrote: "The exterior of the houses is dirty, the architecture shabby, and all strikes as very low and confined." Charles Küttner, a German traveler, noted that "a great portion of Stockholm is composed of wood, and even of miserable huts, inhabited by persons in the most indigent circumstances."

In view of the rigorous northern climate and the inhospitable soil, squeezing out even a marginal existence must be scored a considerable achievement. But the basic natural difficulties were accentuated by a rising population (up roughly 50 percent from 1810 to 1850) in a static economy. Hunger crises were frequent. A by no means untypical year was 1838, when (1) the 1837 recession in the United States was reflected in falling demand for Swedish iron ore, (2) the harvest was poor, and (3) the winter was unusually harsh. The result was massive misery; crowds of famished country dwellers jammed the cities in search of food and work—both scarce. A newspaper remarked: "As sparrows in the countryside are seen coming to the house in quest of food when the woods are covered with snow, one can now see in the cities these troops of needy folk coming to seek bread and jobs." In that year a sardonic work called *The Meaning of Swedish Poverty*, by the poet C. J. L. Almquist, was published. "In Sweden," wrote Almquist, "there is no question of *seeking* poverty. It is a dowry from nature.... And when Christ says: Blessed are the poor ... the pronouncement is most especially addressed to the Swedes."

Retarded politically, as well as economically, Sweden was governed by a parliament, of four estates—nobility, clergy, burgesses, and peasants. But crusty, autocratic Charles XIV John (the former French Marshal Bernadotte named King in 1814), held most of the reins in an iron grip. The tenor of the regime could be seen in an official investigation of poverty around 1840, when the principal recommendations were for expanded prisons and a strengthened police force. Hopes for liberalization rose in 1844, when the young Oscar I, who had shown some interest in liberal thoughts, took over the throne. His liberal ideas proved easily abandoned, however, and brutal repression of popular emotions was common. Public demonstrations inspired by the Paris riots of 1848 were cruelly suppressed, with nine persons killed. In 1851 silent, passive protest marches against the government were staged for six consecutive evenings in Stockholm; on the seventh they were abruptly crushed by the police and numbers of marchers arrested.

By the mid-nineteenth century the first faint stirrings of the Industrial Revolution began to be felt. For one thing, sharp cuts in British import duties spurred Swedish timber exports. Too, the forest industries were stimulated by invention of the steam engine. Instead of hauling cut wood over the rugged countryside from sawmills located adjacent to inland water-power, the whole logs could be floated down the rivers to steam-powered sawmills conveniently—and profitably—located on the coast. Abolition of the rigid guild system, which had held back commercial development in a vise of cartelized rules, also spurred economic progress. Perfection of the Bessemer steel-making technique (by a Swedish engineer) made possible the production of high-quality steel and ushered in the modern steel age. These and other technical advances acted to vitalize Sweden's slumbering economy, and output jumped rapidly as small, inefficient units were replaced by larger, more economic units. In the 1820's the average annual production of pig iron was 80,000 tons, but it rose to 145,000 tons by 1850 and to 205,000 tons by 1865.

The impact of the changes was felt slowly, and the average citizen was untouched by the revolutionary transformations taking place around him. At least one traveler—a Frenchman named Albert Vandal, who passed through in the 1870's—found much to praise in the country's backward state: "In a Europe which is being more Americanized every day, the Swedes have been able to conserve the traditions of our old and aristocratic societies."

The pangs of poverty were most keenly felt in rural areas, where the bulk of the population increase took place and where economic conditions were least tolerable. Through hard-won improvements in agricultural productivity Sweden had become more or less self-sufficient in grain by the middle of the century and was even able to register modest exports. Nevertheless, poor harvests could still cause chaos in the 1860's and 1870's, and American and Russian grain exports, facilitated by advances in transportation, could crack farm prices and cause trouble of a different sort. In the 1850's, for example, Russian grain exports stopped abruptly because of the Crimean War, and many farmers took advantage of high world prices to feed their grain into the lucrative export markets; at other times it was more advantageous to divert it to the profitable business of distilling. Throughout most of the century violent demonstrations and hunger riots were common.

The infant industries willingly absorbed some, but only a minuscule fraction, of the discontented country dwellers. The explosive economic factors at work manifested themselves mainly in emigration to America—a gigantic wave of threadbare humanity, swelling at times to the proportions of a flood. At its height, in the 1880's, the exodus was carrying well over 1 percent annually of the population out of the country and toward America's streets of gold. In all, more than 1,000,000 Swedes left for the United States between 1860 and 1910.

Some Swedes look on the mass emigration as a shameful and catastrophic chapter in the country's history. It is probably true that it was costly—the emigrants were to a great extent drawn from the young and vigorous. But one can question how vigorous they might have remained had they stayed at home to accentuate the widespread misery. As one emigrant wrote: "Mother Sweden can be compared to a mother who has too many children; she is too poor to feed and clothe them."

Personal testimony of the emigrants gives a vivid picture, not only of the country's grim poverty, but also of the iron-bound class structure, religious oppression, and lack of democracy. One of the earlier emigrants wrote: "As for me, I have missed Sweden but little. I long realized the oppression of her less fortunate citizens . . . the undue power of the upper classes, the disregard and harshness with which they used to push down the poor. . . ."

The most common reasons for migrating were summed up by one of the refugees: "(1) The terrible long working hours and meagre food . . . and the poor pay, (2) the priests' self-appointed guardianship over the people and the pettiness that the people are subjected to ... and (3) the upper classes' contempt for physical labor and those who are engaged in it." Another said he left Sweden "mostly because of fear of poverty and starvation, which I experienced too much of during my childhood." A former resident of Jönköping told his story: "Although it was poor in our home, I never starved, though occasionally we had nothing to eat but potatoes, which we dipped in crushed salt or sour crushed lingonberries and ate with coarse bread. Sometimes we had it better, however, and we were certainly better off than most farmers in our neighborhood."

One emigrant left a bitter story of an apprenticeship, intended to last 6 years, with a sailmaker; the normal workweek was 78 hours, and meals consisted of a bit of raw herring for breakfast ("I've seen swine fed better"), pea soup for lunch (made from the shells only, since the peas themselves went to the gentry), and porridge for dinner ("Sometimes we got skim milk with the porridge, and that was a feast"). The pay was 20 kronor (about $5 at exchange rate of the time) annually, to rise gradually to 30 kronor in the fifth and sixth years. The chronicle concluded with the summation: "I have seen slaves since in Africa and Australia, and they were treated better." A great many of the emigrants had similarly poisonous opinions of Sweden. "God preserve us from Sweden!" wrote one, and another remarked: "It's astonishing to me that Sweden still has as many inhabitants as it does."

The critical factor for many was Sweden's rigid class structure. A woman emigrant told this story: "I left home at the age of eighteen and worked as a servant for many fine families. They were army officers and employers and even noble by birth. But heavens, I could cry when I remember how it was. We servants were all like slaves, and were so happy when we weren't scolded. If we didn't bow as politely as they wanted they glared at us as though they wanted to tear us apart. And they were fine people, educated people...." A man comments: "When in America you tell how in Sweden a servant had to hold his hat in his hand when he talked to his master, you can't even get an Irishman to believe you...."

As Sweden was a late bloomer in other respects, so she was retarded in the development of radical social movements. Scattered interest in rebellious sentiments began to show up around the middle of the century but had little impact until much later. One of the first Swedish radicals was a used-book dealer named Per Götrek, who founded a short-lived radical paper and organized left-wing study groups. He was mainly a follower of Saint-Simon and Cabet, rather than of Marx, and was regarded as relatively harmless by the authorities. He was arrested on suspicion following the riots of 1848 and whiled away the time during his brief detention by attempting to convert the police chief to Socialism.

At about the same time small workers' study groups were formed (some later developed into labor unions), but no real surge of radical activity took place until the 1880's. A wandering tailor named August Palm, who had picked up the new Marxist ideas in Germany, came to Sweden, and a meeting he organized in Malmö in 1881 was the first public manifestation of Marxism in Sweden.

The labor movement was barely in its formative stages. Sporadic, poorly organized strikes had broken out starting in the 1850's; but goals were often obscure, and the strikes most often failed. Unionism's progress was slow in great part because the bulk of the major industries—forest products, iron, and steel—was located in isolated villages, each dominated by a single all-powerful company. Since the workers were dependent on the company for jobs, welfare, and housing and since adhesion to the labor movement was often flatly forbidden, union activity called for a good deal of courage or ideological conviction. Unionization was also hobbled in the 1880's and 1890's by legislation granting legal protection to strikebreakers and forbidding strikers from attempting to persuade their fellow workers to strike.

Nevertheless, the radical movement limped uncertainly, but

doggedly, ahead. It got its first stable newspaper, the *Social Democrat,* in 1885. The Social Democratic Labor Party was founded in 1889; it established a close connection with the labor unions. In 1896 the Social Democrats managed to elect their first member of parliament—one of the party's founders and a strong figure in its history for many years, Hjalmar Branting.

The years from 1890 to 1915 were a period of tremendous growth for Swedish industry, and many of Sweden's notable technological triumphs date from this time. Real national income just about doubled in the twenty-five-year period, and Sweden was at last moving full steam ahead. But progress had its price. The first years of the twentieth century were scarred by a hard-fought struggle between the Social Democrats and their union allies, on the one side, and the employers' Establishment and the ruling Conservatives, on the other. The unions had formed a united front, a national confederation called *Landsorganisation* (LO), in 1898. The management forces countered four years later with two employers' groups (later merged into one), and the two sides were thus well organized for the bitter battles that lay ahead.

An important stumbling block to the progress of the Social Democrats was the lack of a universal franchise. In 1866, Sweden had made a large stride in the direction of democracy when the old four estates parliament abolished itself and set up a two-chamber replacement in which the members were chosen, either directly or indirectly, by popular vote. But voting rights were based on moderately elevated property and income requirements, and in 1900 only 7 percent of the population had the vote. The acid antagonisms aroused by the voting issue blended with and intensified the conflict between labor and management. A three-day general strike was called as a protest in 1900, and the continuing bad feeling aroused by this issue was echoed in the numerous labor disputes that followed.

The first decade of the century was virtually an unbroken plague of friction between management and labor. A chain of lockouts declared by one of the new management groups in 1903 led to, first, protracted negotiations with the unions and, finally, two years later, to mass worker walkouts that touched off more lockouts and five months of idleness for more than 200,000 workers—a dispute finally settled only by government intervention. In 1906 a pulp mill in Mackmyra in the north was unionized. The owners immediately evicted 200 persons—workers, wives, and children—from their company-owned real estate; after six months of argument the union won the right to exist. Among the strikes of 1907 was a harvest strike in the south, which touched off severe reprisals and which failed. More memorable was a scuffle at a pair of sawmills in the north, beginning with dismissals of union members and culminating in a walkout, battles between workers and strikebreakers, and sentences against the workers of up to eight years at hard labor. In 1908, worker wage demands combined with a burgeoning recession were sending employer blood pressure up, most dramatically epitomized in a strike against shipowners. During the midst of the struggles, a ship named the *Amalthea*, loaded with strikebreakers from England, was bombed in Malmö Harbor by a trio of young Socialists, killing 1 strikebreaker and injuring 20 others.

In 1909 the struggle reached its high point, in a dispute that has since become known as the Great Strike. The recession was continuing. The employers, now united in the national Employers' Confederation, were becoming increasingly incensed at worker demands for higher wages. They carefully planned a massive attack in an all-out effort to crush or at least seriously to cripple the movement. In the early summer, while a number of tiresome negotiations dragged on in various industries, the board of the Employers' Confederation issued an ultimatum: if by August 4 satisfactory solutions to the points at issue had not been found, a wide-ranging lockout would be declared, and it would be successively expanded "to the extent that the board may decide." The employers suggested they would do all possible to prevent the formation of a "Socialist monopoly" of the labor market. The union issued a counterultimatum—that if the lockout were carried through, a general strike throughout the country would be called.

As expected, the negotiations failed, the lockout was declared, and the general strike materialized. By the middle of August, 200,000 workers, plus an additional 100,000 unorganized sympathizers, and even a good part of the professional strikebreakers (who had their own organization), had walked off the job. More than 11,000,000 workdays were lost.

The strike was a momentous demonstration of union power, and management learned that it was not going to be possible to destroy the unions. But the strike was no triumph for the unions (the issue at stake were eventually settled one by one). Numbers of workers were jailed or blacklisted, and for several years thereafter union membership dropped off.

Despite the violent nature of many of these disputes, some of the underlying tensions in Swedish life were at the same time being smoothed out. After years of discussion and parliamentary shuffling, universal franchise was enacted early in 1909, though applying only to men and only to the second chamber. The first chamber was chosen by local officials, who were elected by those who could meet certain income requirements and who were entitled to up to 40 votes, depending on financial standing. Nevertheless, the discontented lower classes had, beginning with the 1911 election, a more effective channel through which to vent their feelings—an opportunity they seized with great élan. The number of Social Democrats in the second house, which had gradually risen from 1 in 1897 to 35 in 1908, jumped to 64 (out of 230) in 1911.

A number of social reforms also made their appearance at about this time. Legislation on industrial safety was passed between 1905 and 1914. A modest form of old age pension was instituted in 1913, and an unemployment commission was founded in 1914. A start was made in granting home loans to lower income groups. A system of government mediation in labor disputes was set up. The Social Democrats, in line with the new prestige accompanying their parliamentary position, assumed a solemnly responsible stance. They worked with the other parties in seeking practicable compromises in parliament and, in 1911, substantially modified the revolutionary fervor of their platform. In other words, in spite of the severe surface strife, some of the basic elements in what would later develop into Sweden's profile—compromise, social reform, and a spirit of cool rationality in approaching problems—were being quietly set in place.

After the First World War the Social Democrats were considerably strengthened. Full democratization of the vote and female suffrage were passed in 1918, and the Social Democrats —despite the splitting off of a pro-Bolshevik group after the Russian Revolution—were the largest political force in parliament.

In 1920, the first purely Social Democratic government—led by the party's founder, Hjalmar Branting—took office. This, Sweden's first left-wing government, lasted only a few months, but the Social Democrats formed two other governments during the twenties. Political life was unstable, complicated as it was by numerous shifting splinter parties: two new Farmers' parties (later combined); a split by the Liberals into wet and dry forces (later reconciled); a Soviet-oriented Communist Party (which itself later split in two); and the already mentioned split in the Social Democrats. Since no party had a majority and coalitions for the most part proved unworkable, various minority governments held or attempted to hold power during this time. In the thirteen-year period 1920–1932, exactly thirteen governments held office.

The overriding domestic issue during the twenties was unemployment, and the manner in which it was handled showed that deep social antagonism still existed. An unemployment commission—the *Arbetslöshetskommissionen* (AK)—had been established in 1914, but since there was little unemployment during the war and immediate postwar years, it had little to do. In 1922 the worldwide postwar depression hit Sweden, and at the beginning of the year an estimated 200,000 workers were unemployed. Conditions improved quickly, and by the following year unemployment had recovered to the "normal" (for the time) figure of 7 to 8 percent, where it stayed during most of the twenties. But the AK had ample opportunity to display its workings—and to become the country's most hated institution. At emergency work projects, pay scales were set at below the going rate for the lowest paid common laborer—regardless of the skills of the workers in question. Because it was considered improper to compete with privately owned industry, much of the work bordered on the useless. Some of the unemployed were set to breaking up stones by hand—considered noncompetitive, since such work was ordinarily done by machines.

The AK also angered workers through its so-called conflict directive. According to this rule, no one involved in a strike or a lockout could get employment assistance. But the regulations were so intricately entangled that in many cases workers who were already jobless when the conflict broke out or who had been employed in an entirely different place, were barred from help. In some cases an entire category of workers was excluded from assistance.

Feelings ran high over this storm-tossed institution, and two Social Democratic governments were toppled when proposals to soften the AK's harsh rules were rejected by parliament.

The worldwide depression which began to accelerate alarmingly in early 1930 had little initial effect on Sweden. Exports held up well, and industrial production in 1930 was down only 3 percent from the 1929 level. In mid-1931, however, economic conditions steadily worsened, and by the middle of 1932 a depression—aggravated by the suicide of the Swedish international financier Ivar Kreuger and subsequent financial panic in Sweden in the spring—was in full swing. By the end of 1932 the number of unemployed had reached 160,000.

As economic conditions deteriorated, so did labor-management relations. In 1931 the gravest incident in Sweden's industrial history occurred in a town in the north called Ådalen. A group of striking workers, spurred on by Communist agitators, stormed a haven of strikebreakers guarded by police and soldiers. The strikers were fired on, and four workers and a spectator—a ten-year-old girl—were killed and several others wounded.

The Ådalen massacre served to focus attention on the plight of the workers, the brutality of employers, and the coarseness of the official assistance offered the unemployed and thus doubtless aided the Social Democrats in the important elections to the second chamber in the fall of 1932.

In the elections the Social Democrats scored heavy gains, though not enough to give them control of parliament. But the Farmers' Party offered to support the Social Democrats if the latter would agree to pay heed to the farmers' poor economic position. As a result, in 1933 the Social Democrats stepped into power for the first time with a solid basis of parliamentary support.

With the exception of the war years (when the other parties accepted an invitation to participate in a coalition government) and other minor exceptions, the Social Democrats have been in power ever since—either alone or in coalition with the Farmers' Party (now known as the Center Party).

The Social Democrats have thus had virtually a free hand in putting their accumulated Socialist theories into practice, and there is indeed a widespread impression abroad that the result is today's "Socialist Sweden." The notion is altogether understandable since the Social Democrats constantly boast of their undying loyalty to Socialist principles and are constantly attacked by the opposition for these Socialist principles. (The confusion is not entirely dispelled by the Social Democratic government's expenditures of considerable funds to explain to foreigners that the country is not, after all, Socialist, at the same time that they are telling Swedes that it is.) The fact is that most of the party's Socialist principles have remained unused. The doctrinaire nature of the party's Socialism was modified many years ago. A Social Democratic government official remarked to me: "Already in the early twenties it was apparent that Socialism was not going to play a major role in the party's development." Rudolf Meidner, a major Social Democratic economist, bluntly declared: "It never has been a really Socialist regime."

Militant elements within the party have on occasion called for implementation of more radical Socialism. In 1944 a firebrand postwar program was whipped together and given the party imprimatur; it called for such measures as government ownership of land and nationalization of insurance companies and other selected enterprises. But these alarming proposals have not proved especially popular with the electorate, and the government has remained resolutely pragmatic—and non-Socialist—in its actions. Some 95 percent of industry is in private hands, and the single major state take-over of a private company —the purchase of the vast LKAB iron mines in 1956—was executed pursuant to agreements stretching back forty years and originally made by a Conservative government. Similarly, the other major state-owned companies—a tobacco company, a wine and liquor monopoly, a commercial bank, and other operations —trace their governmentalization to Conservative governments. Basically, it is a free enterprise economy, with a strong commitment to competition and free trade.

But one Socialist principle has been carefully retained by the Social Democrats—at least in principle—and this is the equalization, so far as possible, of incomes. Aside from a steeply progressive income tax, which has the effect of relieving the rich of some of their monetary burdens and distributing it to the less fortunate in the form of subsidized education, medical care, and other social benefits, little real action along this line is within the government's powers, and progress toward equalization has been unsatisfactory, in the opinion of many Social Democrats. Nevertheless, the idea remains extremely popular in Sweden, particularly among intellectuals. Kjell-Olof Feldt, Undersecretary of Finance, emphasized to me: "This is one principle that I don't think will ever be abandoned." It undoubtedly has some effect on policies, even though the impact is sometimes difficult to detect, and the whole thing is often omitted from discussions of Social Democratic policy designed for foreign consumption.

The most apparent result of the Social Democrats' mix of pragmatism and Socialism is what might be called a system of welfare Socialism, whereby social services designed to assure a modicum of protection against the hazards and misfortunes of life are provided, under a state monopoly, for all citizens. No doubt the hot-voiced revolutionaries of the nineteenth century would be aghast at the doctrinal impurities and hopelessly middle-class values embodied in this creation of their spiritual inheritors. Yet even though the construction of the system has been so gradual and orderly as to deserve to be called the sleepy revolution, the process has nevertheless meant a wholesale transformation in the life of the poor, marginal Sweden of only a few decades ago.

IV

Welfare, Swedish Style

When the Social Democrats finally came to power in 1933, they had ample supplies of problems on which to try their skills. Sweden's fragile economy having been badly crippled by the worldwide depression—unemployment hit an all-time peak of 40 percent in March, 1933—they turned first to the immediate crisis. Sven Aspling, present Minister of Social Affairs, explained to me: "We needed to do something at once for the poor people." This meant primarily jobs, and emergency construction projects and other make-work operations kept an average of 45,000 persons employed throughout 1933 and 1934 —with the total rising to as much as 70,000 at times—compared with around 25,000 during the worst parts of the decade-earlier depression. It wasn't a total solution to the depression, but it was a start. Moreover, recalling the bitterness engendered by the old relief work schemes, the Social Democrats took care to pay the workers standard going wages.

But the government was faced with a no less urgent social ill of a different nature—a declining birthrate—and the attention it devoted to this problem served as a base on which was later built the far-reaching structure of social benefits. The birthrate had been dropping since the late nineteenth century, but under the pressures of overcrowded housing and the depression it began to sink alarmingly in the thirties. It dropped from more than 25 per 1,000 population at the turn of the century to under 15 in the thirties; the number of births, which had averaged 130,000 annually in 1913–15, plummeted to 87,000 annually in 1931–35.

Public attention was drawn to the question by Gunnar and Alva Myrdal's book *The Population Crisis,* published in 1934. This enormously influential volume painted a terrifying picture of the drawbacks of a low birthrate: depopulation, unexploited natural resources, declining living standards, and the increasing burdens carried by a proportionately dwindling group of the young and able. One immediate result was the establishment of an official population commission, one of whose members was Gunnar Myrdal, which ground out an uninterrupted flow of reports and recommendations over a four-year period.

Some of the proposals were promptly put into effect: free prenatal and postnatal care for mothers, free medical care for children for one year after birth, free obstetric services, and a cash payment to mothers at the time of delivery. But one of the most heartily welcomed innovations was noneconomic: a flat ban on the cruel, but common, practice of discharging female employees when it became known they were pregnant or sometimes at the news of marriage or even engagement.

The birthrate turned up in the second half of the thirties, only to falter again at the end of the decade, spurring appointment of another study commission in 1941. But action on all such matters was halted by the outbreak of World War II, when the full attention of the Swedes focused on a familiar difficulty: survival.

During the war the theoretical wheels continued to spin, and the coming of peace found the Social Democrats bubbling with fresh ideas. Consequently, new social benefits were added as rapidly as political feasibility and economic resources would permit. In 1946 the old age pension, first weakly formulated in 1913 and often revised, was reorganized, expanded, protected from inflation, and made almost completely independent of need. Free school lunches were established, and a system of financial assistance to students was set up. In 1947 housing subsidies to families were instituted. In 1948 child subsidies were overhauled. The eccentrically discriminatory tax-deduction technique (similar to that now in force in the United States) which permits a certain amount to be deducted from income and in effect gives maximum government subsidy to precisely those parents who need it least, was abolished. A flat cash child contribution was set up instead, the same to everybody, payable quarterly to mothers. In 1951 a statutory three-week annual vacation was passed. In 1955 a long-planned compulsory universal health insurance program was put into effect. The last major benefit was added in 1959: an enlarged supplementary pension plan.

With that, all the spectacular measures the Social Democrats could think of seemed to have been taken care of. Subsequent legislation has taken the form of improving and expanding existing programs (such as the increase in the statutory vacation to four weeks in the early sixties) and simplifying the administrative side of the operation.

The basic philosophy of the system has shifted somewhat during all this time. At first benefits were available only to those who needed them. But there has been a gradual trend toward giving everybody the same and, in much recent legislation, toward giving bigger benefits to those who earn more. As one official explained to me: "The idea is that no one—[that is, not even the relatively well off]—should be penalized by misfortune."

Even a quick glance at the more important social benefits can give the impression that every conceivable situation has been foreseen. The process starts before birth. During pregnancy a mother-to-be receives free prenatal care, tests, courses in baby care, and gymnastics at special centers or, when her condition prohibits personal visits to a center, home visits from a nurse. She receives free dental care during pregnancy and for 270 days after giving birth. When the baby is born, all hospital services are free, and she receives a cash payment of $175. If her absence from the home causes difficulties, free home help can be furnished. If she is employed, her job is guaranteed for six months, and during that time she receives regular sickness compensation, scaled according to income. If, after the birth of the child, the mother has no place to live, she can often be accommodated at a mother's home, where she can stay a maximum of one year, three months without charge and thereafter at a low rate, according to income. There are also a very few homes (one in Stockholm) where she can stay until the child is four and others where she can stay until the child starts school. For working mothers, subsidized day-care nurseries charge according to income. The child contribution—increased several times and now at $175 annually—begins immediately after birth. (For handicapped children the amount is about $675.)

Every child is entitled to free periodic checkups at child health centers. There are about seventy such centers in Stockholm alone, and more than 95 percent of children are taken to them. After the child begins school, he gets free health supervision at school facilities. He gets free dental care up to the age of fifteen.

Children also benefit from a comprehensive network of playgrounds with organized activities (more than 100 just in Stockholm); three-hours-a-day kindergarten at a charge, depending on parents' income, of $1 to $5 monthly; after-school centers for working mothers' children from seven to twelve, where they can study, play, and get a snack, costing $2 to $7 a month; similar centers for children twelve to fourteen years; and evening hobby centers, where a nominal membership fee is charged. In the summer some summer camps are operated, and free transportation can be provided to them and others run by private groups. If, in spite of all these facilities, the child has emotional or other nonclassifiable problems, counseling at child guidance clinics is available free.

Approximately as extensive a range of benefits is available for the aged as for the young. The basic pension now amounts to about $700 annually for a single person and $1,000 for a married couple, calculated according to the value of money in 1957; this means it is actually about 50 percent above these figures and will go on rising as long as inflation continues. The supplementary pension, which goes on top of this, will be in full effect in 1980, at which time it will pay out an annual income roughly equal to two-thirds of the pensioner's average annual earnings during his best fifteen working years (up to a maximum of about $5,000 annually in 1960 prices). Most pensioners receive a rent supplement, which may amount, on average, to $20 a month. Further benefits available, according to circumstances and—sometimes—financial need, include home help, free or at a nominal charge; low-rent pensioners' dwellings; and foot care, at a nominal charge if the pensioner can afford it, otherwise free.

Almost all education—in secondary schools, universities, and vocational schools—is free (adult education, while not free, is heavily subsidized). In most cases, free lunches and free school-books, up to the university level, are provided. Students on a higher level receive an allowance of $15 monthly ($35 if they are attending school away from home), and they may obtain low-interest government loans if they wish. One official summed up the objective: "One of the chief aims is that education should not depend on the income of parents. I think it may now safely be said that no one need refrain from higher education because his parents' income is too low."

One unusual benefit is the housewife's vacation. Kate Wennerlund, in charge of the Social Welfare Information Office in Stockholm, explained to me: "The law in Sweden says that everyone who works gets a four-week vacation. But the housewife is not employed." Therefore, any housewife whose family's income is below a certain (only slightly below average) level is entitled to one free round trip anywhere in Sweden once a year. But this provision is only of value, of course, when the lady has a place to go to. "We also have housewives' vacation homes," says Miss Wennerlund. "They pay a small fee, or it can be free.

They should have low incomes and have at least two children under fourteen, but these rules are flexible. There are three homes near Stockholm, owned by the city, with room for about three thousand guests a year."

In addition to the main benefits, an almost infinite range of other services is available—to alcoholics, people with family problems, people with sex problems, people with legal difficulties, the crippled, the blind, the neurotic, and most other groups.

Probably the most discussed aspect of the welfare system—doubtless because it is the largest single item of social welfare, accounting for about 40 percent of all welfare spending and about 5.5 percent of the gross national product—is the sickness insurance system.

Its guiding principle was pinpointed for me by a medical official: "The policy is that everyone should have medical care when he needs it—without regard to ability to pay."

The basis of the program is a compulsory insurance plan, contributions to which are made along with regular income taxes. In return, anyone can visit a doctor or the outpatient clinic of a hospital as often as he likes; 80 percent of all charges are reimbursed by the state. All care requiring admission to a hospital, including surgical and all other charges, is free (in public wards; private or semiprivate rooms carry a small extra charge). The cost of prescribed medicine is also reduced by 80 percent through reimbursements. Certain especially vital medicines, such as insulin, are free. Some special services—X rays for tuberculosis, polio shots—are often free. In short, almost all medical services are fully or largely covered. There are exceptions—preventive shots taken before voyages to exotic climates and oral contraceptive pills, for example. Dental care is not included, except for pregnant women and children, but the government has promised to bring this in as well.

During illness, whether one is confined to a hospital or not, a daily cash stipend is paid, scaled according to income. Since

1967 the payments have ranged from $1.20 a day for those earning from about $350 to $500 yearly (as well as housewives) to a ceiling of $10.10 a day for those earning more than about $7,600. These payments, which are reduced slightly for those confined in hospitals and raised somewhat for those with small children, go into effect after a one-day waiting period.

The system has a certain amount of flexibility. For one thing, the possibility exists of choosing one's own doctor—at a price. A doctor in Sweden may be in one of three categories. First, he may work in a hospital, usually run by either the local government or the state (a very few are private). Second, he may have a strictly private practice. Third, he may be a county medical doctor, who is in many respects independent, but he covers a defined geographical area, enjoys the use of facilities belonging to the state, and must conform to certain fixed requirements. Almost all such are in rural districts, often remote areas which otherwise would lack medical service. Of the approximately 8,500 doctors at the end of 1965, about 1,200 were private, and 700 were county medical officers. Only the private doctors are free to set their own fees, the others being ruled by a centrally fixed schedule. The importance of the schedule is that reimbursements to the patient are based on it. Gunnar Ohlin, editor of the *Swedish Medical Journal,* explained to me: "In general, private doctors charge more than the schedule. But some—especially older doctors—stick to it. Some younger doctors charge double or more the official rates."

Thus, the free choice has a substantial cash significance. A service carrying an "official" rate of, say, $5 means that the patient's cost is only $1 since he is reimbursed by the state for $4; if the same service is rendered by a private doctor, the charge may well be $10, but the patient still receives a refund of only $4. In order words, his cost may be six times as much.

In hospitals, one is normally not permitted to choose one's own doctor, but most people understandably prefer it anyway. For this and other reasons, the free sector, as they say in Sweden, is steadily shrinking. Dr. Arthur Engel, former head of the

National Medical Board, says: "Five or six years ago one-third of medical consultations were in hospitals, one-third in offices of the county medical doctors, and one-third with private practitioners. Now about half go to outpatient departments of hospitals, and I expect this to increase further." But this is also due to the doctors' own attitudes. Editor Ohlin pointed out: "It's not so popular to be a private practitioner. It's much more convenient to be in a hospital with all the modern equipment, specialists, and so forth." He says the Medical Association wants very much to retain the free group, partly because: "When negotiating for higher fees, the doctors in hospitals can strike, and the private doctors can take over." The Medical Association is a trade union which bargains for its members—not on wages, but on the fee schedule—and it has strong feelings on this subject, said Ohlin: "If a strike should occur, the patients must not suffer."

Dr. Sture Jernmark, association president, gloomily described the problem: "The purpose is to give young doctors the courage to go out in the field. It's difficult. They don't want to accept risks." To encourage them, the association offers financial and other assistance to doctors setting up group practice. But Dr. Jernmark is not optimistic. "I think the government wants to reduce the free sector even more," he said. "The tendency is clear." Dr. Engel, of the Medical Board, denied this when I spoke to him. "We have a Socialist government," he said, "but a liberal Socialist government. It is leaving room for private enterprise without reluctance—as long as it doesn't interfere with the organized state care."

Despite relatively low earnings (most doctors earn between about $10,000 and $18,000), doctors in Sweden appear to be content. The Medical Association has no important objections to the system. "Most Swedish doctors," said Dr. Jernmark, "are in favor of the program in principle, but there are discussions over details. The program has burdened doctors with lots of paper work—a waste of doctors' valuable time. The evolution is toward more and more bureaucracy. Before, we were occupied with pure medicine; now, with so many other things. But one can do nothing about that, can one?"

The medical system often draws harsh criticism from the Swedes, not for the plan's objectives, but for the way it works out, or doesn't work out, in practice. Most commonly, complaints are directed at the maddening bottlenecks that appear at every turn. Anyone seeking help at a hospital outpatient clinic must often be prepared to wait hours, even after making an appointment. It is frequently necessary to telephone in advance just to arrange for a later telephone conversation to make an appointment for a still later personal consultation, at which time one must expect to wait a considerable time again. Every medical facility's telephone hours are noted in the telephone book—often only half an hour a few days a week—and calls made at other times don't get answered. Waiting times for certain operations and other forms of treatment extend up to two years. Dr. Peter Heiman, a Swedish doctor who has been an outspoken critic of the system, remarked: "Waiting in line has almost become an accepted part of medical care."

One of the reasons is that with the price of medical care hovering just slightly above zero—or even below, considering that one is actually paid for being sick—many people find the temptation to fall ill irresistible. Fradley Garner, American medical writer, quoted Dr. Ragnar Frykholm, a noted Swedish neurosurgeon, as saying that emotionally disturbed people exploit the opportunity to invade hospitals, but only during the winter months when other amusements are minimal. "The existence of numerous neuroses is a typical welfare phenomenon," Dr. Frykholm said. Dr. Engel conceded that there is some truth to the charge: "It is so comfortable to go to a hospital for a checkup."

Another reason for the bottlenecks is Sweden's small number of doctors: about 100 per 100,000 inhabitants, which compares with about 140 in the United States and is lower than in such less developed countries as Italy and Greece. The problem is partly balanced by a higher proportion of hospital beds than most countries—around 1,600 per 100,000 inhabitants, compared with about 900 in the United States—which, by bringing the patient to the doctor instead of vice versa, has enabled Sweden to increase medical "productivity" remarkably, but not enough to completely offset the doctor shortage.

The production of doctors is being expanded rapidly. The number of beginning medical students rose from about 300 per year in the early fifties to about 600 in 1965 and will rise further to about 900 by 1969. The number of doctors has risen by 75 percent in the 1950–65 period, and the plan is to score a 40 percent increase—to 11,800—by 1975.

The system is also vulnerable to criticisms of excessively strict bureaucratic adherence to rules and red tape. For example, if you want to go to a hospital, you must go to the one in the district where you are registered; if you should by chance attempt to penetrate another, you will be turned away unless you are on the point of death. Another common cause of irritation is the practice of calling a patient back to a hospital for different forms of treatment—and being forced to work one's way through different waiting lists for each phase of treatment. This process is aggravated by having the patient examined at each stage by a different doctor, who is unfamiliar with the case history.

Dr. Peter Heiman has written: "Health care . . . has developed into a powerful administrative apparatus. We must constantly be on the watch for over-organization, administrative tyranny, waste of money, and a development toward impersonal and mechanized care."

This sort of complaint, as well as the criticism (frequently voiced by foreigners) of the cold, inhuman manner of the doctors, is frequently directed specifically at the medical system. But I do not believe this is quite right. The knots of bureaucratic involutions in the health system can be excessively irritating, but they are not appreciably worse than the cold-blooded indifference displayed by retail-store clerks, dry cleaners, repairmen, telephone operators, or any other Swede one is likely to come into contact with.

The many operating problems in the health program have become so noticeable that they have even come to the attention of the authorities. As yet, the reaction has not been altogether what one might hope. A Council for Efficient Hospital Operation has been established; but it has, in the typical Swedish fashion, fixed its attention on such matters as automation, hospital design, use of computers and the like, and there has not, so far as I am aware, been any effort to attack the human problems.

But with all its grave lapses, the system works. One hears constant complaints about the human indifference of the machinery, but one also hears—if one pays attention—frequent tales from low-income families about the painstaking medical resources that are readily available in the pinch. On the whole, the system may be said to fulfill with truly remarkable precision the goal; everyone does indeed "have medical care when he needs it—without regard to ability to pay."

Anyone who has problems not specifically covered in some program can ask for special help. Greta Grenander, at the Central Social Welfare Board, told me: "You have every right to claim additional public assistance if you need it. You can go to court and demand it." What help is to be provided and how depend on the circumstances and, to some extent, on a particular community's policies. Mrs. Grenander said: "We try to make municipalities understand that people who accept public assistance are not inferior. It is sometimes very difficult." In order to make it easier, the name of the assistance—*fattigvård,* which means care for the poor and which had a long history of unpleasant connotations—was changed some years ago to *socialhjälp,* which simply means social help.

I asked Mrs. Grenander if this meant anyone could insist on being supported by the state instead of working. She answered: "No—only if you are old, sick, under sixteen, or have children under sixteen. If you are a healthy man out of work, you can ask for public assistance; but you have no right to it, and if the community does not want to give it to you, you cannot do anything. Several years ago I worked in the north, and many communities gave unemployed forestry workers just enough to eat and nothing more. It could happen that a single man got about a dollar a day. We believe that no community will let people *starve*, but beyond that there are great question marks."

During 1964 a total of 129,906 cases of emergency assistance were processed, a slight (1.5 percent) decline from the previous year. There has not been any growth in the amount of money disbursed in this way for the past several years, because of the refinements added to the more specific programs. Mrs. Grenander said: "With the amendments that are added every year, fewer and fewer people have to ask for public assistance."

To get an impression of the mechanics, I visited Social Bureau Number 7 in Stockholm (there are a total of fourteen in the city), located in a shiny new office building in Bromma, a placid, relatively prosperous residential area on the city's outer fringes.

The bureau's director, Birgit Florin, a friendly fiftyish lady, explained that anyone was free to telephone for help or information between 8 A.M. and 9 A.M. or to come in person between 9 and 11. The previous month a total of 256 persons had come to the office, and at the present moment approximately 335 cases were in various stages of investigation or action. The staff consisted of, besides the director, a group leader, 3 social workers, and 3 clerical workers. Attached to the same office was a separate 4-man group dealing exclusively with helping older people obtain help in the home—at a cost of slightly under $1 an hour, if they have it or nothing, if they don't. "This is a very small bureau," explained Mrs. Florin. "Some have three times as many cases."

Very often the bureau functions merely as an information service; this suggests how complex the welfare system has become. "The public seems to have the impression that everything is taken care of here," said Mrs. Florin. "That's not so. For legal questions we send them to the Legal Assistance

Bureau. If it's children, we refer them to the Child Welfare Board. For family problems we get in touch with the Family Counseling Service. For housing questions they must go to the Housing Exchange."

But the social bureaus are left with a bewilderingly wide variety of human misery. To give me an idea of the problems, Helen Brolin, one of the social workers, pulled out her card file and told me about a few typical cases.

The first was a woman who had come in that morning. "Her husband abandoned her and their four children. After several months—this was a few weeks ago—he was found, but now he has disappeared again. Meanwhile, his family has nothing to live on. He has alcohol problems, and this kind of thing has happened a number of times. Every once in a while his wife tries to work, but it never lasts. Last month she got a job, and it lasted one day. A few years ago she decided to get a divorce, but nothing came out of it. Anyway, we must help her with money so that she can live. We gave her $25 today and will mail her another $25 in a week. She is supposed to tell us if the man turns up, and she must contact us every week. I don't know how long this will go on."

The second one was simpler. "This is a pensioner whose only income is his basic pension—he lives in an old people's home. He needs a summer coat. No alcohol problems, no psychological troubles, just someone who needs a little money for a coat—perhaps $30 or $40. He will most certainly get it."

The third was a complicated history of an eighteen-year-old girl who had long been oscillating between various kinds of instability. "Earlier she worked as a domestic servant in Finland," said Mrs. Brolin. "Then she worked in a hospital, which also gave her a place to live. She first got in touch with us when she contracted a venereal disease and her sickness insurance didn't cover her living expenses. Then she lost her job and her apartment at the same time. When she got fired, she disappeared. She worked as a waitress in railroad dining cars and lived here and there with acquaintances. Her parents are in

Stockholm, but they don't want to have anything to do with her." Despite this unhappy background, Mrs. Brolin was not giving up hope. "We think she's a gifted girl, and we are trying to get her a place to live and vocational training. She's interested in hospital work. If we can get her to accept it, she can get free training and cash payments of $100 to $125 a month. But we can do nothing if she won't cooperate. We must give her motivation. We don't just want to keep giving her money. Over the longer term we want her to take care of herself."

The fourth case did not involve money. "A woman asked if she could get help. Her husband has a good income, but he is an alcoholic and doesn't want to get in touch with the Temperance Board." Mrs. Brolin pointed out that individuals with alcohol problems can obtain help in complete secrecy. "We discussed the problem, but there is little we can do. We always discuss things. Sometimes it's a help just to know that there is someone here who will listen."

The last card told a tale of a couple with two small children who had been receiving social help "off and on for the last four years." They had drifted into marriage when the woman had become pregnant and since then had traced an unsteady course through life. Mrs. Brolin had previously referred them to the Family Counseling Service. "At least now they can discuss things with each other. That's something positive. The man has a good income, but there are always problems with money. They keep buying things on credit—a refrigerator, clothes, furniture. They couldn't pay the telephone bill, so the telephone is now shut off." Mrs. Brolin sighed. "It's possible we may give them a loan to combine their debts. But they don't actually *need* social help. They should be able to get along by themselves."

Mrs. Florin explained that this type of case was particularly prevalent in this relatively prosperous neighborhood: "That's the backside of the welfare state. People try to live up to a standard they can't reach. We didn't have this kind of problem fifteen years ago; now it's very common. They think they must have help. We probably will give it to them. But we would rather give them a feeling of independence and self-reliance."

Housing may not seem part of a welfare system; it is not, in fact, included in official information tabulations of welfare activities. But in Sweden the government has taken over almost complete control of housing, and it is one of the benefits Swedes have come to expect from the state.

For various historical reasons—including distressing poverty, difficulty of enlarging cities outward because of poor transportation and problems of terrain, and financially rapacious landlords—growing numbers of city dwellers were stacked closely on top of one another in the nineteenth and early twentieth centuries, and by the 1930's Sweden's housing supply was in a miserable state of overcrowding and decay. In 1933, 76.9 percent of all Stockholm housing units consisted of two-rooms-and-kitchen, or less, and official investigations showed a large portion of them to be seriously dilapidated.

As American economist Leonard Silk has written, "building for profit" had not given the Swedish people adequate housing, and in the mid-forties "the Swedish Social Democratic government virtually nationalized the planning and financing of residential building, though it has not taken over the actual construction work or the ownership of the completed dwellings."

Accordingly, the share of housing production attributable to private enterprise has sunk from 88 percent in 1939 to about 20 percent today (not counting one-family houses, which are a small part of the total); the rest is built by the state, communities, and nonprofit cooperative groups. The private builders are squeezed out through discriminatory treatment in the allotment of building assignments when local authorities plan new areas and through the higher subsidies (in the form of low-interest loans) granted to their competitors. But private or nonprivate, it all is controlled by the state, which decides how much housing is to be built every year and directly or indirectly arranges the financing.

Since the government has accepted the responsibility for housing, it must also accept the blame for the truly scandalous housing shortage. In the Sweden of today, obtaining an apartment within a reasonable time—without the aid of a friend or relative in some helpful position—is virtually impossible. Central waiting lists are maintained in most communities, and the one in Stockholm (population about 700,000) has more than 120,000 names at this writing. Waiting times of ten years and more are not uncommon. Family members often must live apart from one another because of the shortage. Industries cannot expand because they cannot offer housing to workers imported from other areas. People who might want to move from one place to another or from one job to another (apartments often come with the jobs) can't because of the shortage. A reasonably satisfactory illegal and quasi-legal market in "furnished" premium-rent sublets and under-the-table bribes has developed, but even ample funds are not always a solution.

Why should Sweden, which has not suffered from war damage in more than 150 years, boast one of the most severe housing shortages in Europe? One reason, as the official explainers never tire of pointing out, was a mass exodus of forestry and agricultural workers to the cities, as victims of automation and other symptoms of progress.

But the chief cause of the crisis has been the tight government grip on the housing market and the housing industry—most important, a system of rigid rent controls originally instituted as protection against wartime inflationary pressures. In the immediate postwar period it was thought the controls could be removed after a short spurt of slightly stepped-up building to make up for the wartime lapse in construction. It didn't work. Assuming the spurt had been too short and too slight, the government therefore diverted massive resources of capital and labor to housing, pushing the number of completed units up from an average of 48,000 annually in the early fifties to about 90,000 in the mid-sixties. By 1963 Sweden was building more housing units (10.7 per 1,000 inhabitants) than any other Western country. (West Germany, with 9.9, was second, Switzerland, with 9.3, was third, and the United States, with 8.6, was fourth.) But no amount of building seemed to help, and although there is considerably more housing now than there was at the end of the war, the slight shortage of 1945 has become a truly critical social problem.

What the planners failed to foresee was that galloping inflation and fast-rising incomes would in effect push the frozen rents down relative to everything else. And when prices drop, demand rises. Thus apartment dwellers paying artificially low rents have had little incentive to adapt their modes of living to their ability to pay. The planners' ineptness has also contributed, mainly by not planning construction in line with real needs; about 70 percent of all the names on official waiting lists are in the three largest cities, but only about a third of the housing gets built in these cities. I once asked the head of planning for the Stockholm region why parliament didn't increase the cities' housing allotments. Referring to the Swedes' well-known attachment to nature, he replied: "It's not politically popular to build too much in the cities." One might have wished the planners had a little less sentiment and a little more attentiveness to the real needs.

Like most things, the housing shortage has not been all bad. Housing standards have improved markedly as a result of the frenzied building activity undertaken because of the shortage. The portion of units with two-rooms-plus-kitchen, or less, which as late as 1945 still accounted for more than three-fourths of the total, is now well under half. Moreover, the total number of units has risen by about 50 percent. Indoor toilets, baths, and central heating, which existed in well under half of all units in 1945, are now almost universal. So whether they wanted it or not, the Swedes possess today a far higher housing standard then ever before—at least some recompense for all the suffering caused by the shortage.

It eventually became brutally apparent that the situation was not going to improve under the prevailing conditions. Increasing numbers of young people, who did not have access to an older rent-controlled unit, were left living with parents or friends or in some other makeshift pattern or, if they were lucky, in one of the newer, far more expensive units. For this and other reasons, the government has determined to take action. A number of economic studies have shown that the only practicable solution is to allow rents to rise to their own market level; this should impel landlords to adjust their rents to the market and tenants to adapt their demands to their ability to pay.

Although the government clearly recognizes the need to liquidate rent controls if the shortage is ever to be eliminated, its determination on this question has not proved to be particularly steady. After many years of preparation, a proposal was bravely submitted to parliament calling for the gradual ending of controls over a five-year period. Nevertheless, the prospect of arousing the ire of tenants enjoying the benefits of the controls apparently became unacceptably vivid, and the proposed legislation was nervously withdrawn at the last minute.

However, despite the dark sides to the problem, the housing saga does illustrate (up to a point) the Swedish passion for attacking a problem as directly and as promptly as available resources of capital, labor, and brainpower permit. Even though the question could, at least in retrospect, have been handled with far greater skill, it is not difficult to think of countries where similar problems have been attacked even more clumsily than in Sweden.

Are there any social problems which have not been attacked? Minister of Social Affairs Sven Aspling sees many. "We have much more to do," he said. But a new stage has been reached: "The purpose of the general reforms is to give everyone security. As in a fisherman's net, the gaps in the system should be as small as possible, so that if someone falls, the net will save him. Now that the basis for the general reforms has been made, we must move toward individual neglected groups. This is the last brick in our edifice."

One important group, he explained, is the handicapped, and progress has been made in, for example, schools for handicapped children. "We have had excellent results with these schools," he said.

The Nävertorp School is one. Located just outside Katrineholm, a neat, sleepy town of 20,000 in the south of Sweden, it gives vocational training to about 190 mentally retarded children (IQ's of 50 to 70) between the ages of four and twenty-three and is housed in a collection of cheerful red-brick buildings dotted about a wooded thirty-five-acre plot.

Stig Vide, who has been connected with the school since two years before it opened in 1956 and is now its head, is fiercely proud of the results. "They didn't believe it would be possible to give such children vocational education," he said. "Before, they were put in institutions, and they stayed there until they were carried out. Here, since 1958, about eighty boys have left, and sixty-five are completely self-supporting. Last year one of them earned 24,000 kronor. Their average income was 11,750 kronor."

All students in the classroom school study from twenty-four to thirty-five hours a week; those who have advanced to vocational school, forty hours; twenty-seven of practical work, three of vocational teaching, eight of more academic theory, and two of athletics. The workshops, whose huge menacing power tools were an obvious source of pride to Vide, produce about $10,000 worth of metal and wood parts annually for neighboring manufacturing companies. In addition, they make a certain amount of furniture to order for the area's residents. "We think it's good for the pupils and good to show people who are paying for all this that we can really produce useful things," he said, showing me a storeroom jammed with chests, cabinets, and bookshelves. "When one item is ordered, they always make a dozen because when Mr. Svensson sees that Mr. Andersson has one, he must have one, too. We always sell them."

It was not without some trepidation that the project was launched. "Everyone had told us it would be terrible; they would cut off their hands, their feet. So I can tell you we were scared. Almost as soon as we started, a boy cut off three fingertips. They took him to the hospital and replaced the fingers.

The next day a boy ripped all the skin off his wrist. They took him to the hospital and grafted the skin back on. The third day another boy tore a big gash in the flesh between his thumb and forefinger. They took him to the hospital, too. That was in October, 1958. Since then we have not had one accident."

Not all the activity is practical. "We have music once a week. We think it's important to listen to music, not only pop, but also to Beethoven. In the beginning they didn't like it, but after a time they realized it really was music and now often ask for more. Their classical favorites are Mozart and Smetana."

The final goal is to give the students a real life. "We think about 75 percent can lead quite a normal life. The others may be only partially self-supporting. At first they weren't willingly taken in by employers, but today all companies will accept them. Every year ten or twelve boys leave. This year [it was then May] out of twelve boys, only three are left that we haven't been able to place. If they can get jobs, we are anxious to get them out."

Dr. Bo Svedberg, the school's psychological expert, told me many more such schools are needed in Sweden. "It is now shown that these people can lead a full life, that they can be made productive; they can mean something in the national economy."

In order to focus more clearly on the problems of the handicapped, a parliamentary committee has been set up. The committee chairman, parliament member Ingemund Bengtsson, explained: "There are two main lines in the welfare system. First, there is money given out when you lose your income or become sick, disabled, or old. That part has been completed. Second is the more difficult job of taking care of people who need it, and in this we have not done so well. The first part—giving money away—is the easiest. But when you solve problems, you always solve the easiest ones first."

Much is already being done for the handicapped, he said. "Every handicapped person receives prosthetic devices free. If he can't use regular transportation he gets $2,400 for a specially equipped car, and he pays no auto tax or gasoline tax.

If you are disabled, and your working capacity is reduced by at least one-third, you get a disability pension. The amount depends on your previous earnings; it takes into account the years you worked and the years you would have worked, but not the higher earnings you might have had later. It is adjusted for inflation, but it's not adjusted for generally rising standards. We have a special investigation into the pension problem."

The committee's first chore, he said, was to learn more about the present state of affairs. "We are asking the municipalities what they are doing. Some have done a great deal, and others nothing. One purpose of this inquiry is to stimulate them to do more." Recommendations for a central state program would come later.

I asked Bengtsson what he thought the total cost of his proposed program might amount to. He brushed the question aside: "It's not a question of money; it's a question of imagination. We have agreed that a handicapped person should live as far as possible the same life as anyone else. That's our goal. The barrier is, not money, but finding out how to reach the goal."

There are still some minor gaps in the welfare system. There is, for example, no compulsory unemployment insurance (although many workers are covered under private plans). An official commission is now studying the advisability of a compulsory plan, but it has not been considered an urgent problem because unemployment has not been a problem for many years. But perhaps even more important, the assistance available to those out of work is not primarily aimed at solving short-term financial problems with a handout but is intended to propel the recipient to become a self-supporting, dignified member of society.

It may be said, in fact, that the real achievement of the system is that it has largely removed the element of fear from the average person's life. The Swede is probably better protected against the hazards and misfortunes of life than anyone else on earth, and this is by no means insignificant. Although everyone in Sweden complains at times of the system's defects, it is undeniable that most Swedes heartily approve of it, and no political party would dare suggest that its scope be reduced, much less that it be dismantled. On the contrary, all the opposition parties compete in charging that the benefits are not being expanded at a sufficiently rapid rate.

But a telling criticism of the system is that it has created what one opposition politician has called a *kösamhälle* (a waiting-list society), in which there are never enough of any of the benefits or services to satisfy the demand, and anyone who wants medical care, an apartment, a place in a day nursery for a child, or almost any other benefit has to put himself at the bottom of a (generally long) waiting list. But if this is so—and it is—the reason is that in their ambitious rush to provide every benefit they could think of almost as soon as they could draw up the legislation, the Social Democrats have usually failed to consider the inadequacy of society's resources to satisfy the extra demand thus created. Encouraged by the low prices attached to the government services, the public has understandably lined up to take advantage of more of them than can be delivered.

Yet in a way, even this defect attests to the Swedes' success in building up the system. It must be remembered that the entire network of benefits has been constructed in the relatively short time that Sweden has attained a certain degree of affluence, and some of the shortages are eloquent reminders of Sweden's sadly underdeveloped state only a few years ago. For example, it is not under any condition possible to register more than very gradual increases in the number of doctors and the number of apartments, and if the present state of affairs in these areas is not wholly satisfactory—after the demonstrably massive efforts in both in recent years—it nevertheless indicates clearly from how low a base Sweden was forced to begin at the end of the war.

In the expanding of the system no expense—literally—has been spared. Spending on items included in official tabulations of social welfare (this leaves out housing and education) climbed from 1.6 billion kronor in 1947 to 12.5 billion kronor (about $2.4 billion) in 1964—an increase of nearly 700 percent. The nation's wealth grew rapidly in that time, of course, and there was much inflation; but even so, the share of gross national product accounted for by welfare spending jumped from 7.9 percent to 16.7 percent. In other words, the average family consisting of two adults and two children received, on average, $1,100 worth of benefits in 1964.

The benefits are not produced by magic, of course. Sweden's taxes are among the world's highest—38.4 percent of gross national product in 1965, compared with 28.6 percent in Great Britain and 27.3 percent in the United States (the figures also include social security payments). A married man earning $3,000 hands over 18 percent of the total to the government; at $10,000, the tax is 36 percent. In addition, a general 11 percent retail sales tax is levied on almost everything, plus excruciating imposts on such items as liquor (a bottle of Scotch costs $10), cigarettes (about $1 a pack), candy (20 cents a small bar), and gasoline (65 cents a gallon).

But the system seems to be worth it. At least the Swedes think so, and it is difficult to imagine that they will change their minds in the foreseeable future.

V

The Organized Society

Sweden's breathtaking complex of welfare benefits is truly impressive, but it is not the only—though perhaps the most dramatic—manifestation of the Swedish talent for organizing, regulating, and systematizing life.

The enthusiasm for organization can be seen even more clearly in another large area—*i.e.*, in the organizations. In Sweden, the word "organizations" carries a very special connotation. If something is said, as it often is, about working toward some end through the organizations, everyone knows what is meant; it is taken for granted that every Swede belongs to whatever organizations are appropriate to his station in life and that if something is to be accomplished, it will be done through these bodies. The very common use of the word in the plural reflects the multiplicity of the organizations and their points of view, as well as the fact that they achieve their importance in actions where all of them—or at any rate a large number of them—are involved. It is natural for the government, in dealing with important questions, to call on the organizations—all or as many as might be affected—to cooperate in finding solutions. Thus, it struck no one as unusual when the government announced in the massive educational campaign being carried out in connection with the 1967 switch from left- to right-hand traffic, the organizations were being assigned a key role in passing the word around.

Gunnar Heckscher, prominent scholar, political leader, and diplomat who has devoted special effort to studying this curious phenomenon, has written:

> Let us take for example an ordinary worker; he probably lives in a building owned by a housing co-operative, or if not, he will be a member of a tenants' association; he buys his provisions at a co-operative store on the corner; his working conditions are fixed by an agreement between his employer and his union; if he wants to study, there is a workers' cultural organization which organizes study circles or courses where he can go and hear lectures; if he likes sports, there is a sports association; if he wants to go out on a Sunday excursion there is a tourist association which will organize everything for him; and when he wants to go on vacation he has only to go to the travel association of the workers' movements. So that all his life, from morning to night, he is surrounded by associations and organizations, and one might say that the only thing in this worker's life that is not organized for him is his sleep. . . .

This description might give the impression that it is only the worker who is laced up in his organizations, but this is not so. If the gentleman in the example were an advertising man, a sculptor, or a farmer, the degree to which he would be bound in on all sides by organizations would be about the same, though the organizations would be different. There is a stunning assortment of occupational, cultural, and recreational groups, so rich in their variations that a different set of memberships can be custom-tailored to fit every subtle shading of personality. If the worker cited above happened to be unusually religious or especially interested in political ideology, his organizations would be slightly different. If he owned a car, he would probably belong to an auto club, and if he owned a car and didn't drink, he might belong to an auto club for people who don't drink. His sports organization might be one thing if he were interested in skiing, another if he were a hiker, still another if he leaned toward gymnastics. There are organizations promoting women's rights, temperance, morality, farmers' interests, and innumerable other more or less clearly definable specialities. Heckscher observes wryly that many of them "seem to have little *raison d'être* other than to provide responsible offices for those unfortunate members of the community whose ambitions could not otherwise be realized," but they are taken with deadly seriousness in Sweden.

Well, what is so surprising about this? Americans generally think of themselves as the most organization-minded people on earth, and De Tocqueville is often cited ("The Americans of all ages and all conditions, and all dispositions, constantly form associations . . . not only commercial and manufacturing . . . but associations of a thousand other kinds, religious, moral, serious, futile, restricted, enormous, or diminutive") to indicate Americans' deep-rooted organization-mindedness.

The Swedish organizations are different. Whereas a great many American organizations exist primarily to facilitate social contacts or to promote the exchange of technical and professional knowledge, neither of these aims is the paramount objective in the Swedish world of organizations, although many do carry out educational activities. As a rule, a Swedish organization exists primarily to promote as vigorously as possible the very concrete interest of its members, and often that is its only purpose.

Nobody knows how many such organizations there are, but it is safe to suppose they number in the many thousands. Some draw their memberships only from single communities or parts of communities. Some cover a larger region, and others are nationwide. The smaller groups—confined to a single locality, industry, or profession—are combined into larger groupings, which in turn are linked in still larger organizations of organizations, and these supergroups are known as top organizations.

As a rule, it is in the top organizations that the power and influence are concentrated.

The organizations fall into two fairly distinct categories: the so-called interest organizations (mainly concerned with furthering their members' economic aims); and the idealistic organizations, which center their attention on more nonmaterial targets. The Federation of Swedish Farmers' Associations stresses chiefly the promotion of the economic position of farmers, while the Society for the Protection of Nature is mostly interested in preserving the beauties of nature which its members enjoy, its only economic activity being what is strictly necessary to perpetuate itself.

Some of the more important interest organizations are the Swedish Confederation of Professional Associations, the Confederation of Industrial Unions, the Employers' Confederation, the Swedish Retail Association, the Bank Association, the National Swedish Farmers' Union, the Consumer Cooperative Society, the National Association of Insurance Companies, the National Tenants' Association, the Swedish House Property Owners' Association, the Federation of Wholesale Merchants and Importers, and the General Export Association. The idealistic classification includes such groups as the Council on Alcoholism, the Sailing Association, the Football Association, the Historical Society, the Bible Society, the Tape Recorder Club, the Equestrian Association, and the National Association for Sexual Information.

Understandably, the economically oriented organizations tend to be the most powerful and influential, but regardless of the type of activity pursued, all the organizations—if they have any members at all—carry weight. (One expert on organizations reminded me: "The sports organizations are very powerful.") Roughly speaking, the influence of a particular organization is dependent on the number of its members and their overall importance in the country's life. Although precise and completely just measurements are not possible, it seems that every organization gets approximately the influence it deserves.

It is not for the most part a question of making great exertions to bring influence to bear; the organizations are firmly locked into the country's political, social, and economic machinery. They doubtless wield their greatest or most obvious influence in the legislative arena. Before an important piece of legislation is put before the Riksdag (parliament), an official investigation is usually carried out. These investigations are extremely thorough and are conducted outside the glare of public attention. They often take several years to complete. The committee members are drawn partly from the ranks of the Riksdag, an attempt usually being made to give each political party a fair representation (especially if the question is a controversial one), but the committees also often include outside experts drawn from various organizations. These outside experts are often nominated at the government's request by the organizations whose interests might be affected. The committee also normally calls on other experts, many of them also connected with the organizations, for assistance on special problems.

This method of conducting the investigations guarantees that the viewpoints of the affected organizations will have been considered in drawing up the final report. A great effort is made to achieve unanimity in the final reports (the majority are in fact unanimous), which of course requires considerable compromise and understanding among the members. But dissenters are free to file a minority objection.

The process does not end here. Before any actual legislation is drawn up, the report is sent out for comment to government authorities, institutions, and, of course, organizations (usually including the same ones that are represented on the committee). If the objections raised at this stage are excessively critical, the whole matter is shelved. Otherwise, a formal bill is drawn up for submission to the Riksdag, including a digest of the outside opinions.

The organizations are thus firmly imbedded in the legislative process, not only at three different stages, but also in three slightly different ways: (1) in the initial composition of the committee, where, technically at least, the members are chosen for their expertise and are not supposed merely to put forward their organizations' viewpoints (it is nevertheless rare, though it does happen, for them to go against these viewpoints); (2) in the work of the experts called on during the investigation, where the assistance is usually of a more technical character; and (3) in the commentaries supplied on the final report, where the organizations are fully expected to push their official, selfishly biased viewpoints. They also have considerable weight in the Riksdag, since many officers and members of organizations are also members of the Riksdag. The power thus exerted is truly immense. Nils Andrén, Swedish expert on government, says that the organizations constitute "a kind of extra constitutional power balance system." He adds: "When the parties in this system arrive at an agreement on some question, the matter is in reality generally decided. The government's function is hardly more than that of ratification."

A typical example of such parliamentary investigation was a study of education for central government employees made by a committee named in 1961. The committee consisted of a high-ranking civil servant as chairman, five members who were also civil servants, plus an officer of the Confederation of Industrial Unions, an officer of the Swedish Confederation of Professional Associations (a trade union for people with university degrees), an officer of the Clerical Employees' Association, and an officer of the Association of Government Officers. The last was also a civil servant, since his group is a union for government employees only. During the committee's research it utilized material and experts provided by these and other organizations. When its work was finished in late 1966, the report was sent out for comment to about fifty government agencies (ranging from the Supreme Court to the Central Statistical Bureau), plus the four organizations represented on the committee. In addition, unsolicited comments were supplied by the Association of Social Workers and the Association of Local Government Administrators. On the basis of the report and the comments, legislation was drawn up proposing establishment of a central administration for the education of civil servants. After presentation to the parliament in early 1967, the legislation was quickly passed and the agency established at midyear.

In a sense, the organizations are a kind of counterpart to the system of lobbyists in Washington, whose efforts greatly affect the drafting of U.S. laws. But there is an important difference. Although anyone with a little capital, a point of view, and a willingness to register with the authorities can become a Washington lobbyist, there is no way for a Swedish organization to be recognized as an important organization except by being an important organization. Vigorous (and costly) beating of one's own drum is not necessary, nor is it worthwhile. Anyone has a right to form an organization to further any cause or selfish interest, and if he can manage to enlist other members, it is likely that the government will, in considering legislation in that field, call on the organization. If you organize a group devoted to the protection of petunias or to the betterment of the economic lot of petunia growers, you can be virtually assured that the next time petunia legislation is up for discussion, you will be asked to help out with the lessons of your experience, the weight of your opinions, and the force of your prestige.

In assessing an organization's power, there are no hard and fast rules. Total membership is not the deciding factor. It is not to be expected that the Association for the Promotion of Skiing and Outdoor Life, with its 200,000 members, would carry the weight of the Federation of Swedish Industries, which has only thirty-five other associations as members (which in turn have 4,300 members altogether). Nor is economic wealth the answer. The Bank Association, whose members exercise close control over industry, as well as finance, is probably less powerful than the Clerical Employees' Association, whose members rank low on the economic scale.

Nevertheless, the organizations do not complain that they are given short shrift in the total scheme of things. In my conversations with officials of various bodies, I have not received the impression that they are dissatisfied with the extent to which their opinions are requested, even if they often (in some organizations almost invariably) disagree with the government's opinion. Even the tiny organization of syndicalists, whose main function sometimes seems to be to complain about being neglected, told me proudly that its insights were frequently sought after by parliamentary committees.

The organizations' role in the legislative machinery is not the only indicator of the vital position they occupy in Sweden. In innumerable ways, their activities are closely interwoven with those of government—so much so that it is at times difficult to tell where the organizations end and the government begins. Quite as a matter of course, functions which an outsider might regard as proper for official bodies are delegated to organizations dominated by private self-interest.

For example, the General Export Association, whose membership consists of approximately 1,200 of Sweden's largest exporting companies can practically be said to manage Sweden's foreign trade policy, and Sweden's bargaining position in international trade negotiations is largely the work of its experts. The National Association of Residential Tenants habitually negotiates the rents which are to be recognized as official in new apartment buildings. Representatives of the organizations whose members' interests are affected are invariably selected as members of such bodies as the Labor Court, the Industrial Injuries Insurance Court, and the Rent Court, which are in the business of making decisions in the areas in which the organizations are involved. Administrative or advisory boards in the government are commonly heavily weighted with representatives of the organizations.

Jonas Nordenson, head of the General Export Association, said to me: "Certain of our activities could well be included in government operations, and in some countries are. We send out questionnaires and collect the information on which bilateral treaty negotiations with some countries are based. We also prepared the material used in the Kennedy Round negotiations. In addition, we act as a central organ for trade commissioners; they are paid by the government, but they report to us. The government not only uses our opinions to a great extent, but we usually participate in the negotiations. Right now we have a man in Rumania following and influencing the negotiations." Nordenson also points out that a government-supported Small Industries Export Bureau is managed by his association.

Some of the most startling instances of this organizational infiltration of the government have been in the agricultural area. In the 1950's representatives of agriculture negotiated on such matters as agricultural price levels and the like with the State Agricultural Board. What was surprising was that two members of the latter were appointed to their positions on the recommendation of the farmers' organizations, so that in effect the farmers' organizations were sitting on both sides of the table. Similarly, the Dairy Associations have taken over administration of distribution of support payments to producers, and are compensated by the government for their efforts.

Nils Elvander, an assistant professor at Uppsala University, whose 1966 book *Intresseorganisationer i Dagens Sverige* (Organizations in Modern Sweden), has thoroughly illuminated the Swedish organizational world, said that the organizations' representation in government bodies is "enormously extensive." One sign of this, he said, is the fact that all but two of the nineteen organizations he has studied in depth "are represented in various authorities, most of them many times."

An equally forceful—perhaps even more forceful—channel of influence is the system of informal contacts that develop between the state organs and the organizations whose area of specialization they are dealing with. This occurs through the day-to-day contacts necessary for carrying out the business at hand, but also through get-togethers of a more social character. A prominent example of the latter was the series of meetings held at Harpsund, the summer estate provided for the use of the Prime Minister and various representatives of organizations—especially those from financial and industrial circles. These meetings came to an end in 1964, mostly because of political criticism of "Harpsund democracy"—whereby the gov-

ernment and small groups of powerful figures were alleged to
have been cooking up sensitive deals in secret—but also partly
because other similar meetings began to appear, and the term
"Harpsund" is still used to refer to them.

Such a system of informal relationships often facilitates the
business of government. Said Hans Grundström, head of an
organization of small businessmen: "By working through the
organizations, you have no prestige factor to consider. In parliament, even if a suggestion is a good one, it might not be politically opportune for the government to accept it. But if I
go to some member of the government, I can have a much more
relaxed discussion, and make more progress." Elvander said:
"The government often listens more to the organizations at
Harpsund than to the politicians in parliament." But the organizations firmly disclaim any intention of taking over the
actual business of government. Otto Nordenskiöld, head of the
central organization of white-collar workers, emphasized to me:
"There must be a line between what the organizations are
trying to do and what the government is trying to do. We
don't want to take over the power of the government, and we
don't want to make the government's decisions. When decisions are made, the responsibility for them rests on those who
make them."

Nevertheless, these informal contacts understandably often
do bring about a significant increase of the government's understanding for the organizations' views. A case in point is the
relations between the National Association of Insurance Companies and the National Insurance Inspection Board, one of
whose duties is to keep an eye on the insurance companies.
During the late forties and early fifties the insurance industry
was at different times threatened with a variety of attacks, such
as campaigns for nationalization and for stricter control over
investment activities. During these moments of crisis, the insurance companies were able to count on the inspection board
as a loyal ally in warding off the sallies of the attacking groups,
sometimes including other branches of the government.

One who comes into contact with the Swedish organizational

phenomenon for the first time is apt to feel that the whole system is thoroughly undemocratic. Just before and during the Second World War, when the system was becoming ever more firmly planted in the country's life, there was much discussion of the dangers of corporatism—that is, of a kind of semi-Fascist management of society through a series of, so to speak, sweetheart organizations.

During the war this fear was not entirely groundless, because the organizations were in fact diverted from their many original purposes and put at the service of the state. The government had to depend heavily on the organizations to carry through various vital policies, such as programs of economic stabilization and campaigns against black markets, and therefore resorted to what were almost coercive measures during this temporary crisis. The effort worked rather well, but apparently only because the crisis was real and the nation in great measure supported the coalition government (the majority Social Democrats having invited the opposition parties to join the Cabinet). But that this was altogether untypical was shown by the failure of the government's efforts to repeat the performance at the end of the forties. Again, there was a crisis —tight import controls had been imposed after the war and the krona had been devalued in 1949—but it was only a financial crisis. After a couple of years of exercising restraint in its wage demands at the government's fervent request, the central labor organization loudly revoked its cooperation in 1952, opining that "it is the government that has the responsibility" for economic stability, not the organizations.

Thus, this attempt, on a rather honorable level, to marshal the organizations' support in order to facilitate the government's task of governing fell flat. In any case, the shift toward corporatism has not yet taken place.

In theory, it would appear possible for the organizations to be exploited in a totalitarian direction, inasmuch as they are repositories of ready-made power, a take-over of the organizations would be tantamount to a take-over of the society. But the very complexity of the system works against this. The organizations are tangled in such heavy and inflexible bureaucratic thickets that it would be difficult to get a grasp on the seat of power. To control a government, one might have to strike at one key point, but to get control of the Swedish organizational apparatus would require a striking at a thousand points. The oft-lamented growth of bureaucracies can have its positive side.

There is, to be sure, a fair amount of authority exerted by the administrators of the organizations, and complaints are made that they act without regard to the members' interests. The administrators do have considerable power over their members. The Employers' Confederation, as an example, lays down certain rules on what types of contracts its members may enter into, and neither its members nor those of the union group have the right to declare a work stoppage without permission from the central body. These restrictions on individual action become especially significant when one considers that in many instances, according to Heckscher: "Although membership is voluntary, the pressure to join is often as compelling as if it were regulated by law." The members thus do not, as a practical matter, have the choice of resigning if they do not like the way things are run.

However, it is doubtful that the organizations could long survive if these restrictions were deeply resented. Where such restrictions are in force—especially in the management and labor groups—solidarity is obviously essential if the groups are to retain their power, and the members accept the realities of the situation.

Democracy in the organizations certainly falls well short of the ideal, a fact most of them willingly confess, but the difficulty appears to lie more often in the members' indifference than in that of the central administrators. Although the latter devote a good measure of effort to explaining, justifying, and persuading on behalf of their own viewpoints, they also attempt to learn the opinions of the members, who, after all, always have the power to discharge the administrators if they become sufficiently disenchanted with the policies being pursued. But sparse attendance at local meetings and congresses and other manifestations of the members' low interest are difficult to combat. This is increasingly true as organizations become bigger, ideological foundations weaken, and the onrush of prosperity gives people more amusing ways to spend their free time.

The organizations' machinery does, in effect, constitute a sort of second government. In the normal democratic process the people elect their representatives in the parliament, who then presumably express the will of the people through their management of the government. In Sweden the people also elect their representatives in the organizations, who then push for the interests of their members in the complex process discussed above. The second government may, indeed, be more powerful than the first one, but it would be difficult to say that it is any less responsive to the will of the people as a whole, especially since the existence of equally powerful organizations expressing opposite points of view means that they act as a check on one another's opportunities to abuse their power. Nils Elvander, the expert on organizations, remarked to me: "There is probably more democracy in the organizations than in the regular government."

A real weakness of the system, based as it is on the dominance of huge, impersonal units in society, is that the individual becomes reduced to an insignificant cog in the organizational machinery, with a consequent tendency toward conformity and a dampening of the personal imagination. There is no provision for any kind of individual influence in government; individuals' views are normally not requested by parliamentary committees, and it is not practicable for a private person to ask a committee to consider his personal viewpoint. A young businessman remarked to me regarding the organizations' importance: "You know, you can't do anything without them. You can't just act alone. You've got to get some organization representative to cooperate with you."

There is an apparent contradiction between the eagerness

with which the Swede embraces his organizations and the individual isolation which is characteristic of him. The organizational system is accepted only because it has proved to be the most efficient and practical way to get things done. The Swedes do not form into groups because they necessarily like one another (such behavior is quite foreign to the system) and their intragroup contacts tend to be on the most formal and impersonal level, so that the organizational life does not really conflict with the isolation of the individual.

In a sense, the organizations actually contribute to the individual's isolation in that they promote conformity. Because it is not customary for the views of a single person to be expressed unless they are fed into the organizational machinery and blended with those of others, this would seem to act as a deterrent to the expression of any individual views. Whether this defect is directly traceable to the organizations or whether it is all bound up with the Swedish proclivity toward the practical is difficult to tell.

But nobody in Sweden—at least none of the many people I spoke to—thinks conformism is a problem, and most people whom I asked about it were plainly perplexed about why I should suspect that it was or that I should question the value of the organizations on such a trivial and abstract basis. A sociologist I spoke to brushed the question aside as of no importance whatever, remarking that it was much more vital to achieve an equitable distribution of economic resources. The head of a grouping of professional people expressed some regret that it was necessary to act through organizations, yet added: "The organizations, through their contributions, can create much more freedom for the individual." I asked Elvander what he thought, and he replied, "In the twenties and thirties some people thought the individual was oppressed by the organizations. But this sort of thing has virtually disappeared from public debate. On the whole, it has no relevance. The great majority of people like their organizations and have confidence in them."

The dangers or potential dangers of an overorganized life

are not discussed to any perceptible degree in Sweden. Questioning analyses of the unattractive aspects of group dominance, such as Whyte's *Organization Man* and Riesman's *Lonely Crowd,* do not exist in Sweden, despite the rich lode of raw material. My experience leads me to believe that this is simply because little importance is attached to helping the individual retain his personal preferences and eccentricities. I once spotted a copy of *The Organization Man* on the bookshelf of a sensitive and intelligent government official, and I asked him if he didn't think the stress on group action and group thought might cramp individual creativity. He didn't, and he didn't think the subject was worth discussing either.

The Swedish indifference to such questions does not mean they are not important, but it does indicate that the passion for efficient organizations through groups tends to override all other considerations. Moreover, one thing is clear: whatever the faults of the organizational systems, they are so firmly woven into Swedish life that it is difficult to see how the country could long survive without them.

VI

The Individual vs. the Organized Society

In a country where no sacrifice seems excessive for the sake of efficiency, where the precise organization of life is a national obsession, and where group action is the norm, there is a certain danger that the rights of the individual could be lost in the shuffle.

The danger would appear all the more real when, as in Sweden's case, there was a rich store of precedents for the brutal suppression of individual rights. In the narrow class-ridden society of the nineteenth century, censorship and other repressive measures were common. *Aftonbladet*, a notably outspoken newspaper founded early in the nineteenth century, was shut down no fewer than twenty-six times between 1830 and 1851 (the full consequences were averted through the clever strategem of reopening immediately as the *New Aftonbladet,* the *Newer Aftonbladet, Aftonbladet No. 4,* etc.). C. J. L. Almquist, one of Sweden's most talented nineteenth-century writers, was dismissed from his teaching post and became virtually unemployable after he published a mildly licentious book. As recently as 1921, Knut Wicksell, one of the country's most distinguished economic thinkers, was imprisoned for blasphemy. As described earlier, labor agitation was ruthlessly repressed, workers advocating strikes were jailed, and employees were virtually owned by their employers (not until 1920 was the employer's right to beat his workers abolished).

But as it turned out, it has been perfectly feasible to marshal the Swedes' great organizational powers to protect individual rights in more or less the same way that they have been applied to other parts of life.

Moreover, the Swedes have for many years had some traditions of independence, so that in spite of everything, they have acquired a certain taste for freedom. They have not ever been under a completely totalitarian rule, the monarchy always having been subject to control from other power groups. Feudalism in the true sense of the word has never existed in Sweden, and Sweden has never been occupied by a foreign power (the domination by Denmark from 1397 to 1523 is classified as a voluntary union, against which the Swedes rebelled when it became overly oppressive).

In addition, the Swedes have become accustomed to the possession of some seemingly minor, but jealously protected, freedoms. One of the most curious of these is the centuries-old *allemansrätten* (everyone's right), which gives the common man the right to swim, hike, camp, and pick wild berries and flowers anywhere in Sweden, regardless of who owns the real estate involved, so long as it is not a farm under cultivation or in the immediate vicinity of a residence. This tradition is still very much a solid reality to the nature-loving Swedes, despite occasional attempts by unsympathetic property owners to post no-trespassing signs (which have no legal significance).

As the modern Swedish system has developed, the traditional freedoms have been retained, polished up, and expanded, and new rights added—with the same efficient touch that is used in any other area—and overall, the legal position of the individual has been greatly strengthened.

Part of the explanation for some of the rigidities in Sweden, as well as for the attention paid to individual rights, lies in the

Swedes' passionate interest in and respect for rules. Birgitta Blom, an official in the Ministry of Justice, explained to me: "In Sweden, we adhere to the rules more than you do in the United States. I think it is part of the Swedish character. We have an expression, *rättshaveri*, meaning very strongly that you have your rights, that the rules must be followed. It may be that the rule is not so very good in a particular instance, but we want the rules to be followed."

The insistence on one's rights sometimes extends to rather trivial levels. For example, if it is raining (as it often is in Sweden), a passing car might splash you. If so, you have recourse. Mrs. Blom explained: "You take the license number down and go to the police station and tell them that fool splashed your suit. If a court finds that he hasn't taken the precaution he should have, he must pay for the damage"—which in this case means having your suit cleaned. Other matters of small apparent importance can also be pursued in the courts. Mrs. Blom said, "In a civil case you can bring suit with no limit to the amount of money it concerns. This is based on the idea that for a poor man 20 kronor [about $4] can be a lot of money. Of course, if he loses, he runs the risk of having to pay the other side's expenses. But he can get financial help from the state to run his case."

Jan Freese, an official in the Stockholm Courthouse, told me about this assistance. The free trials, in which court costs (which the loser of a case usually must pay) are waived, date back to 1919. "It's something like social welfare," he explained. "Anyone with a low income should have the right to go to court even if he has no money." The eligibility ceiling on the plaintiff's income is usually about 12,000 kronor ($2,400), but it can be higher if it is a very complicated and expensive matter. A recent proposal has recommended that the income limit be raised to about 20,000 kronor. "If a person who has a free trial gets a lot of money, later on it is possible the state will ask to get its money back. It seldom happens, but it's possible."

Karl-Erik Rosén, an official who is much occupied with this

sort of proceeding, told me about a typical case. It concerned Alice Sofia Broman, who was suing Sven Axelsson, a welder. "She says that last year Axelsson telephoned Mrs. Broman—he was going with her daughter at the time—and asked to borrow 400 kronor. She didn't have any money at the moment, but managed to borrow it, which she gave to her daughter, who gave it to Axelsson. Axelsson said it was true he had had an occasional date with the daughter, but that he had not borrowed any money from either the mother or the daughter. After hearing Mrs. Broman, as well as Axelsson and the daughter, the court approved the complaint and obliged Axelsson to pay immediately the 400 kronor, plus 6 percent annual interest from July 1 last year to September 28 this year." Mrs. Broman's lawyer got 450 kronor from the state, and Axelsson had to pay costs for the free proceedings, which, at 450 kronor, were slightly more than the judgment. It seemed to me that some of the cases are so trivial that if it weren't for the free trial, one would hardly bother to bring them to court. Rosén agreed: "It is said in Sweden that the only people who can go to court are the very rich and the very poor."

Another official told me: "When a person who has no money at all sues someone who has a little, or even where neither has any, the litigation never stops. They go on and on because it doesn't cost anything."

Not every obscure individual with difficulties needs to go to court, but he can get whatever attention he requires at the Stockholm Legal Assistance Bureau (*Stockholms Stads Rättshjälpsanstalt*).

This unusual establishment was organized in 1921 and is managed by a gentleman named Bror Wahlström, who has been connected with it since 1933. "We are exactly like a private lawyers' bureau," he said. "People come and ask for assistance; they get a lawyer assigned to them, and he follows the case to the bitter end—to the highest court if necessary. Except that here it doesn't cost anything. There are sixteen such institutions in Sweden. A person who lives where there is none available can go to a private lawyer, and that lawyer will be paid by the community." There is an income ceiling for those who are helped: about $3,000 for a single person and slightly higher for a married man. But a married woman can come regardless of her husband's income. "We sometimes tell a man who makes too much money to send his wife; then it won't cost anything." The bureau gets more than 15,000 cases a year, some of which are merely a simple question; about 4,000 become court cases. Some of the people who get free help from the bureau also get free trials. In those cases, the lawyer's fee that is paid by the state to the plaintiff, if any, goes into the bureau's general funds. The rest of the bureau's income comes from the state and the city of Stockholm. "We even have trials against the city of Stockholm," said Wahlström, "even though they pay our salaries. We are completely independent."

About half the cases involve some aspect of family law: divorces, paternity cases, and the like. But some can be quite dramatic. Wahlström related one such: "There was a man living with his lady friend, but after twenty years he had a child with another woman. So he bought a house for the first one to live in and moved the second one, along with their daughter, into his own home. But the first one was his only love—they saw each other every day—even though his child was by the second one. When he died, a sealed envelope with his will inside was found under his mattress. It divided his estate between his first love and his daughter—and nothing for the daughter's mother. But in that will someone had crossed out the name of his first lady friend. He had left a copy with his lawyer, and in that one nothing was crossed out. The mother of his daughter said she didn't know anything about it. The lower court said that what was crossed out should stay crossed out—that is, the whole estate should go to the daughter. The appeals court said the same. At that point his first love came here. We sent the envelope in which the revised will had been found to a chemical laboratory, and they found that the saliva was not that of the deceased; it couldn't have been. Could have been that of his second girl friend, but it wasn't certain. We went to the

Supreme Court; it reversed the lower court and gave the man's first—and only true love—her half of the estate."

The bureau attracts a fair number of eccentrics. "One man came in," Wahlström said, "and wanted us to write to Queen Elizabeth. He said she owed him 5,000 kronor. But we had to listen to him. No matter how crazy they seem, there could be a grain of truth somewhere."

The clientele is, in fact, endlessly variegated: "Anyone who lives in Stockholm has the right to come here. Lots of foreigners come—in the summer lots of tourists. We send them to the embassies, but the embassies often send them back. There are so many people we are not really obliged to help, but there is no one else to help them, so we do anyway."

The careful respect shown for the individual's rights is well illustrated by practices in criminal proceedings. Ragnar Gottfarb, a criminal lawyer, told me: "As a rule, the position of the individual is very weak here; it's very difficult for the individual to make his voice heard. But in the courts, he is in a very strong position." As a jocular aide in the Stockholm Courthouse remarked, "Sweden is a wonderful country in which to commit crimes."

When a person suspected of a crime is taken into custody, an application for an order of detention must be submitted to the court by the following day (under especially unusual circumstances this may be extended to five days), and a hearing must be held within four days. It is odd that in a country where most things are done with agonizing slowness—where you cannot even get a suit cleaned in a reasonable time—a person suspected of a crime is usually brought to trial within a week of his arrest. In cases where more time is needed for investigation, an extension of the holding period may be granted, but only under exceptional circumstances and after application to the court.

The suspect is also supplied with a public defender, whether he wants one or not. Ragnar Gottfarb explained: "The law says that as soon as a man is arrested, they must tell him he is suspected of a particular crime, that he is entitled to get a lawyer at once, and that he is not required to answer any questions without a lawyer." The suspect can specify any lawyer in Sweden he wants, and an effort is made to comply with his wishes. Gottfarb, one of Sweden's best-known lawyers, explained: "When a suspect says, 'I want Mr. Gottfarb,' the court calls me and asks if I want to defend him. My principle is to ask only when the trial is going to be. I never ask—and neither do my colleagues—what the man is suspected of. We feel everybody should have a good defense. If I can't make it, the prisoner has a choice of waiting or choosing another lawyer." One official told me: "Those suspects who come back every year— we call them subscribers—have their own favorite lawyer, whom they always use."

Trials are conducted before a judge, plus seven to nine lay assessors—that is, ordinary citizens who have no connection with the legal profession and who serve about twenty times a year for six years. The judge's decision alone carries, unless all the assessors (or at least seven if there are more than seven) disagree. The accused does not, indeed cannot, testify under oath, although he is permitted to make a statement regarding the case if he wishes.

Swedish trials tend to be quiet affairs. Folke Schmidt and Stig Strömholm, in their *Legal Values in Modern Sweden,* state:

> High-flown eloquence and appeals to sentiment are almost completely unknown in Swedish courts ... the absence of jurors (who might conceivably influence the demeanor and tactics of counsel), the absence of special rules as to what material may be produced as evidence, the lack of outward pomp, and possibly —if such an explanation may be ventured—the somewhat phlegmatic temperament of Swedes in general tend to make trials, even in very serious cases, rather undramatic.

Further, the prosecutor is obliged to help ascertain the truth, not merely to obtain the conviction. He is required to produce any information that might favor the accused. Gottfarb said: "The prosecutor is very objective. He is supposed to be something of a judge. The prosecutor doesn't want me to go around saying he is not objective, so he is anxious to be objective."

The trend has been toward more protection for the accused, and many of the features of the present system were devised in a Code of Procedure adopted in 1948, which drastically altered the previous almost exclusive reliance on written material. Now the case is decided on the basis of whatever transpires during the final court hearing, and if no written material is referred to, it is not considered. This tends to help the people who are accused of crimes, who often are unable to cope with the complexities of legal writings.

If the accused is convicted, he is considerably better off in Sweden than in most countries. Sentences tend, by American standards, to be light (most sentences for theft are four to twelve months, for manslaughter six to ten years), and most sentences are reduced by a third (some by a half) through parole. There is no capital punishment, and "life" imprisonment (extremely rare) usually works out to not more than twelve years. If a fine is levied, it is always in the form of a day-fine, a certain multiple of a figure based on the income of the accused (in practice, about a third of his daily income). Thus, twenty day-fines would be one thing for a rich man, quite another for a poor man. If the sentence is imprisonment, the prisoner has the comfort of knowing that Swedish prisons are world-famous, the explicit aim being to reform, not to punish or take vengeance. Numerous "open" prisons exist, and as this is being written, the prison administrators are experimenting with allowing some prisoners to receive overnight visits from their wives and sweethearts and to permit others to have their entire families live with them in the prison.

No doubt the most famous Swedish innovation in civil liberties is the *justitieombudsmannen,* who protects the average man from public officials ("the citizen's attorney against the bureaucracy," as one expert said) and who has become known in English-speaking countries simply as the ombudsman.

Actually, "ombudsman" is a common Swedish word, as the

present *justitieombudsmannen* (JO), Alfred Bexelius, explained to me: "It means a representative—one who speaks for another. If you cannot attend a meeting, you send an *ombud*. So the JO is the representative for parliament or, one can say, for the whole Swedish people."

The office of the JO was included when the present constitution was written in 1809. At the time it was chiefly a means for a suspicious parliament to keep an eye on the government. The JO is still appointed by parliament (for a term of four years at a time), but there is at present no conflict between this office and other branches of the government.

Technically, the JO does not have great influence. As Bexelius said: "The powers given to the ombudsman are not impressive. He cannot change a decision already delivered by a court or administrative agency." Although he has complete freedom to investigate, suggest, recommend, and persuade, he cannot personally change anything. And the limited power he does have is hardly ever used. Originally it was intended that he should recommend prosecution of officials who acted wrongly, but today he does this in only half a dozen cases a year.

But like other institutions in Sweden depending on reason and voluntary cooperation, this one works quite well. Bexelius said: "You see, people don't want to be criticized, so the criticism is just as effective as prosecution." Pointing to the 700-page annual report detailing all the officials who have been found at fault during the year, he said: "No official wants to have his name in this book."

Any citizen is free to examine the background of official actions if he wants to determine whether a decision is or is not proper, because all official documents are public unless they bear on a person's private life, with extremely few exceptions. But even so, as Bexelius pointed out, "the average citizen is hardly qualified to judge whether or not a particular ruling is legal."

Bexelius told me of a case where this right to examine documents itself was at issue: "Last month I decided a case where a high government official had denied a newspaperman the right to examine some documents. He was angry at the news-paperman, but the newspaperman wrote to me about what had happened. After I investigated the case, I wrote to the official and told him he had committed a punishable fault. But I am allowed to omit prosecution. In this case I believed he would never do this again, so I merely explained to him how important it was to let the newspaperman see the documents. Then last week a newspaper association complained that the ombudsman had been too kind. Well, everybody has the right to express himself."

Even where there is no clear-cut fault in evidence, the JO sometime brings up an issue anyway. Bexelius related: "In one case a court had ordered an arrested person to pay the costs of his own return from the U.S.A. to Sweden for a trial. The party complained to the ombudsman on another aspect of the case, but in the review I discovered that the complainant had been wrongly made to pay his own transportation. Since the law was not clear in regard to transportation costs, the judge could not be held responsible for the error. But the ombudsman wrote to the government and requested that the man be reimbursed. This request was granted."

The ombudsman receives about 1,200 complaints a year, but many investigations—about 200 a year—are conducted on his own initiative, on the basis of newspaper reports or from data collected during his inspections of prisons, mental institutions, and other government facilities. "Last week, I inspected a home for alcoholics," he told me. "I took six members of my staff with me who helped me inspect documents. There were eighty-seven people confined there. When I explained that they could complain to the JO, about fifteen did. But I quickly understood there was no reason for complaint, except in two or three cases. These will be investigated. As long as there is any possibility of a fault, I investigate."

The ombudsman occasionally investigates administrative practices. Bexelius explained: "I'm just now working on the question of explaining administrative decisions. It's a very difficult question. The agencies themselves don't want a law on this point. For example, certain agencies have the right to recall drivers' licenses. But they should spell out their reasons so that if the license holders want to appeal to a higher authority, they will be able to do so. This question must be solved. I think it is undemocratic for the authorities to act as if they were gods."

Bexelius says that only about ten percent of the complaints received turn out to be justified, but he does not regard the other investigations as wasted. For one thing, everyone must have the right to have his complaints looked into if the system is to have any value. Furthermore, the JO's worth cannot be measured with statistics, since one of the very important aspects of the office is the widespread knowledge among civil servants that any misstep may result in their inclusion in the JO's annual report.

In recent years the ombudsman has received increasing amounts of attention throughout the world, partly through the result of the considerable amount of publicity that followed Denmark's adoption of the system in 1955. Ombudsman systems have also been set up in Norway and New Zealand, and as this is being written, Great Britain and Nassau County, New York, are establishing similar offices. Bexelius himself has obligingly helped spread the word and has traveled to the United States to explain his work to eager and fascinated audiences. "I never dreamed anybody could be so interested in anything," he remarked to me.

Bexelius has no reluctance to criticize high officials if the need arises. In mid-1966 he admonished Dr. Arthur Engel, the head of the National Medical Board, for acting as a consultant to a private insurance company without the government's permission, although there was no hint of wrongdoing. He also often defends obscure and powerless minorities, as in this case he told me about: "This was a case concerning the Lapps who drive their reindeer from one place to another. They have done this through many years, and nobody has ever wanted this land for any other purpose. But now they are beginning to use it for mines, airports, and highways, and the Lapps have to make detours on their journeys with their herds of reindeer.

So some of the Lapps wrote to me and objected that the authorities had taken their land without asking them. When I studied the question, I found that the Lapps were indeed not consulted in advance and that, furthermore, the government's compensation for the land is not paid directly to them but into a fund here in Stockholm, which is used for their benefit. So I wrote the government and told them that as long as we are so concerned about the way other countries handle their minorities, we must make sure our own minorities are protected. The government appointed a commission to work out a new law. We have only about two thousand such Lapps who are living from their reindeer, so it is perhaps not so important. But it is an important principle that they must have the same rights as other citizens. The Lapps were very grateful; they even came down to Stockholm to thank me personally."

The JO's office gave birth to an offshoot in 1915—the *militie-ombudsmannen*, the military ombudsman (MO). He handles the same types of cases as the JO, except that he deals exclusively with the military service.

Hugo Henkow, the present MO, explained to me: "We don't get too many complaints now—eighty or ninety a year or so. We have about seven hundred cases in all, and the others I take up on my own initiative. I spend about thirty or forty days a year on inspection tours, and over a five-year period I cover all military units in Sweden. About half the complaints are from conscripts—circumstances of service, length, leave, and so forth. Sometimes they complain about the officers: they have been drunk or have assaulted or insulted the conscript. Many complaints are from civilians, whose property has been damaged during maneuvers, for example."

Like the JO, the MO has the power to recommend prosecution but, also like the JO, usually doesn't use it. "I prosecute in only about ten cases a year," said Henkow. "In the others, I merely issue a comment if any fault is found. But often I find nothing is wrong."

A great deal of the MO's efforts are devoted to protecting

the conscript against injustice. Henkow related a typical case: "A conscript had been sentenced to ten days' confinement because he had been drunk. But we found that he had not been drunk. He had drunk ten centiliters of liquor [about two average-size drinks] plus a bottle of beer. The policeman who had picked him up while he was in town had not been questioned by the commander who sentenced the conscript. But I did, and the policeman said he had interfered with the conscript because he was following some girls, but was not drunk. I prosecuted the commander, as well as his legal adviser, and they both were fined."

Is there a danger that the MO's office interferes with military discipline? Henkow said: "Earlier, officers believed it was good for the soldiers to have a hard life, but nowadays they don't think that way. They understand that a soldier has his civil rights—that he is in uniform only for a short time and that military matters can be dealt with in much the same way as civil matters." Sometime ago it was proposed that the MO's office be changed, a suggestion that met with stern resistance from the MO, as well as from the military establishment itself. Henkow said: "The commander in chief of the Army said he felt the office should not be altered; he felt that this office had done much to build confidence between officers and conscripts and the public."

Actually, both the ombudsman institutions grew out of an even earlier, but lesser known, office—that of the *justitiekansler,* the chancellor of justice, commonly known in Sweden as the JK. Founded in 1713, this office has a number of duties connected with its status as the legal representative of the crown, and one of these is to keep an eye on civil servants. Thus, the government is in a sense watching itself, and it was primarily distrust of this system that motivated parliament to agitate for its own watchdog, the JO, about 100 years later.

Sven Rudholm, the present JK, explained his position to me: "I work in very much the same way as the JO. But if the JO has eleven to twelve hundred cases a year, I have three to four hundred. If I receive a complaint against a civil servant and it turns out to be justified, I point out to him that this is not proper behavior. If he disagrees with me, then we can go to court. But if he admits his error, we usually do not prosecute. We can also prosecute the administration of the courts, if, for example, a judge bullies his witnesses, or doesn't hold hearings within four days after a man is taken into custody, or doesn't pronounce sentence within a short time after the trial is over."

Really sensational corruption is virtually unknown in Sweden, but milder forms of official wrongdoing occasionally occur, and some of these come to the JK. Rudholm said: "I instituted a prosecution of a chief of an administrative board which was constructing some buildings on an experimental farm. This man owned some timberlands, and he sold some timber to the state. There is a requirement that different suppliers must be asked to bid on such purchases. He didn't do this; he just asked himself. He said he charged the standard price, but he's not allowed to do it anyway, so he's being prosecuted."

Doesn't the JK's work interfere with that of the JO? "There could be a clash," said Rudholm. "The same man can complain to the ombudsman and to me. But we try not to make double work. When I read something in the newspaper that should possibly be investigated, I ask the ombudsman first, so that we don't take up the same case. A man who isn't satisfied with the JO's decision can come to me; I'm not bound by his decision. I have had a few cases where I simply wrote to the complainant, 'I note that you have been to the JO, who rejected your complaint, and I quite agree with him.' "

Like the JO, the JK is much concerned with the rights of unimportant individuals. "We had a case about a year ago: a girl who was fifteen or sixteen years old doing housework in a family was suddenly fired. She went to the social bureau for help in finding another job. A social worker talked to the girl, gave her lunch money, and told her to come back later. Then he called a hospital to arrange to see if the girl was pregnant and also to check on her mental state." When she came back that afternoon, two civil servants were waiting to haul her off to the hospital, where she was kept for two days. The doctors found her all right, and her parents came to pick her up. The civil servant was prosecuted, convicted, and fined. Said Rudholm: "He just wanted to help the girl. But he was a little too helpful. I sent information about the case to the Central Social Welfare Board and suggested that it should be sent out to local boards in all parts of Sweden. I didn't want this to happen again."

Another of the JK's duties is to administer Sweden's Freedom of the Press Act. Sweden's first press-freedom law was passed in 1766—said to be the world's first—but actual freedom has often fallen short of the ideal. During the early stages of World War II individual issues of anti-German newspapers were occasionally seized, and dissatisfaction with such action was the main force behind a strengthening of the act after the war. At present no censorship prior to publication except that relating to the very few public documents classified as secret is permitted. Otherwise, those responsible for printing material that is treasonable, libelous, or indecent or that promotes racial prejudice can be prosecuted and all copies of the offending literature seized—but only after publication.

Rudholm is in charge of all this: "If a suspected crime in the freedom of the press area occurs, I can prosecute." Generally, he acts on the recommendation of the Minister of Justice.

The manner in which the press law has been applied in the field of pornography is an excellent example of how the Swedes' practical and sensible approach has been applied to a question of freedom. A few years ago an enterprising publisher named Bengt Forsberg had the decidedly unoriginal notion of publishing a series of pornographic books. But his series had a couple of unusual twists: he got some of Sweden's top literary artists to contribute under their own names, and he frankly labeled his books as pornography. Hiring an unconventional novelist, poet, and translator named Bengt Anderberg (who once achieved a modest fame by donating the proceeds of a literary prize established by the royal family to a group devoted to the abolition of monarchy) to edit the series, Forsberg brought out the first two volumes, entitled *Kärlek 1* and *Kärlek 2* (Love 1 and Love 2) in early 1965 at the rather fat price (for slim paperback books) of $3 each. The first edition sold out within minutes of publication, and demand was so heavy that for some time copies were nearly unobtainable. In the first two years they sold some 150,000 copies each, and were followed by further volumes up to, at this writing, *Kärlek 8.* Although they were well written, entertaining, and frequently funny, their scabrous quality is not to be denied—not convincingly anyway.

Since this breakthrough, which the authorities made no effort to prevent, a large vogue for pornography has developed. Certain newsstands are clogged with salacious books and magazines, and specialized pornography shops have been established to purvey the titillating literature. Rudholm is not especially disturbed by this sequence of events. "Actually, there has been a steady trend in this direction for about the past ten years or so," he remarked to me. "The people involved in *Kärlek 1* said pornography is good for some people. Anyway, the Minister of Justice decided not to prosecute, and I agreed with him. I do not believe that ordinary good pornography is harmful, and I have never heard any responsible medical opinion that it is. Of course, it is hard to say what is ordinary and what is good. But in general, we have better uses for our courts and our police."

In mid-1967, sometime after I had spoken to Rudholm, during which time the pornography became even more daring and pornography shops even more ubiquitous, a number of publishers were prosecuted for their salacious material. I therefore talked to Carl Libdom, an official in the Ministry of Justice, who is concerned with, among other things, examining pornographic literature to see if it oversteps the permissible limits. (Technically, copies of all periodicals published in Sweden are supposed to be submitted for examination after publication, though in practice most are not; this requires the authorities to make the rounds of pornography stores to see what is being sneaked onto the racks.)

Libdom said about fifteen publishers had been prosecuted, only one for fiction (a brutally sadistic novel), the rest for magazines specializing in pictorial features on sadistic sports or other imaginative entertainments involving several unclad participants of mixed sexes. Had the official attitude taken a more restrictive turn? Libdom said no: "I can assure you there has been no fundamental change in policy; we have the same liberal laws as always. But the pornography industry has changed quite a lot, and the publications have become more and more obscene. The Minister of Justice can interpret the laws very liberally; but he must act in accordance with existing legislation, and when the publishers themselves are becoming so bold, there comes a point at which he must interfere." Libdom said that if the legislation should be revised along the lines of current thinking, much or all of the literature against which the authorities had acted would become legal. "We think that in the future legislation should be directed only to the advertising and methods of display. As it is now, it is openly shown in the shopwindows and on posters, and it is difficult to avoid. We have no means of interfering with the advertising methods. If people want to read obscene literature, they should have the right to do so (it is not the place of the state to tell an adult what he must or must not read), but people who are offended by it should not have to encounter it on the streets." He explained that a committee was studying various aspects of this question and would eventually recommend new legislation. Some press reports, followed a widespread tendency to blame most unpleasant events on the United States, had attributed the pornography crackdown on pressure from American postal authorities; was that true? Libdom said: "Naturally, we are embarrassed that so much pornography is exported; it's not good propaganda for our country. But we have no intention of changing our freedom of the press laws to satisfy the customs of others. There are two international conventions directed against the circulation of pornography, but Sweden has not ratified either of them, and does not intend to." What about the possibility that pornography could lead to crime? "I can say we know absolutely nothing about it, and if you don't know with certainty that pornography is harmful, you can't very well act on the basis that it is. You might have a feeling that it incites crime, but someone else might have the opposite feeling."

The pornography boom is the most sensational manifestation of press freedom in Sweden, but the same freedom exists in other spheres. Sven Grönhagen is another official in the Ministry of Justice, whose job includes the examination of potentially inflammatory political writings. "What I read is mostly extreme papers—extreme right-wing or extreme left-wing," he told me. As in the pornography department, the practice is to interpret the laws as liberally as possible and to interfere only in particularly outrageous instances. The last prosecution occurred many years ago against a notorious anti-Semite. "He was prosecuted three or four times, I believe," Grönhagen said. "The last time he was sent to prison for two months. There was some protest because he was so old, but according to the law, we had to do something." Grönhagen was in favor of letting things pass, when in doubt: "People must have the right to express their opinions. They shouldn't hesitate to say what they think through fear of being prosecuted. You know, nothing is scrutinized here before it's printed. Occasionally someone asks us to look at something before publication. We have to say we're sorry, but we can't."

The Swedish welfare apparatus is frequently criticized for ignoring the individual. Alfred Bexelius, the JP, told me that he gets occasional complaints on the snobbishness and unfriendly demeanor of social workers, but that such complaints are hard to pin down. I have no doubt that many such complaints are well founded, especially considering the Swedish fondness for strict decorum and respectability. But so far as I personally have been able to investigate or to experience the system, I have found that usually as much attention is paid to the individual as could be expected and that those in charge often make great efforts to do more than is strictly required.

More important, when the effectiveness of programs depends on adapting them to the needs of the individual, they can be constructed in such a way as to satisfy that demand, showing that the Swedes can, when necessary, design a good deal of flexibility into their systems after all. A prefabricated house with so many numerous optional extras that it can meet any combination of individual preference is still basically a prefabricated house, and a bureaucratic system with numbers of choices built into it is still a bureaucratic system. But it can still be very satisfying to the customer.

An outstanding illustration is Sweden's active labor market policy, which is a form of social benefit, as well as an instrument of economic management. Its basic purpose is to promote labor mobility—to prod workers to move from areas where jobs are short to others where labor is short. Obviously, people cannot be imperiously shuffled about the country merely for the sake of efficiency. Persuading people to move is not easy, even when the economic benefits are clear-cut, and the Labor Market Board goes to lengths to increase the willingness of people to move where they will be most useful to the economy, as well as to themselves. Every year it provides tens of thousands of people with assistance in retraining, relocating, and job finding (private employment agencies are prohibited). And its success in this tricky enterprise depends in great measure on fitting its services to individual requirements.

Switching from a twenty-year career as a farmer in one part of the country to a job as a skilled lathe operator in another might seem an unusual feat for a man of small means, plus a wife and five children, but a forty-year-old Swede named Börje Vogel pulled it off, hardly shifting gears in the process. Discouraged with the increasingly difficult life of the small farmer in his area of central Sweden, he inquired about the help offered by the Labor Market Board. First, he was given a thorough two-day series of aptitude tests free, at a private testing organization. Because he suffered from a childhood back injury; he was sent to a Stockholm clinic, where he was given physical tests lasting a month. The clinic's services were free, and his transportation, board, and lodging, plus a small family allowance, were paid. On the basis of all this, several future occupations were suggested to him, and he picked that of metalworker. He was offered free training in this field and was given the opportunity to make a one-day inspection visit to a metalworking school in Västerås, about 200 miles north of his home, for which he received round-trip train fare and an expense allowance for himself and family of about $28. He approved of the school, and when he started the initial three-month course, he received $100 as "start help." He received a salary during this phase of about $1.15 an hour. After three months the Labor Market Board found him an apprentice job at ASEA, the electrical equipment manufacturer, also in Västerås, at which time his salary rose to about $1.55 an hour. He still continued school in the evenings, for which he was paid $1.15 an hour. After about eight months he became a regular lathe operator at a wage of about $2 an hour. Because he at first left his family behind, he received a family allowance of $115 a month for the first three months, $75 a month for the next three months, and $40 a month for the next three months. Once a month he was given a round-trip train ticket for a visit home. After about eight months he moved his family to Västerås; moving expenses of about $200, plus train fare for everybody, were paid. If Vogel had come from one of the especially depressed areas of the far north, he could have received an additional bonus of $400, and if he had owned a house in an area so depopulated there was no market for houses, the government might have, depending on circumstances, offered to buy it. As it was, the Vogel family received about $2,000 in cash outlays, plus considerable amounts of free medical, educational, and counseling services. But it wasn't only a question of spending money. If every element in the program had not been painstakingly tailored to fit Vogel's needs, he might very well have dropped it, as he was free to do at any time, or decided to move back home after it was all over, as he was also free to do, and the whole effort would have been wasted.

This may seem a lot of money and a lot of effort to expend on one relatively unimportant family, but the system is designed to provide massive doses of medicine specifically prescribed for this one individual. As a result, it is improbable that Vogel will ever again be a burden on the state. Not everybody, of course, needs as elaborate a set of measures as Vogel, but in order to make the program work, the authorities have to be ready with a wide selection of possibilities to fit every case. How does Vogel, who still misses his farm, feel about it? "Sometimes I regret the move," he said, "but when payday comes around, I feel pretty good. The state does quite a lot for the people in Sweden."

It can happen that facilities set up with the express intention of functioning within the organizations can, in some cases, adapt themselves to an individual's needs. One example is the Labor Court, which is chiefly supposed to handle disputes between unions and employers' organizations. Bengt Hult, chairman of the Labor Court, explained to me: "The usual rule is that an organization brings up the case. But an individual worker has the right to bring it himself if the organization refuses. We have to be sure the organization did refuse; we can telephone them and ask to make sure."

But it does happen. Johan Lind, secretary of the court, tells of one case: "There was a system where the employer was to deduct part of the workers' pay and send it to the union, which then paid it out to the workers at vacation time. But in this case the company didn't make the payment when it should have, and this particular worker didn't happen to have any money at the time and was unable to go on vacation. When he finally received the money, it was too late, so he sued for damages.

When the case came up, his very own union came to court and argued against him. But he was awarded 100 kronor, plus interest for late payment of his vacation money. It wasn't much. But he won his principle."

All this evidence of the attention paid to systematizing the individual's rights is indicative of a distinct awareness of the tendency to grind up the individual in all his organizations. This awareness is also occasionally shown in efforts by the organizations themselves to improve the position of the individual. The Employers' Confederation speaks of the increasing attention being given to this area: "It is a new trend, still at a questing, experimental stage, but it is there. Evidence of it crops up repeatedly to challenge the impression that the contribution of the single worker, the initiative of the individual employer, the personality of the private citizen have been quite lost sight of, if not submerged in, the Swedish system." Examples are greater stress on training foremen in the arts of human relations, as well as in technical matters, and the establishment of a Council on Personnel Administration by the Employers' Confederation to make psychological and sociological studies of work. The LO, Labor's Confederation, for its part, has sponsored a technical study of *Individen och den Industriella Miljön* (The Individual and the Industrial Environment), as part of its extensive survey of the effects of technical progress released in 1966. On the whole, these are small signs but are hopeful indications for the future.

There is no disputing that the Swede is still firmly enmeshed in his world of organizations and is constantly subject to various visible and invisible pressures to conform to the group. As a matter of fact, the group emphasis appears to enjoy wide support among the population as a whole, and it would not be proper to speak of large numbers of discontented individualists struggling to break out of the entanglements of the group. It is true, of course, that a particularly individualistic person might be excessively irritated by all the stress on group action and not be at all placated by the knowledge that his legal rights and basic freedoms will be protected under any circumstances and however obscure his station in life. But to the extent that official action and carefully designed systems can promote freedom and secure individual rights, the Swede is probably better off than anyone else in the world.

VII

The Initiative Question

Surely the most frequent charge leveled against the Swedish system is that it dulls the willingness to take risks and destroys initiative: the combination of comfortable security, full employment, high taxes, and emphasis on acting through organizations is said to make the individual ever more reluctant to chance an expression of personal ambition.

Not surprisingly, a great many Swedes reject these arguments with indignation. A typical comment is one by Ian Lagergren, an official in the Ministry of Social Welfare, on the question of too much security: "We believe this is utter rubbish. How anyone can seriously claim that the system can make you lazy is beyond me. On the contrary, it stimulates you, you don't have to worry about your family and other responsibilities."

If only because of the frequency with which the accusation is repeated, no book dealing with up-to-date Sweden can gracefully avoid the issue (despite its obvious vagueness), and I have accordingly made an effort to examine it. I am inclined to think my conclusions, which will be unveiled shortly, are as soundly based as could be expected, but I cannot claim to have discovered any final truths on the subject.

There is a distinct dearth of solid, measurable evidence that initiative is on the decline. To the extent that such a thing might be measured by statistics, the trend is quite the contrary. When the new pension program was launched in 1960, a financing fund was set up to receive the premiums, not for actuarial reasons (the pension system is not organized on actuarial lines), but because it was assumed private savings would drop with the increase in security that the new pensions promised, and some sort of capital formation was felt to be necessary. As far as can be deduced from available statistics on the rate of saving (which, as is the case with similar statistics in the United States, are not entirely satisfactory), this has not happened. People appear to want to save as much now as they did before. Moreover, insurance in force has continued to rise steadily.

Too, many people have been impelled to work harder despite the cushy security and other discouraging influences. The proportion of married women holding jobs has risen from 19 percent in 1950 to about 30 percent currently and is still rising, despite substantial tax disadvantages connected with double bread-winners in the same family. (Unlike the United States, where married couples can combine incomes and be taxed on a lower basis than two independent single persons, Sweden requires married couples to combine incomes and to be taxed on a higher basis—a drawback that remains after a slight, but very slight, modification of the rules in 1965.) The high taxes seem in some cases to spur people to work harder; a high percentage of workers in Sweden holds second jobs. Until 1967 almost all retail establishments in Stockholm were required to shut down at 6 P.M. most days, but special 10 P.M. privileges were granted to a small number of downtown stores. An executive of a company that operates one of these stores told me that the flood of applicants for after-hours jobs was so great that no advertising for evening workers had ever been necessary.

If a passion for education can be said to reflect initiative, then it has been increasing at a dizzying pace. The number of students in universities and other advanced institutions just about tripled in the 1956–66 decade, and it is expected at least to double in the following decade. This thirst for knowledge is, in fact, so widespread as to be almost a mania. Alan Trei, an American advertising man attached to the Stockholm affiliate of his agency, who took a generally dim view of the Swedish worker's ambition when I spoke to him, nevertheless said: "I've never met any group of people so intent on improving themselves. Even experienced account executives take night courses. We have started evening seminars ourselves; there's no compulsion to come, but surprisingly many do. If you tried to do that in the States, I don't think anybody would show up. The very existence of the Sales and Advertising Club here is something not known in the U.S.: it offers lectures, courses, talks, and so forth —there's very little social activity." Sometimes this thirst for education is carried to absurd lengths. Yves de St.-Agnès (in a somewhat eccentric but fascinating study called *Les Suèdois*) tells of an Italian university student, vagabonding through Sweden, who worked for a time as a dishwasher in a restaurant and who one day remarked to a female fellow worker that he was a student. "Oh, so am I," she said. "I'm studying to be an assistant cashier in a restaurant." The point is that in line with the stress on systematizing life to the extent possible, Swedes do not generally attempt tasks they have not been specifically trained for and quite naturally regard formal education as the proper preparation for any activity. An American friend of mine living in Stockholm who happens to be exceptionally friendly was once working among some Swedes, and one awed girl finally summoned up the courage to ask if it was customary for Americans to take formal courses in methods of conversation.

If the Swede evinces in many respects an admirable perseverance and steadiness of purpose, he does not make a big fuss about it. The Swedes have long shown a reserve, bordering on listlessness, which may reflect, or may be mistaken for, a lack of initiative, and which complicates any attempt to study the effects of the events of the past few decades. Edward Daniel Clarke, an English traveler in Sweden in 1799, commented: "In their disposition, the Swedes are naturally mild and obliging: being rarely provoked to anger, or passionate when disputing with each other." Joseph Marshall, also a British tourist of the eighteenth century, opined that the Swedes were possessed of many fine qualities, without, however, being "a noisy bustling people that are one moment in grief and the next laughing; they have not so much vivacity as the French. . . ." J. T. James, who followed in 1813, noted that the Swedes were, on the whole, "of a tranquil, modest demeanor," and complained of the "humility" of the Swedish soldiers who customarily "entered a liquor-shop . . . with their caps off, and their money in their hands, bowing in a mute and quiet manner, totally unbecoming the mien and character of a man of arms."

The Swede of today is still a tranquil soul and most often chooses not to speak up if there is an option of remaining silent. If you telephone someone at his job and he happens to be out, the telephone operator is likely to reply that he doesn't answer. If you want to know when or if he will come back, you must formulate a special question to this effect. If you want to talk to whoever takes care of the absentee's responsibilities when he is out, you will have to make a special request along this line, too. The operator, who quite properly regards herself as a telephone operator and not as an information bureau, will not volunteer any information, since that is out of her department. At a department store combination shoe-repair and key-making (while-you-wait) facility, you might wait patiently while the man at the counter replaces a heel for the lady ahead of you, so that you can get a duplicate made of the key you are ostentatiously clutching in full view of the repairman, but if it turns out—as it will—that he is only the shoeman and that the keyman is off duty that day, do not expect him to inform you of the fact unless you specifically ask him. To the Swede, who is accustomed to being enmeshed and isolated in his own special system, this is a perfectly natural way to behave.

The calmness of the Swedes is excruciatingly noticeable to

anyone who associates with them for any length of time, and American students in Sweden often remark on what is to them this irritating characteristic among their native colleagues. A Swedish report on a group of fifty U.S. college students, who were brought together for a meeting just before their return home, said they had found the natives to be "dull and a little stiff." The report said: "After their nine months' stay ... they especially missed, in Scandinavian youth, American initiative, eagerness to discuss things, and more independent opinions." An Englishman named Terence Howard, who studied at Uppsala in the early postwar period, wrote: "The students here, too conscious of being serious specialists, are willing but rarely to commit themselves outside their own special fields or to indulge in the rich irrelevancies of a general discussion." One American student complained to me: "They are great here on facts. They are fanatic about facts. But once they have them, they don't seem to be able to do anything with them; they're not so interested in making judgments." A Swedish professor who had taught in America gave me the reverse of this coin: "Intellectual curiosity is higher among American students in that they want to learn about many things—but not too many facts. They are much more willing to discuss things they know nothing about."

In Swedish schools it is not customary to ask questions. A young Swedish woman told me that when she attended elementary school in the mid-1950's, one of the pupils was a boy of Swedish parentage who had lived with his family in the United States and who had gone to school there. He asked incessant questions, a habit that did not make him at all popular with his schoolmates. "Everyone thought he was crazy," she said. A university professor with U.S. teaching experience remarked: "There is a definite reluctance to ask questions in class here; we are trained not to ask questions. The difference struck me very much in the U.S. It's the same at a professional meeting. In the U.S. the chairman always invites questions and always gets them. In Sweden, if you are clever, you will telephone a friend in advance and ask him to bring up a question after you have finished your talk." A similar phenomenon can be seen at

press conferences in Sweden. In some cases those who are scheduling press conferences make a special effort to coax foreign
journalists to attend, since, unlike the Swedish reporters, they
can invariably be depended on to make nuisances of themselves
to a satisfactory degree. This lack of curiosity, or unwillingness
to express it, is no doubt a contributing factor in the poor quality of the Swedish press.

In some ways, therefore, the vigorous exercise of individual
initiative has long been foreign to the Swede's basic nature. And
this fact is reflected at many points in the Sweden of today. A
case in point is the heavy emphasis on the group. Oloph Hansson, a labor relations expert with Swedish Radio, told me about
an industrial study he had taken part in: "Many workers said
they had been asked to take better jobs as foremen, but they
had refused, because, 'If we take those jobs, we can't go back to
our comrades.' If you take that step, you are out of the group;
belonging to the group is very important." There is a strong
and rarely resisted pressure on workers to join the union
(though there are no closed shops). Along the same line, a piece-
rate worker who produces more than is considered to be an acceptable average will be politely informed by his colleagues that
such behavior is frowned upon—advice that is usually accepted.
    Gunnar Heckscher, the expert on Swedish organization life,
has written: "It is not surprising that Swedish society is far from
competitive in character. The individual is more inclined to
better himself by improving the position of the group to which
he belongs than by moving into another."
    The sentiment for the group is accompanied by a strong and
widespread egalitarian sentiment, presumably deriving from the
spread-the-wealth Socialism of the Social Democrats, and one
result has been a stigma for the person who stands out. As Paul
Britten Austin, an English journalist, has written: "If there is
one thing more dangerous, in Sweden, than to fail, it is to succeed." Erik Lundberg, the noted Swedish economist, remarked
to me: "The American view is that a rich man is a good man.
Here a rich man is a man who has been stealing." A Swedish

lady I met who had lived in San Francisco said to me: "In America, if you take a trip to Tahiti or some such place, people will say, 'How nice!' or something like that. Here they would only say, '*H-m-mp*,'" meaning, she explained, that you must be a tax cheat or other form of disgraceful character.

A great part of the population thus seems involved in a mass drive toward a gray middle-class status, where differences are small and where the famous Swedish reserve or, as they say, *stelhet* (meaning stiffness, but including the idea of a particularly obnoxious stuffed-shirt smugness and unimaginativeness), is particularly strong. One sometimes gets the impression that the Swede's idea of the perfect Swede includes a large element of the kind of stodgy, unambitious respectability that is often identified with the civil service. Sune Carlson, a professor of business administration at Uppsala (who would doubtless disagree with my overall characterization of the middle class), explained a traditional Swedish attitude to me: "The best people went into civil service because of its high standing. It's changed somewhat, but it is still quite high. Sons of working-class parents who get an education still want to go into the civil service."

In other words, the prestigious position remains one where great amounts of initiative are not necessary. But if a large number of people are striving to reach this level, not so many are eager to push beyond it. The idea of egalitarianism should presumably include equality of opportunity, as well as equality of status, but there is not yet much indication that those on the bottom of the heap are climbing to the top. In 1959, Rune Höglund, a vice-president (now president) of Svenska Handelsbanken, spoke of the changes that would occur in the ranks of top executives, traditionally drawn from the upper classes, as educational opportunities became more widespread: "It is rapidly changing. . . . In ten years, you will find an entirely different picture." As this is being written, the ten years are not yet up, but the development so far seems to be quite the contrary. A survey of backgrounds of company presidents in mid-1966 showed that more of the newer top executives (those under fifty-six years of age) came from the upper classes than the older ones (70 percent against 52 percent), and fewer came from lower-class backgrounds (zero against 20 percent).

The apparent tendency of Swedish workers to strive industriously to reach a certain moderate level, but not to care particularly to go beyond it, has been invariably confirmed in my talks with foreign executives in Sweden, who maintain that the ordinary Swedish worker is not possessed with any burning, aggressive ambition. (It must be pointed out in this connection that Swedish employees are rarely fired. This practice, which arises in part from an employer's reluctance to be known in labor-short Sweden as unjust or overly demanding, is not a formal part of the welfare system but is nevertheless a real and very strong element in the overall feeling of security.) Alan Trei, the advertising man, said: "People on the lower echelons look on themselves as functionaries. They have found a niche where they are comfortable and protected. It never crosses their minds that they might be president of the agency one day." Trei excepted from his criticism higher-level employees, who he said are satisfactorily ambitious, a fact he attributed to the emotional rewards of the advertising business. But he said: "Americans in other businesses feel Swedes do what they need to get by and not much else." Another American executive, who had been working in the U.S. subsidiary of a Swedish company and had been transferred to Sweden for several years to introduce American efficiency methods, confessed: "I have not become enchanted with the Swedes. The problem of finding suitable candidates for promotion is exceptionally aggravating. And they don't want to promote aggressive people. There's too much question of 'Will he rock the boat?' If so, out with him. In the U.S., they very often don't want you to rock the boat too much, but here not at all. It's exceptionally difficult to arouse any enthusiasm about the progress of the company; this is true not only of low-level people, but also of department heads." On the other hand, many American executives admire the Swedes' industriousness and the seriousness with which they take their work. One head of a small Swedish subsidiary of a large U.S.

company said of his employees: "They work hard, and we have many people who take work home." But he added: "I think the factor of initiative is hurt by the welfare state. People are not subject to the risk of insecurity. That little extra burst of enthusiasm is lacking."

An energetic Dane named Erik Bil-Nielsen, who manages the Swedish subsidiary of a Pittsburgh management consulting firm and who claims to know personally the presidents of 200 Swedish corporations, told me that, in his opinion, the *present* Swedish executive is no more lacking in aggressiveness than anyone else: "If you take the good executive of this country and the good executive in America, they are very much alike in making decisions and in taking action—same ambition, same drive, same ability. I don't think the tax situation bothers the Swedish executive. The fact that his income is taxed at 80 percent does not affect him—favorably or unfavorably. I think the welfare state has influenced him in a positive way; it has relieved him of pressure. I worked in Chicago for a time; every executive was haunted by insecurity. Incredible the pressure they were under!" Bil-Nielsen is, however, less optimistic for the future of those now growing up under the system: "Among the youth, it is killing initiative. There's a tendency to go from risk takers to caretakers." As far as the lower employees are concerned, he agreed with other observers: "The Swedish salaried employee is very rights-conscious. If he contracts to work from eight to five, he works precisely from eight to five—much more so here than in the States."

One place that a drop in initiative would be expected to have an impact is in entrepreneurial activity—the willingness to launch small businesses. Sentiment for small business has always been stronger in the United States than it has in Sweden, which, like most of the rest of Europe, has been more hampered by the force of tradition, a rigid social order, and powerful cartels. I believe it is still unquestionable that the establishment of an independent business by a small entrepreneur occurs a good deal less often in Sweden than in the United States and that when it does occur, the success is much more modest.

Furthermore, small business appears to be on the decline. Erik Dahmén, an economist who has studied the question, said that the total number of manufacturing companies shrank by 10 percent from the mid-fifties to 1962 and that "the entire drop, which presumably has continued since, was concentrated in the group with fewer than twenty employees."

It is one thing to notice the weak position of small business and quite another to pin it with any confidence on a decline in initiative. Hans Grundström, head of the Swedish Crafts and Small Industry Organization (*Sveriges Hantverks- och Industri Organisation*), a grouping of 35,000 small companies, pointed out to me: "The general increase in wealth and the development of business has given job opportunities to people who twenty years ago might have started their own businesses. On the whole, they are now more free to choose the field they want to work in. Another barrier is that a firm must be larger today than before to be profitable. A long time ago a man could start with one helper, but now the business must be on a certain scale, with expensive equipment, in order to survive. It requires more capital now than it once did."

Sweden's severe shortage of capital is a serious bar. When money is tight, as it has been almost constantly for many years, smaller enterprises, as well as would-be entrepreneurs, bear a disproportionately large share of the inconvenience, as what capital is available tends to go to larger and more stable companies.

But small-business activity is probably also held back by a general lack of enthusiasm for this kind of thing. In discussing the policy—expressed by labor and government, among others —of spurring mergers of companies into ever greater units for ever greater efficiency, I asked Lillemor Erlander, a labor economist, if there weren't some social values in smaller companies, both from the point of view of the owner (who might appreciate being independent even if it meant a less secure existence) and from the point of view of the employees (some of whom might prefer not to become enmeshed in a huge organization, even if that might also mean less security). She didn't think so: "The important judgment must be from the worker's side. Smaller businesses are more vulnerable to technological change. Also, it is usually easier to obtain a good wage in a larger firm. There are more disadvantages than advantages with smaller businesses." When I mentioned this to Kurt Söderberg, an economist and small-business expert at the Federation of Swedish Industries, he was not surprised. "Labor thinks about this purely from the economic point of view," he said. "The government probably would share their opinions, although that's not to say they would express them so openly." Söderberg pointed out that official government encouragement to small business is slight. Smaller corporations do not, for example, benefit from a lower tax rate, as in the United States: "The shares have to be valued every year by the authorities and the fortune tax paid. The owner has to pay on income, dividends, and fortune, plus an estate tax at death. I'm quite sure these taxation problems have induced many smaller firms to sell out to their large competitors. The tax system does not favor small enterprises at all. Quite the contrary."

Legislation designed to protect small business has been almost nil. "We have nothing here corresponding to the Robinson-Patman Act [i.e., the U.S. law that bans price cuts by suppliers for companies that purchase in large quantities]. The big stores here are quite entitled to make whatever deals they can." There are a couple of part-government-owned credit institutes for small business, local trade development boards which can offer small amounts of management assistance to small business, and a government-supported Small Industries Export Board geared to assist small companies in entering overseas markets. But the total importance of these entities is marginal.

As Söderberg said, the government has a hardheaded view of the matter. Rune Johansson, Minister of the Interior, commented on Sweden's struggles in world competition: "In order for us to meet this competition, we must build up companies so that efficiency and the degree of utilization of equipment is as high as possible. Obviously, these larger companies are able to attract more workers and more technical expertise, and many smaller companies are squeezed. I don't think there is much one can do about that." He did express an affection for the idea of small business: "What we must aim for is to make possible the development of small companies with competitive products. Society must see to it that the possibilities exist. . . ." But he added pointedly: "That is not to say we will interfere with a natural trend which can force smaller companies to shut down. . . ."

Erik Dahmén pointed out that although the direction of recent economic development has reduced the number of ambitious smaller businessmen by creating so many "other, and often better, alternatives to choose from" and has made things tougher in many ways, it has opened new opportunities as well. "This evolution," he said, "has meant more chances for even quite small companies to specialize in new products, where sales possibilities are not sufficient for real mass production in a large factory." He also said that smaller companies can often make use of the research results of larger firms. On balance, he concluded that all the relevant factors together "have not brought with them a significant worsening of conditions for small business." On the contrary, the decline in small-business activity has occurred, he believed, because "the general *inclination* to launch one's own business is on the downgrade." This low inclination is confirmed in my observations. A number of people I spoke to spoke glowingly of the health of small business in Sweden and mentioned as an example the network of 1,800 subcontractors used by Volvo. Yet when I spoke to Per Eriksson, Volvo sales manager, he did not seem to think the company's experiences in this regard illustrated the viability of Swedish small business. "It is very difficult to find small suppliers," he remarked. "We have to take the initiative in building up a network of subcontractors. We have had to build an upholstery plant ourselves, even though we would much rather buy from someone else if possible. We would rather invest our money in the development of our main products. Small business is not supported in this

country. The policy of the government is to create large enterprises. We need the large companies to compete internationally,
but I think we lose a lot of individual initiative."

The view that the initiative required to engage in independent business is shrinking—under the pressures of too much security, among other things—is extremely common among Swedish
businessmen, economists, and other authoritative observers.
Even if one makes a large discount for the natural tendency of
businessmen to grumble about the government, the prevalence
of this opinion is surprisingly widespread. Grundström, head
of the Crafts and Small Industry Organization, said: "Many
people with initiative and capability prefer to go into a big firm.
They are interested in a feeling of security. They are perhaps
less willing to take risks than their fathers were." Erik Bil-Nielsen, the management consultant, stated flatly: "I think the days
of the entrepreneur will be soon over." Sven Langenius, vice-
president of the Industrial Association (*Industriföreningen*), a
small-business group, said: "People feel good where they are."
Kurt Söderberg summed up: "There's so much government supervision for business, and taxes are growing all the time. And
at the same time you are getting better and better off all the
time, with a four-week vacation, a forty-hour week soon, and all
the social welfare on top of that; you may judge that the compensation for taking the risks is not adequate."

One small businessman I spoke to most emphatically dis-
sented—Åke Öberg, president of a Stockholm company called
Perfex International, established to manufacture a machine
used in producing business forms and still in its formative stages.
Principal financing had come from an American investor, but
Öberg had a substantial piece of the equity.

"I have strong feelings regarding this matter," he told me. "I
don't think this Socialized life we lead in Sweden has killed
initiative. If there's an *apparent* lack of initiative, it's due to
other things. For example, the trend to bigger units. A super-
market manager doesn't start his own store because he knows
it's not possible. But that's not a lack of initiative. There's a lot

of ambition in this country to start independent businesses, but they are stopped now mainly by the difficulty in getting money. Recently we even had one of our own milling men who left to go on his own."

Thor-Plast AB, a plastics firm in Stockholm, was in its second year (with sales running about $400,000 annually) when I talked with Nils Verner Thorsen, president. He was the principal contributor of brainpower to the company and shared ownership with two others, who had contributed the capital. He didn't believe the necessary drive to succeed was often to be found in Sweden. "Many people in Sweden talk about starting their own business," he told me. "But they don't really mean it, they only dream about it. It's very difficult to do anything with only a dream. They don't want to leave the security of a good job. Maybe they have a house, a car, a motorboat; they don't want to risk all this to start something so uncertain." He did not believe the high personal income taxes are a barrier, because they are balanced by tax breaks for business: "When you have your own firm, it's easier to arrange not to pay much tax. I don't think this business of taxes has so much importance." But he thought others were missing something by not going on their own: "It's much more stimulating to have your own company. It's the same as jumping into cold water; once you're in, it's all right."

Småland is a lovely forested area in south-central Sweden and is the traditional center of small private industry. There I found considerable pessimism on the future of small business. Two brothers, Karl-Erik and Berndt Granstrand, who own a furniture factory in Skillingaryd, making inexpensive chairs on a mass-production basis, had started in 1955 and had sales about $700,000 a year. Although they were satisfied with their experience, things had deteriorated since, and not a single new business had been launched in four years in the town. "We couldn't have started if conditions then had been as they are now. Costs have risen tremendously, and the administrative side has gotten much more complicated. Initiative is certainly disappearing.

Today you would think not twice, but a hundred times, before starting your own company."

Sven Olofsson, president and sole owner of AB Form-Trä, in Värnamo, which since its founding in 1952 has captured the lion's share of the Swedish market for wooden coat hangers (and built sales to nearly $1,000,000 annually) with a new efficient manufacturing process, was equally gloomy. "Starting a business today without quite large resources is difficult—the capital shortage, taxes, tough competition. If society wants small business to survive, they've got to change the government's policies. As it is now, they're keeping private enterprise down. New businesses come up much more seldom now. Only one other manufacturing company has started in Värnamo in the past five years."

Thure Berg, a salty fifty-four-year-old businessman in Lagan, grew up on a tiny farm with eleven brothers and two cows. In 1946 he started his own company by borrowing $4,000 on the collateral of two machines (which he neglected to make clear to the borrower were purely imaginary). After a couple of years he sold out for $9,000, started another company, which he also later sold for $18,000, and started the present firm, Bergs Säng-kläder AB, producer of quilts and pillows. In 1951, his first year, he had sales of under $40,000; when I spoke to him in 1966, volume was running at over $1,500,000, plus an expected $1,000,000 or so in a new plant in the Netherlands, plus licensing in Finland, and investigations were under way for further expansion in England, Germany, and other countries.

But Berg, who cheerfully invited me to join him in a morning glass of whiskey when I visited him, did not think the future of small business in Sweden was especially promising. "An employee who might want to start his own business today would think it over carefully," he said. "He has it pretty good—pension, holidays, sickness insurance. If you start small, you can't expect to earn more than an ordinary employee at first, and you have to work much harder. The pressure has been building up little by little—taxes, salaries, pension benefits. If I hadn't earned money in the first years and got a plateau to stand on,

I wouldn't have survived. Today salaries are high, and possibilities for profit in your own business are not. The welfare state works against private enterprise." In addition to his other activities, Berg was building a restaurant adjacent to his plant, partly to give the employees a place to eat and partly to provide the surrounding area with a first-class restaurant. He hoped to get a liquor permit with the backing of other businessmen of the area. "I wouldn't start my own business today," he said. I reminded him of his many expansion projects, including the restaurant. "That's only to keep the tax collector away," he said. Well, in any case, it didn't appear that private enterprise was completely dead. "No," he agreed, "but it's ready to die. If I were younger, I'd move to another country." A few months after I spoke to him, I read in the paper that the liquor permit had been denied, and he had halted construction of the restaurant.

On the basis of my conversations and my observations of Swedish society, I have concluded that initiative does indeed suffer in Sweden. However, I do not believe this can be blamed on the vast panorama of welfare benefits; in fact, I find the idea completely absurd. As extensive as the welfare programs are in protecting the citizen against the unkindnesses of fate, they do not easily permit him to live without working, much less to attain the above-average rewards that an ambitious person might covet. On the contrary, they should in some degree contribute to his aggressiveness—by improving his mind through free education, improving his body through free medical care, and widening his choice of activity through free vocational guidance and job-finding assistance. Nor do I believe much of the blame can be laid at the door of the high tax rates. The Swedes are accustomed to their tax rates (even if many people do not like them), as they are accustomed to the relatively low incomes that upper-level executives earn (low, that is, compared with U.S. salaries). As a matter of fact, I have noticed that income rewards that are by American standards decidedly on the modest side (especially on an after-tax basis) seem nevertheless to be well admired in Sweden.

More important are the general prosperity in which the Swedes are drenched, making it unnecessary to exert oneself greatly in order to enjoy a comfortable existence, and the effect accentuated by the government's policy of promoting full employment. But these tendencies, in slightly varying degree, are true of most industrialized countries.

As I see it, the real influence working against individual initiative is simply a pervasive anti-individualistic spirit in society, undoubtedly deriving in great part from the Swede's traditionally passive nature and reinforced by the emphasis on the group and the interest in egalitarianism. Although the Swede experiences a fair amount of isolation, he is nevertheless not much interested in independence, and there is no strong desire to attain individual distinction. To be sure, the equality doctrines pushed by the Social Democrats play a role in holding back initiative; but there is, after all, no law against being aggressive, and the doctrines could not strike such a responsive note if there were not considerable receptivity among the populace to begin with. Conformism may have a bad reputation in some countries, but the overwhelming majority of Swedes find it perfectly natural to conform to the group and to accept society's norms. The typical dream of a young person is to obtain a respectable job where he may wear a white collar and exercise a modicum of authority over his colleagues, not to construct an independent existence geared to his own peculiarities and preferences. He is not taught—nor does it occur to him—that individual aggressiveness has any particular value.

If a single culprit must be found for this situation, I would recommend the reluctance of employers to fire their workers; this most certainly does far more to increase an individual's cozy sense of security than any state-sponsored system of welfare benefits.

But does it really matter? The statements about the decline in Swedish initiative do not make it clear just why individual initiative is so essential. One might agree that the ragged men outside the mosques in Istanbul who sell two-and-a-half-cent handfuls of corn for tourists to feed to the pigeons display a high degree of initiative and self-reliance, but it is not altogether certain that this contributes measurably to their own happiness or to the overall good of society. The initiative that the great majority of people are capable of is of little use to anyone.

In the United States, it is widely accepted that promoting the vitality of small business and therefore encouraging the exercise of initiative are worthwhile, but this is by no means to say that it is necessary. Erik Dahmén argued that it is at least desirable: "From a socioeconomic point of view you lose something—the opportunity to make innovations. The bureaucracy in big companies means a difficulty in carrying through original ideas. I think small business has a real role to play in a dynamic society. If you think competition is a good thing—new products, new ways of doing business—there is a definite risk in having only big companies." But Dahmén admitted that his own studies do not support this; in an extensive investigation of Swedish industry between the wars he found that most innovations actually came from larger companies. However, he insisted that the very existence of the small companies spurred their larger competitors on: "There is the question of *potential* competition, which exists as long as the giants can be threatened by smaller enterprises." Perhaps so, but it still remains to be seen.

There is no evidence so far that the economy has suffered from low initiative. Postwar growth has been rapid and steady and actually accelerated in the late fifties and again in the early sixties. If declining initiative were to have any economic impact, surely it would affect foreign trade; yet Sweden's share of world exports has been growing at a satisfactory clip, and she can now boast that with one four-hundredth of the world's population, she accounts for one-fortieth of exports—up from one-fiftieth in the mid-fifties. Rudolf Jalakas, chief economist at Svenska Handelsbanken, said: "You can't say that businessmen who are lacking in initiative could do that well." One important point is that even if individual initiative is down, group initiative seems not to be. The technological capacities of the large companies are on a high level, and one can conjecture that those who under different circumstances might have started their own businesses are now energetically developing new and improved products in the research groups of large corporations. The economic effects of the lack of initiative seem to be, in short, nil. As Jalakas said: "If we are able, with minimum initiative, to reach the highest standard of living in Europe, then we must be very clever."

Moreover, where individual initiative is absolutely demanded, it seems to appear. In contrast with the lack of spark among lower level employees, a great many top executives display a great deal of vigor. In fact, having found American business executives, of whom I have met a great many, to be on the whole a drab lot, I have been surprised to discover that some of the most stimulating and alert people in Sweden are businessmen. This applies especially to those in exporting industries, since they are forced to keep up with developments throughout the world and are constantly being challenged to prove their competitive powers. Curt Nicolin, the hard-driving head of ASEA (Sweden's second-largest company), said: "There will always be people who will work hard regardless of the money reward." One ASEA employee told me that Nicolin demands—and gets—120 percent of capacity from every member of the staff.

There is also the possibility that initiative is being reduced through mass emigration of aggressive people. Folke Lindberg, head of the Association of Family-Owned Companies (*Familje-företagens Förening*), painted a grim picture for me of the effects of government policies on private enterprise and said: "Many wealthy people are leaving Sweden; they sell out their companies to large firms and go to other countries." It is well known that there is a tiny colony of Swedish tax refugees in Switzerland, but none of the people who worry about such things seems to know just how many such people there are. Lindberg said: "We have very poor statistics on who is leaving Sweden." Sweden has had some brain drain of scientists and engineers leaving for the United States, but so has virtually every other country where emigration is free, because of higher salaries and better research facilities in the States. But Sweden's experience on this score has not been, according to studies that have been made, particularly alarming.

To sum up, it is probably true that individual initiative is not as fully developed in Sweden as in some countries, yet it probably does not matter very much. I am positive that the Swedes do not believe it makes them any less happy. While one can agree with the spirit expressed in, say, Antoine de St.-Exupéry's philosophy that one becomes a man only by meeting and overcoming a challenge, one must admit that one's enjoyment of this sort of thing is largely a question of personal taste. A lack of individual assertiveness may irritate or depress non-Swedes, but the Swedes cannot reasonably be expected to shape their society for the amusement of foreigners.

It is, of course, entirely conceivable that the effects of various initiative-limiting elements in Swedish society will eventually have clearly harmful effects. But as long as one is speculating about the future, one can also speculate that the Swedes will see such a development coming and will modify their system to avoid any serious damage.

VIII

The Great Labor Peace Apparatus

Two of the most powerful entities in the Swedish organizational spectrum are the Employers' Confederation (*Arbetsgivareförening*), or SAF, which represents management in labor negotiations, and the Confederation of Industrial Unions (*Landsorganisation*), or LO, which fulfills the same function for labor.

Needless to say, the two organizations, being unambiguously dedicated to the furtherance of their members' selfish ambitions, work from approximately opposite philosophical positions, hold sharply different opinions on almost everything, and have extremely good reason to be locked in perpetual conflict.

All the more odd, then, are the frequent, jointly sponsored lunches for visiting journalists and the like, where representatives from the two sides provide the entertainment by congenially hashing over the jolly old times at the bargaining table. Abroad, awed hosts of the groups are diverted by touring companies good-naturedly running through the same performance. In many parts of the world, a Swedish labor-management tandem recounting its remarkable tales of mutual friendship has become a standard curiosity, the business world's counterpart to the bearded lady or the three-headed calf.

The reality behind the vaudeville is, of course, Sweden's incredible record of labor peace. In 1962 Sweden lost a total of 2 man-days per 1,000 employed persons through work stoppages, meaning that labor relations in Sweden were 152 times as peaceful as in the United States, 146 times as peaceful as in Britain, and 74 times as peaceful as in France. The comparisons are much the same back to 1945.

Briefly, here's how the peace machine works: Every two (or sometimes three) years, bargaining committees from LO and SAF go through a ritual of meetings, public statements, expressions of despair, accusations, and counteraccusations over a period of a few months; this culminates in the general outlines of a wage agreement, which is then worked out in detail by the unions and employers' organizations in each industry and further still on the local level. The LO-SAF agreement also usually sets the pattern for the white-collar unions, which begin their negotiations only when LO is finished. There is nothing to prevent a strike (and there was a teachers' strike in 1966), but the parties almost always agree—at least since 1945, when the last major strike occurred.

The record is so obviously too good to be true that a modicum of skepticism is excusable. Yet an effort by a suspicious investigator to uncover the truth beneath the surface amiability and mutual respect is apt to come upon a solid core of amiability and mutual respect. There does not appear to be any influence more sinister than a gravely serious desire to cooperate and avoid conflict. I asked Bertil Kugelberg, who until mid-1966 was head of SAF, what he thought of the enormous strength of LO, which has organized something over 90 percent of its total potential membership. "From an employer's point of view," he said, "it is of interest for the employees to be organized. If something happens in the plant or there is unrest among the workers, the union representative can help smooth things out. It's of great advantage to an employer to have a strong union and to have a sensible man in charge. You know, we have very sensible men in charge of our unions." I also asked Arne Geijer, head of LO, if it was true that he and Bertil Kugelberg were on such good terms. "Yes, we are good friends," he answered. "It's an important part of what we call the Swedish system. Our negotiations are often very hard, but why should we be enemies?" I asked Otto Nordenskiöld, head of TCO, a large but not especially powerful group of white-collar workers, if the great might of the organized employers was troublesome. He replied: "When we start to organize a company, it usually immediately joins SAF. So if a difference comes up, the employers' group comes into it, and that helps us. They know what the normal practice is, and our union knows also. This makes the atmosphere much calmer."

In groping for an explanation for this peculiarly peaceful atmosphere, some experts have opined that the lack of differences in race and religion between the two sides is the key. Perhaps, but if that is so, there is no clear reason why it should not have applied in the twenties, when Sweden's racial and religious makeup was even more homogeneous than it is now, but when her work-stoppage record was considerably worse than in most other countries.

The first traces of the present-day sweetness and light appeared in the 1930's. It was becoming apparent that the stormy labor relations of the twenties were a costly and useless drain on society's energies. Since one of the Social Democrats' principal intentions was to cure hard social problems through an increase in centralized government power, the thought of calming the labor storms through legislation was unavoidable. It was made all the more so by a bitter ten-month strike in the building industry in 1933–34, a time of great economic peril. This action gravely frustrated the government's major antiunemployment instrument—heavy public works spending. Public feeling was running high, as was public receptivity to the idea of putting both sides under strict government control. LO, closely allied with the Social Democrats, could not gracefully object to the legislation, but it understandably suspected that legislation might restrict its freedom of action.

At the same time, employers, to whom dealing with a Socialist government was a new and by no means welcome experience, had little reason to expect gentle treatment in any newly devised system of state-directed labor relations.

But there was one thing the Social Democrats liked better than legislation: it was avoiding legislation when the desired result could be achieved some other way. Thus, a parliamentary commission, named in 1934 to suggest methods of government intervention, recommended that labor and management be first given the chance to try a once-and-for-all settlement of their differences.

Results of previous efforts to cooperate had been less than sensational. A start had been made in 1906, when SAF obtained LO's approval of the so-called Paragraph 23 (management's right to "hire and fire workers, to manage and distribute the work and to use workers belonging to any union or to no union"), a clause that is still demanded in all contracts of companies connected with SAF. In return the workers were guaranteed the right to organize and granted immunity from reprisals as a result of union activity.

This promising beginning was followed by twenty-five years of strife. Toward the end of the 1920's, under the influence of labor peace movements in Britain, a few feeble efforts were made to get the two Swedish parties together again, but nothing came of them.

Nevertheless, all hands were game for another try, and in the spring of 1936 SAF and LO began a series of talks. Two and a half years later the Basic Agreement was signed between LO and SAF at Saltsjöbaden, a placid resort village near Stockholm. It is from this agreement that Sweden's peaceful labor atmosphere is said to stem. As a matter of fact, the "Saltsjöbaden spirit," by which is meant a willingness to settle thorny disputes through negotiations, cooperation, and compromise, has often been cited as a central cause, or symptom, or result of the Swedish social system as a whole.

Anyone who has heard of the Basic Agreement's magical effect may be surprised not to be able to find in the text anything that would seem capable of accomplishing the wondrous feats attributed to it. Its contents can be briefly summarized. First, it makes negotiation of disputes obligatory and sketches a detailed procedure to be followed. It bans coercive action, discrimination against individuals on grounds of religion or politics, retaliation after settlement of a dispute, and secondary actions against "third parties"—that is, persons not involved in a dispute. It sets out procedures for laying off and rehiring workers, though without—in accordance with Paragraph 23—disturbing the employer's right to make his own decision in such matters. Settlement of disagreements on all these points is relegated to a Labor Market Council, consisting of three members from each side, specifically established for the purpose. One section of the agreement is devoted to the special problems involved in essential public services.

This is the entire agreement that took two and a half years to draw up. It does nothing to prevent the two parties from disagreeing. It preserves both parties' full right to attack with all their traditional weapons—strikes, lockouts, blockades, and boycotts. Both the organizations retain their original principal purpose, which is to fight with all means at their command for the selfish interests of their members.

In all probability, the key to the agreement's success was the strong faith shown in negotiating. Like a cleverly designed alarm system, a requirement that matters be negotiated is shrewdly placed at every point of potential dispute in labor-management relations, and it is virtually impossible to stumble into open conflict without stumbling over a requirement to negotiate first. In fact, considering the Swedes' well-known incommunicativeness, it is astonishing how much faith the agreement places on getting two parties into the same room in the hope that problems can be solved through talk. The negotiations may be broken off at any time by either party, and resort may then be had to attack with an economic weapon. For example, management must listen, if the unions so demand, to the workers' side of the question when deciding on lay-offs and must give a certain amount of notice, but management still has the last word. The union may, if it feels strongly, appeal the case to the Labor Market Council created by the agreement. But even if the council sides with the workers, its decision is not binding, and management can do as it pleases anyway. The assumption is that somewhere in this process the two parties will come closer to each other's viewpoints.

This dependence on discussion is in a way a logical outcome of the marathon conferences at Saltsjöbaden that produced the agreement. Kugelberg, the former head of SAF, has described what went on between management and labor representatives: "They had their meals together, spent their evenings together, and, as they got to know each other better, talked openly and amicably about many things. The employers learned a good deal about the trade union movement's aims, structure and activities. The workers learned a good deal about economics, management, and business. And so there was born a . . . new attitude . . . a willingness to listen, to understand. . . ."

Thus, the success of the Basic Agreement probably does not lie in the agreement itself, but in the talk that accompanied its production. And having once discovered that talk could be constructive, the parties had little difficulty in settling on a method for solving future disputes: more talk. In the discussions that have followed through the years, the antagonists have continually assimilated something of each other's viewpoints.

As a happy result of Saltsjöbaden, the threatened legislation never was passed, and there still are very few labor laws. The principal ones have established a state mediation system, which can do nothing besides make suggestions (1906), recognized collective contracts (1928), and assured the rights of association and collective bargaining (1929). Overtime is limited to 200 hours annually (an additional 150 hours may be worked with special permission), the 45-hour workweek is statutory (though contracts can provide for longer weeks), night work is prohibited (though exceptions are freely granted), most types of underground work are prohibited for women, and child labor is restricted. But there is no minimum wage and no law on over-time pay.

The atmosphere has been so calm in subsequent years that some of the machinery provided to handle disputes has hardly ever been used. Union complaints to the council about layoffs have numbered only two or three a year. Disputes over the ban on action against third parties, calling for consideration by the council, plus an impartial chairman, have numbered but two since 1938. The procedures for settling conflicts in essential public services have been required but once—in 1953, when a threatening strike in the electric power industry was smoothly avoided. An arbitration panel for the settlement of disputes over time-and-motion studies, set up in 1948, has never been called into action.

A good part of the agreement's impact was unintentional. The committee that hammered out the original treaty was intended strictly as an *ad hoc* body, to be dissolved when its work was completed. But the idea of labor-management co-operation now seemed so promising that the group was kept alive, and it has continued to meet more or less regularly. No idle piece of window dressing, it has continually churned out new agreements which have helped smooth over potentially troublesome areas. It has, among other things, established a a Joint Industrial Safety Council, which arranges educational activities, draws up safety standards, and supervises plant safety committees; a Joint Industrial Training Council, which in much the same way encourages better vocational training; and the Joint Female Labor Council, which helps promote women's rights.

One of the products of the committee's deliberations is a system of labor-management councils. Any company with fifty or more workers can get a factory council if either side insists on it, and more than 90 percent of eligible companies have them. These councils consist of management representatives, production workers, and white-collar workers and meet at least every three months. They are supposed to be informed of all management plans, as well as of financial results, and are expected to give management their opinions and advice. It should not be assumed that the main purpose of these councils is to improve working conditions. Both management and labor are deeply interested in achieving maximum production at minimum cost, and this is the councils' first assignment. A booklet published by SAF explains their function: "To encourage maximum production ... also promote job security and contentment." LO puts it this way: "To improve conditions of production and work." Both put production first. In commenting on the idea that the councils are an effort at promoting industrial democracy, T. L. Johnson, well-known British expert on Swedish labor, wrote: "In discussion of this theme in Sweden there has never been any great preoccupation with fundamental philosophical or moral concepts based on the Dignity of Man ... Swedish industrial democracy has a strong economic basis."

An incidental—and in the long run perhaps more important—function of the councils is their promotion of that favorite Swedish labor-relations nostrum: discussion. A prominent management consultant in Sweden pointed out to me that as far as industrial democracy was concerned, the councils, which have no power, have only "created the illusion of partnership." But he regards them as constructive anyway: "They provide more information, thus increase understanding, thus expand the areas of agreement. Do you follow the logic?"

Having read and heard a great deal about these councils and having become familiar with the Swedes' taciturnity and passivity, I had naturally assumed they were merely an empty ceremonial designed, indeed, to give the workers an illusion of participation—until I attended one. In the spring of 1967 a company called Facit AB (maker of typewriters and other office appurtenances) invited some foreign journalists to its headquarters in Åtvidaberg in southern Sweden. The tour included visits to the factories, interviews with the executives, a couple of immensely enjoyable dinners, and a sit-in at the management-labor council, which happened to be holding its regular quarterly meeting at the time. The company's annual report was being readied for release at the same time, and the company's president, Gunnar Ericsson, and half a dozen other top executives made an exhaustive explanation of the results, as well as the company's plans for the coming five years, for the thirty or so workers present. The management forces were making a particular effort to transmit the message that the workers' lives would likely be intimately affected as the company prepared its defenses for the tough battles coming in the international markets (Facit exports about 50 percent of its production). It also frankly conceded that current conditions were not ideal (the year's profits had been slightly off) but expressed hope for the future.

In the question period the workers were no less exhaustive (and exhausting—the meeting lasted well over three hours) in presenting their viewpoints. Tool workers, machine operators, and clerks asked probing questions about, among other things, the effects of the Kennedy Round on the EEC markets, a rumored decline in production resulting from shifting product assignments from one factory to another in search of greater efficiency, insufficient investment in machinery in some areas, lack of coordination in research efforts of various divisions, the quality of technical management, the reason behind the decline in profit margins to the lowest level in five years, the adequacy of allocations of funds to the tax-free investment funds companies are allowed to accumulate, and why long-term liabilities had risen on the balance sheet. One long wrangle took place between Sven Mojlanen, a young tool worker, and Gunnar Ericsson, president. Mojlanen read a lengthy screed attacking the idea of take-home work, whereby workers can, if they like, take home certain simple piecework jobs for their wives to do. His general thesis was that giving such extra work out was ill advised when business was bad, and he ended with the appeal "We demand that take-home work be abolished immediately." Ericsson was no less blunt in informing him that he was off base and give him an equally lengthy monologue on why the practice was good for morale, had been okayed by the union, and did not represent a threat to jobs because things were turning up anyway. The practice, he said, would definitely be continued. Mojlanen calmly unfolded his paper and said, "Perhaps you didn't understand. I said, 'We demand that take-home work be abolished immediately.'" Ericsson, not surprisingly, had the last word, but Mojlanen did make his point (as it turned out, he was wrong; things did, in fact, turn up).

After the meeting Ericsson explained to me that he did not mind such an exchange but that the real value of the council was to get his viewpoint across to the workers. "This is a marvelous management tool," he said. "It's the best opportunity we have to inform the people. It's good to talk to them before we do something, so they don't come later and ask why we didn't do such and such instead. If someone is going to be moved to a new machine, it's only polite to tell him. This way he's prepared. But they are not going to make management decisions. If they could do that, we would hire them as management people." But occasionally their opinions do come in handy: "I had the idea to build a factory without windows, so I discussed it with them. They said they wanted to be able to see if it was raining outside. I think it was a very good criticism. The plant is now finished and looks much better with the windows."

In many ways, no doubt the councils are an illusion, but an illusion of great value.

A key element in the evolution of labor-management understanding has been the peace-loving nature of LO, the top organization of about forty industrial unions with, in all, just over 1,500,000 members—about 20 percent of the entire population and more than twice as many as all other unions combined. LO's ability to keep the peace depends in part on the powerful weapons it possesses to keep its member unions in line. If a union strikes without permission from LO, it cannot receive its economic support and risks being expelled from the confederation. LO has grown even more powerful since 1956, when the present centralized bargaining began.

The president of LO is Arne Geijer, a self-educated former forest worker. Upon meeting this labor leader, easily one of the most charming gentlemen in Sweden, one understands better how the employers can be so consistently talked into granting fat annual wage increases. Geijer does not regard the cooperation between management and labor as particularly extraordinary. "With the development of modern society," he said, "you need more and more cooperation to solve the problems."

LO is not burdened with complicated philosophical principles. Its single overriding objective is higher wages. To this end it pursues what are sometimes considered peculiar patterns. One of them is its welcoming attitude to time-and-motion studies, in which industrial engineers time the workers' movements in order to work out more efficient routines. The picture of workers walking off the job at the first sight of the man with the stopwatch is well grounded in reality. LO has enthusiastically joined with SAF in forming a Time and Motion Study Council. A council statement remarks, with considerable understatement, that introduction of time studies in the twenties "was not infrequently greeted with distrust and resistance on the part of the workers." However, not only does LO accept the time studies, but it and its affiliated unions have also trained thousands of their members in the techniques in order to promote better understanding of their value.

Such policies have a clear rationale, Geijer explained: "A company's profitability and its ability to pay wages are closely connected. Therefore, it's a union necessity to show interest in a company's internal efficiency, as well as conditions for the workers." The same applies to LO's stand on automation, which, like time studies, not only radically alters jobs, but often also abolishes them. LO has often found itself urging the idea of automation on management. In 1966 it completed a massive four-year study of technical progress and published a 600-page report reaffirming its faith in the beneficial effects of such progress:

> One of the labor movement's most important tasks is to work for an improvement of the member's material welfare. Within the labor movement we have long been conscious that a vital condition for the success of this effort is a progressive increase in efficiency . . . continuous introduction of new technical methods and organizational innovations. . . . The labor movement not only has passively accepted such changes but has shown in words and deeds its willingness to actively cooperate in shaping this development.

LO does not overlook the workers who are dislocated for the sake of higher efficiency, and the report makes clear that technical progress must be accompanied by social measures (retraining, relocation, and the like) to combat the personal inconveniences that arise as a result. Eric Petterson, an LO economist who worked on the report, explained to me: "If the negative effects of changes are too great, negative attitudes will be built up. We must make sure that society is willing to accept change."

Five years before the study on automation, LO released a study on structural rationalization—that is, the process of making the economy more efficient by combining small, marginal production units into big, profitable ones and taking other wide-ranging steps to increase the economic power of big business. It not only wholeheartedly favors the process, but also has often called on the government to prod businessmen to speed up their creation of more viable business units.

Because of LO's feelings on efficiency, featherbedding does not exist in Sweden. Since LO does not challenge the employer's right to hire and fire, there is no union shop or closed shop (though there is heavy pressure from coworkers to join the union). Over the years a strong trend has developed toward vertical unions—*i.e.*, a single union including all workers in the same industry, meaning there is one union at each plant—so there is a minimum of jurisdictional squabbling.

LO's single-minded concentration on efficiency—and on higher wages—is not to everyone's taste. A journalist for a left-wing French paper was appalled at what he found during a mid-1966 visit to Volvo's Göteborg plant: an efficiency system (darkly noted as "of American origin") whose introduction the workers had failed to fight against. He was stunned when a union leader blandly explained: "We regard the organization of the work as the employer's business. Ours is to see that the worker is well paid." The horrified conclusion: "An air-conditioned hell."

In order to keep the members' attention fixed on the main objective, LO operates two schools. "On average, two representatives from each local go through our courses every year," Geijer told me. "They deal with time and motion studies, production, financial problems, factory councils, and how to work with employers. We take it very seriously." On a visit to one of the schools I was surprised that so much of the instruction was concentrated on the business side, rather than on union problems, and I remarked on this to one of the officials. "If you mean 'accept the employers' views,' no," he said, "but if you mean 'cooperate,' then you are right." Lars Starkaryd, a young LO economist, told me: "If our members don't have an education, they will put problems to us that have no solutions, because they don't understand what the real problems are. We are a democratic union, and we must do what the members tell us; but the only way to make sure they are acting responsibly is through education."

Some of LO's emphasis on responsible behavior may be traced to its relationship with the Social Democratic Party. There is at present no formal link between them, but they identify rather firmly with each other. The head of LO is a Social Democratic member of parliament and the party's programs are signed by him, as well as by the Prime Minister. Furthermore, the deficits run up by the Social Democratic newspapers are covered by LO. The connection is also manifested in block affiliation—*i.e.*, entire union branches vote to adhere to the party, and about a third of LO's members are thus affiliated. The blocks naturally include a fair number of people not in sympathy with the Social Democrats and protests, partly because part of the union dues goes to the party, are not uncommon. Technically, any individual member can opt out of the affiliation, but few (less than 1 percent) consider it worth the effort.

Needless to say, a close identification with the government has advantages. The pressure that LO can apply to parliament or to the Cabinet is quite large—not only through the voting strength of its membership, but also through the day-to-day contact between government officials and LO experts. The connection is so close that, to exaggerate somewhat, the process sometimes appears to be a dialogue in which the same entity plays both parts: making requests while wearing its LO costume, which it then exchanges for its government costume in order to grant the request it just made to itself. LO has the option of pushing for its aims through contract negotiations (such as the four-week vacation it won in 1962) or through legislation (such as the new pension program of 1959), depending on circumstances. As one expert has remarked, "It reaps the best of both worlds."

But LO's government connection also carries certain obligations: it must behave itself, lest it embarrass the government and lose votes. Nils Elvander, the authority on Swedish organizations, told me he thought LO might change tactics if the opposition took over the government. "LO might become more active," he said. "The government now is in a position to dictate to LO."

A factor of some importance in LO's operations is solidarity. This term expresses a good many ideas, but to some extent it is a matter of simple social justice. The reasoning is admirably logical: obviously, the poor wage-paying ability of certain industries (*e.g.,* textiles, shoe manufacturing) is not the fault of the workers engaged in them, and there is no real reason they should be penalized for it. Because almost everyone in Sweden is organized, the wages of all workers are pulled up simultaneously, but those in some high-profit fields tend to float up faster than the others. As a partial remedy, LO has often secured extra-large wage increases in low-wage industries. But the appeal for solidarity is also used as a rallying cry to maintain LO's unity, including its power to fight employers, but also sometimes to combat both the tendency of other unions to grab for greater wage increases than those LO members get and the pressure on workers to support the organization even though they might prefer not to. Geijer said: "Naturally, there is social pressure to join, but if there were a general feeling against the union, the pressure would be in the opposite direction. People often protest, but isn't it a human right to protest?"

Much of the criticism against LO's dominance of the industrial field comes from an organization known as SAC (*Sveriges Arbetares Centralorganisation*), a syndicalist workers' movement founded in 1910 under the ideological influence of Bakunin, Proudhon, and Kropotkin. Membership, which hit a peak of nearly 40,000 in the 1920's, is now under 25,000. But the movement still has a measure of vitality, provides an outlet for discontents, and publishes one of Sweden's most lively weeklies—*Arbetaren*, with a variety of articles on world affairs and the arts.

The movement's general secretary, Herbert Anckar, described SAC to me as "a labor organization with an ideological program," roughly comparable to the old American IWW. SAC opposes the state as a matter of principle: "We are flatly opposed to state influence; the less state, the better," said Anckar, "and the movement does not support any political party."

SAC is strongest in forestry and the building industry. It negotiates locally in some cases, but never nationally. Anckar complained: "We have great difficulty gaining new members, because we are so often not represented in the negotiations." The movement commonly asserts that its members are discriminated against in various ways, and occasionally it hints that LO has become virtually an official body. "Our members are often harassed for not being members of LO," Anckar said gloomily. "How things might turn out if we should get high unemployment I don't know. It is very possible that our members would

be in a very difficult position. You might say that we are outsiders in society—but not because we want to be." Perhaps not,
but I had the impression that Anckar enjoyed his role as a nonconformist—one of the few I have met in Sweden. "Sweden is
too much on a single track," he said. "Everybody has to think
alike."

A similar criticism—in a harsh and bitter form—is contained
in a highly tendentious novel called *Skiljevägen* (The Cross-
roads), by Kurt Salomonson, published in 1962. The story is of
a young man who, reluctant to join the union, has been falsely
accused of stealing and fired from his job, and has—when the
novel opens—traveled to the north to work as a construction
laborer at a damsite. His coworkers learn of his previous record,
and when he reiterates his opposition to the union, he is again
forced out of his job, a procedure in which the employer heartily cooperates. The book is full of loyal union members who
spend a great deal of time expressing their views in the most
depressing possible terms. Some bits of conversation: "What is
all this talk about the individual and individual freedom worth?
... I mean, as if we didn't have it good enough in this country.... We can trust the workers' society, and the workers' authority. We can be damned sure that any time a decision is
made it's the right decision. It's obvious that the individual
must subordinate himself...." "I mean, what the hell is freedom? What the hell is justice? As a worker in a welfare state you
have a unique chance to live a pretty wonderful life—just get
yourself a little surface morality." At a union meeting: "The
thing has been discussed on a higher level, and the proposal—
that is, the extra assessment—was unanimously agreed on, and
the proposal has been passed on to us with perfect freedom to
answer yes or no. But ... that freedom does not mean, of course,
that we will vote down the proposal."

Unquestionably, such writings express an opinion held by
some workers, but it is difficult to say how widespread it is. An
American who has lived in Stockholm for some years and who
has been in a position to observe closely the labor market, gave
me his opinion: "I'm certainly not any more alarmed by this

development in Sweden than in the U.S. There's an increasing bureaucratization everywhere. The idea that the organization is so complete that the individual gets crushed is, I think, exaggerated."

Arne Geijer seemed able to regard SAC with a certain amount of detachment: "We don't attack them." But if one expected Geijer to recognize the value of a competing organization for those who are dissatisfied, one would be disappointed. He said firmly, "I don't believe in a split organization."

If there is danger in the overpowering influence of a single massive organization, it is more than counterbalanced by its positive points, at least in the Swedish view of things.

Although LO is the largest and the loudest part of labor, it is not the whole thing. Sweden, like other industrialized countries, has experienced a strong expansion of white-collar workers. As their number has grown and as their status as an elite group has declined, they, too, have become increasingly organized. Legislation enacted in 1936 assured them the same organizing rights that LO had enjoyed since its 1906 agreement with SAF. The first white-collar organization was born the following year, and growth has since been rapid.

The largest organization is TCO (*Tjänstemännens Centralorganisation*), which is a grouping of about 30 unions with over 500,000 members. The next largest is SACO (*Sveriges Akademikers Centralorganisation*), a collection of employees with, in principle, degrees from institutions of higher education; its 30 unions have a total of 75,000 members. The smallest of the white-collar groups is SR (*Statstjänstemännens Riksförbund*), which comprises 42 organizations covering 18,000 military officers and higher civil service officials employed by the state. A Basic Agreement for white-collar workers—similar to that for LO members—was signed by SAF and two of the TCO unions in 1958. Most of the friction in Swedish labor relations arises in these organizations. The solidarity of LO is totally lacking here, and none of the white-collar unions is politically oriented. Not only do the different organizations differ rather sharply with one another (and with LO) about general goals, but the unions within each organization also often bicker with one another and with the central organization. The largest TCO union is the Union of Clerical Workers in Manufacturing (SIF). It accounts for about a third of TCO membership and often acts on its own initiative without notifying the central organization. Occasionally, SIF has threatened to leave TCO, so severe have the strains become. In early 1966 the second-largest TCO group, SALF, a group of supervisors and foremen, did abruptly sever its connection with TCO in a dispute over how the dividing lines among different unions are decided.

Raiding by one union on another's territory is a particularly serious problem in the white-collar area, where dividing lines are hazy and the number of unions large. TCO, for example, has a "vertical" state civil service union, which can conflict both with SR and SACO, as well as with a small civil servants' union affiliated with LO covering the lower grades. But it can also conflict with, among others, "horizontal" TCO unions of, say, teachers or hospital personnel.

The white-collar workers' top organizations do not carry out heavily centralized wage bargaining as LO does, and there is no suggestion of giving low-wage groups extra help. I asked Otto Nordenskiöld, head of TCO, what he thought of the idea of solidarity. He smoothly replied: "We prefer to speak about a differentiated salary policy. It's a basic difference in philosophy."

SACO, the grouping of about 30 professional unions (teachers, architects, psychologists, librarians, and even business executives), is perhaps the most curious feature of the labor landscape and illustrates even better than most other groups the solidarity problems that can arise. It was formed in 1947 precisely as a defense against what it considered the unfair advantages being taken by the less educated but better organized segments of the population. The organization points out that by the mid-forties "people with academic qualifications had suffered an absolute lowering of living standards, not just a reduction in comparison with other groups, and this was in a period . . . when all other groups were able to raise their standard of living."

It seems somewhat odd for intellectuals to form unions, and I asked Jan Carl Almquist, SACO president, if it wasn't difficult to organize such people. "Of course, many of them would prefer not to organize," he said. "But if all other groups act collectively, they must act collectively as well." He added philosophically: "The more complicated society becomes, the more difficult it is to keep one's individuality." A booklet directed primarily to potential members justifies the collective idea: "Most professional people are individualists. But one can very well be an individualist in one's opinions and way of life and nevertheless recognize the necessity of a common organization to safeguard one's economic and professional interests."

After many years of preparation SACO announced, prior to the 1966 contract expiration, that its teachers' unions would ask for a 20 percent annual wage increase. This demand carried extra weight because a new law granting state employees the right to strike went into effect at the beginning of 1966. Negotiations dragged on month after month, and in October, 1,200 upper-level teachers and school administrators walked out, an event which was closely followed by a lockout called by the state for 20,800 other SACO members. The teachers stayed off the job for precisely four weeks, after which an agreement was signed giving them an average increase in 1966 of 19 percent, plus 5.5 percent in each of the two following years. After thus successfully breaking Sweden's labor peace in vigorous pursuit of its members' interests, it was again able to concentrate on one of its more customary activities—a war with TCO on recruitment among each other's memberships.

One of the permanent fixtures in Sweden's labor peace apparatus is the Labor Court. It began in 1929 to decide disputes about collective contracts, whose legal existence had just been recognized.

Although the court occupies a vital and sensitive position in the labor field, only a minority of its members are state officials. It is, in fact, an outstanding example of the infiltration by the organizations in critical state organs. Only the chairman, the vice-chairman, and one other member are civil servants; the other five members are laymen (two from employers' associations, two from LO, and one from TCO).

Originally, the workers fiercely resisted the establishment of the Labor Court, but so just have been its decisions that opposition quickly disappeared. A union man named E. D. Karlfeldt was one of the strongest opponents to the court when it was set up, but by 1953 (by which time he himself had become a member of the court) he was able to say of its functioning: "It has worked perfectly from the start, and no voice is now raised in favor of its abolition." The court's success has been due partly to the custom of appointing well-known individuals of high prestige to the court and partly to the spirit of complete impartiality in which decisions are made. Although the lay members receive their appointments precisely because of their position as organization men, they do not promote a particular viewpoint in their decisions. In 1941, Oscar Karlén, a labor representative on the court, became highly indignant when he thought he was being pressured and said he would refuse to serve if the members were "the sort of puppets who were expected to make up their minds when prompted by a telephone call from a union."

The court's main task is to interpret collective agreements (which according to the law must be adhered to by both sides) in order to decide if an agreement has been violated and, if so, what penalty is to be awarded. Deliberations are informal, and decisions are rendered rapidly. Bengt Hult, chairman of the court, said: "The case begins with, for example, a presentation by the union in which they explain what they want. Then the employer's association comments—one comment from each side. We have a preparatory meeting before the court, then a regular court session, with lawyers, witnesses, and members of the court. Then I write a decision based on a discussion in which every member expresses his view of the case. If a member disagrees with the majority, he can make a reservation. But as a rule we come to the same decision." Indeed, despite the mixed composition of the court, about 90 percent of the decisions are unanimous.

Over the years the court's activities have declined. "We get about fifty or sixty cases a year," said Hult, "but many of them are settled by the parties themselves. We issue about thirty-five decisions a year. In the beginning of the thirties there were about two hundred cases a year." Hult attributes the decline in the court's activity to the widespread study of its earlier decisions. The court attempts to stimulate readership of its decisions through avoidance of excessively legalistic jargon. "We really do try to write as clearly as we can," said Hult. "Union officials, who as a rule are not lawyers, are very interested in our decisions, which they use for guidance when disputes come up."

The cases that do come to the court nowadays tend to be complex. Johan Lind, secretary of the court, told me of one dispute: "A company in the south of Sweden was producing prefabricated houses and had a contract to build about four hundred houses outside Göteborg. They wanted to send men from their factory to Göteborg. But the building workers' union in Göteborg said it was a job for building workers, not for factory workers. The factory workers brought the case up, and the court had to rule on whether they were required to obey the factory's orders. The court ruled they were. But then the building workers in Göteborg started a blockade with the plumbing workers, and they couldn't get the houses finished. The employers' association sued the building workers and said they were trying to monopolize the work and that it was illegal to start a blockade. But the court ruled against the employers and said that the building workers had the right to start a blockade in an attempt to get more work, because there was no contract in force between them and these particular employers. Whether they would actually succeed in getting more work was another question."

Complaints have often been lodged against the court by organizations not represented—most vociferously by SAC, the syndicalist group. Lind explained: "They want the right to have SAC represented. When the Labor Court started, it was important that labor should be represented, because special knowledge of factories was needed. But it was very carefully stated that every member should feel himself a judge and not merely a representative for his organization. A proposal has been made in parliament that any organization which has a case before the court should have a representative on the court. But in the long run it wouldn't be a court any longer; they would no longer be independent. Take the case of the houses in Göteborg. It was considered to be a very important case for the employers' group. But the two members from SAF voted against their own association."

If the court (which is, of course, an instrument of law) seems to deserve some of the credit for Sweden's labor peace, Hult disputes any such view. Each case is decided on its own merits, and the court has not built up any particular philosophy over the years. "Interpreting agreements is our only job," Hult said. "We have no other powers. We only interpret. We do nothing else." Lind agreed: "You mustn't overestimate the effect of law on labor peace; that is primarily the work of the organizations. If they didn't cooperate, there would be nothing the law could do."

IX

How to Run an Economy

The Swedes' vast talents for dealing with machinery, science, and other such matters have found an excellent outlet in the department of social engineering most susceptible to this mechanistic approach—economics. In fact, a great many of the Swedes who have achieved international distinction in this century have been economists: Knut Wicksell, Per Jacobsson, Gunnar Myrdal, and Dag Hammarskjöld.

As early as the mid-thirties these gifts were put into action combating the depression. From 1929 to 1933 industrial production had dropped by more than 20 percent, and unemployment rose at times to more than a third of the labor force. Yet by 1935 industrial production was 25 percent above 1929 and two years later was 50 percent above the predepression level. Aside from a small reversal in 1938, the recovery roared ahead throughout the decade.

The recovery attracted great interest abroad, not least because of the existence of a school of Swedish economists who, as if precisely in preparation for the moment of crisis, had been registering notable advances in economic thought. The best known was Knut Wicksell, whose major contribution was a discussion of the relation between market and natural interest rates and how interaction between the two could powerfully affect savings and investment—termed a "pioneer formulation" by the American economic historian Howard S. Ellis. As economist Robert Lekachman has written, Wicksell "anticipated many Keynesian doctrines" and many authorities believe his work formed a vital stepping-stone for Keynes' later theories. Wicksell died in 1935, but Gunnar Myrdal and others built on his thinking. In 1933, Myrdal's recommendations to the government on deficit financing of public works were enthusiastically put into practice— three years before publication of Keynes' revolutionary *General Theory* and long before countercyclical deficit spending became an accepted economic nostrum.

Economists in other countries were impressed by the remarkable recovery and by the active participation of professional economists in the government process. Throughout the world admiring books and articles were churned out on the triumphs of Swedish economic thought. Richard A. Lester, an American economist, admiringly wrote: "Most of the younger economists have maintained very emphatically that large-scale borrowing to finance public works in bad times is a sound policy. They seem to have convinced the people of Sweden of this. Practice apparently has proved their contention correct—at least for Sweden." An English writer, Brinley Thomas, wrote: "Primarily the recovery is due to internal action, based largely on the theories of Gunnar Myrdal. . . . Sweden's contributions to economic science have been of a significance out of all proportion to the size of the country."

The only difficulty with this flattering view of Swedish economic genius is that it is not true. It is indisputable that (1) Sweden's recovery was extraordinary and (2) the intellectual fertility of Swedish economists was extraordinary. But later study has shown that the one had but little bearing on the other. The economists' advocacy of deficit spending was, to be sure, a bold departure and is by no means to be denigrated. But the prevailing opinion in Sweden today is that it was a rather timid and clumsy view of things in comparison with the more scientific theories later developed by Keynes and his followers. Arthur Montgomery, a Swedish expert on the period, holds that the key reason for the successful recovery was the fortuitous devaluation of the krona when the gold standard was abandoned, a move that followed by a few days the similar action of Great Britain. Monetary policy (in the form of pegging foreign exchange rates, which helped keep prices stable) also played a role. "The reason Sweden's policy was more successful than that in other countries," Montgomery explained to me, "was that the devaluation was bigger [this, by giving Swedish goods a highly competitive position in the world market, proved a strong stimulus to exports and swung the economy out of the slump]. The devaluation was not planned. In fact, the politicians fought against it, and only gave in to the inevitable when it was shown to be impossible to obtain foreign borrowings to protect the krona." Montgomery concluded: "The Swedish unemployment and financial policy did not play any very conspicuous part in actually bringing about the upturn." The economist Erik Lundberg agreed that the quite unconscious impact of the devaluation and the subsequent expansion "were certainly prerequisites for success," but named as another vital factor in the recovery an even less conscious development: "The most praiseworthy feature of the Swedish economic policy during the revival of the 1930's . . . is that many of the mistakes that were made in many other countries were avoided in Sweden. There was no attempt to embark on such ambitious exchange and price policies as those associated with the Blum experiment in France or with the New Deal in the U.S.A. Sweden did not introduce protectionist and bilateral trade policies as did Switzerland; she avoided the imposition of import regulations as in Denmark or of a clearing system of trading as in Germany."

Swedish economists are, of course, pleased at the high reputation of their abilities that was, in a sense mistakenly, spread abroad. This reputation has doubtless been of some weight in the numerous grants, visiting professorships, and similar honors that have been accorded them as their profession has become advantageously identified with their country of origin, somewhat the same phenomenon that has occurred with, say, French chefs, Swiss hotelkeepers, and Russian ballet dancers. It has also created a certain amount of embarrassment. Badly informed observers often tend to expect Sweden to experience perpetual economic bliss. Thus when a New York *Times* writer reported on some of the (not terribly serious, as such things go) consequences of Sweden's overheated economy in 1965, he gravely emphasized the shamefulness of the situation, considering that Sweden had been "long regarded as a paragon of fiscal management."

Though rather exaggerated at the time, the Swedes' gifts for economic management were real enough, and the country continues to benefit from a superior quality of economic thinking; but misconceptions still abound.

Most of these arise from the peculiar nature of Swedish Socialism, which foreigners often confuse with more orthodox Socialism. There are some traces of Socialism present, as the Swedes define the term; but the structure of the economy is still essentially capitalist, and the sporadic rumblings from more radical elements within the Social Democratic Party have mostly failed to find expression in actual policies. One period of agitation for more centralized state control occurred just after the war. Kjell-Olof Feldt, Undersecretary of Finance, explained to me: "Ernst Wigforss, the Finance Minister at the time, wanted to transfer the experience of the war years [when numerous economic controls had been necessary] to peacetime. He was in favor of planning for peace—especially in foreign trade and in directing business investment." But, Feldt added, "nothing happened." This was partly because the more talk there was of strict state planning, the less enthusiastic the voters became for the Social Democrats. The image of planning also suffered from the caustic criticism of many economists and from the embarrassing nonappearance of the widely heralded postwar depression, whose ill effects were to have been the planners' first object of attack.

The actual course of events was in the opposite direction. Most price controls, import controls, and other such leftovers from the war were gradually abolished. A decisive break occurred in 1955, when a man named Per Åsbrink was named president of the Riksbank, the central bank. Åsbrink was a good Social Democrat, but he had his own thoughts on the traditional Socialist belief that low interest rates are good. His first action was to hike the discount rate from 2.75 percent to 3.75 percent. Having neglected to inform the government of this rash move in advance, he was savagely attacked in parliament. But he stuck to his principles and, in the following two years, pushed the rate up to 5 percent. Åsbrink is still the Riksbank's president, and the discount rate has been transformed from an emotional shibboleth into a normal tool of monetary control. Low interest rates no longer possess any special charm. LO has stated: "A higher rate of interest is one of the prices of full employment and a price worth paying for the vast majority of the population."

Any visitor to Sweden who has heard of the Socialist or half-Socialist economic system is apt to be surprised to find the Socialists joining business groups in singing the praises of free enterprise as if they were so many fervent followers of Adam Smith. One businessman explained to a foreign audience: "If there is one fundamental opinion on which we and the Socialists seem to be able to wholeheartedly agree, it is that competitive, capitalistic free enterprise is the most efficient system of organization for an economy such as ours."

The government has consistently turned down all demands that it take more aggressive steps to take over business, and 95 percent of industry remains in private hands. I ventured to ask Gunnar Lange, Minister of Trade, why the Socialists didn't care to take over more of industry. He replied: "We would be afraid of building up a state bureaucracy, which I don't think would be very efficient. We have been pragmatic in our approach. We have never felt the important thing was who owns industry, but rather: Is it efficiently managed? Does it promote growth? Are the employees properly treated? Is it good for the consumer?"

An integral part of the belief in competitive free enterprise is a belief in free foreign trade. Because Sweden depends heavily on such trade for her high standard of living, she is invariably an eager and vociferous participant in international efforts tending toward more international cooperation—GATT, OECD, the Kennedy Round, EFTA, the IMF—and has backed her beliefs with a schedule of customs duties that are among the lowest in the world.

The low duties expose home industries to brutal international competition, particularly where low labor costs in other countries give them a distinct advantage over high-wage Sweden —*i.e.*, textiles, shoes, ready-to-wear clothing. But this is precisely the idea. Companies unable to withstand the competition are supposed to shut down so that capital and labor can shift to areas where they can be used more effectively. Whatever comes out of this policy is a natural product of the underlying forces at work. The state does not attempt to decide which companies deserve to survive and which do not. It is an almost ideal picture of the "invisible hand" of Adam Smith's capitalism.

The constant changes taking place as a result of the play of market forces and the central role occupied by foreign trade in the process have considerable impact on overall policy. The economic disturbances—the numerous shutdowns that have taken place in, for example, the textile industry—are welcomed as part of the price of progress. But businessmen are permitted, in fact urged, to arm themselves against foreign competition by automating, doing away with nonessential employees, and merging to form larger, economically powerful production units (monopolies if necessary)—*i.e.*, the structural rationalization mentioned in an earlier chapter.

Although many workers are hurt by the process, the labor unions heartily favor it. As a matter of fact, the unions are not above giving the "invisible hand" a nudge—particularly in forcing wage increases on companies which cannot afford them (and cannot raise prices because of foreign competition)—on the theory that companies incapable of paying a fair wage do not deserve to survive.

Despite the dislocations resulting from free trade, it remains firmly supported by all important groups. Åke Englund, head of the commercial department in the Ministry of Trade, firmly told me: "The government has made it clear that we have had and will continue to have free trade." LO declared: "It is difficult to find any tenable arguments in favor of Sweden pursuing a protectionist policy." Erick Stackelberg, a foreign trade expert of the Federation of Swedish Industries (*Industriförbundet*), said: "One rather fantastic aspect of Sweden's trade is that industry has always been in the forefront in fighting for less protectionism."

The objectives of economic policy in Sweden are more or less the same as in other countries: full employment, growth, price stability, and balance-of-payments equilibrium. And the tools used to speed up or slow down the economy in pursuit of these goals are the standard neo-Keynesian equipment in use almost everywhere: monetary policy to control interest rates and the money supply and fiscal policy to control the impact of taxes and government spending on the economy.

But in Sweden's case there is one large difference: the key determinant of economic policy is full employment (in contrast with Britain or the United States, where it is often sacrificed for international payments balance or price stability). A Social Democratic policy statement emphasizes: "Full employment is the central task of economic policy." In case someone doesn't understand what is meant by "full," the party spells it out: "We do not accept any percent of unemployment."

In practice, this has meant running the economy at full blast almost constantly, through continuous stimulation of demand for goods, which in turn spurs employment. Unemployment has, in fact, been kept low (often under 1 percent). But the difficulty with this practice is that it puts a considerable strain on the country's resources and, by reducing the incentive to hold prices down or to resist aggressive wage demands, leads directly to inflation. However, a bit of inflation is considered a fair price to pay for full employment. The Finance Minister has put the "acceptable" amount at "2 to 3 percent a year." The actual rate has rarely been that low: the consumer price index just about doubled in the 1949–65 period and rose by 5.5 percent in 1966 and 4.3 percent in 1967. But the insistence on full employment and disregard of the inflationary consequences continue in force.

While foreign observers are often shocked at this calm acceptance of what in many countries is a matter of grave concern, the Swedes would be even more shocked at the calm and deliberate destruction of jobs (as in Britain and America) as part of an effort to protect price stability. When one considers what is really at stake, the Swedish system has much to recommend it. For the centralized money managers, the creation of unemployment is merely a question of pushing numbers around on a piece of paper, but it is a brutal reality for those who are thrown out of work and who unfortunately often lack the sophistication to realize what a constructive service they are performing for the economy. One might feel more sympathy for the money managers if they themselves were required to take a cut in their own salaries every time they pushed through policy changes intended to take jobs away from others.

Anyway, the acceptance of inflation is considered the less unpleasant alternative in Sweden. To a great extent, the economy is built to withstand the strains. The virtually total unionization and highly centralized wage negotiations mean that almost everyone gets a yearly wage increase (invariably larger than the loss through inflation). Moreover, pensions are protected from inflation. Those living from fixed-interest investments are hurt, but they are not numerous. Conservatives have persuasively argued that what with the fortune tax, income tax, and inflation, wealthy purchasers of the state's bonds actually lose money on their purchases—without so far arousing the government's compassion. It could well be argued that the bondholders are in a better position to survive the ravages of inflation than marginal workers are to overcome the effects of losing their jobs.

Moreover, there is not only an acceptance of inflation, but also a positive admiration for it in many circles. For one thing, it is favored because it helps in the even distribution of economic growth. As Krister Wickman, Minister of Industry, has pointed out: "Completely stable prices would require that workers in industries with relatively slow productivity increases receive more gradual wage increases than those in industries where productivity is increasing rapidly." And this conflicts with LO's (and the government's) principles of solidarity, which hold that a worker should not be unduly penalized because he happens to be stuck in a stagnant industry. In other words, the only way for a cabdriver (who cannot easily increase his productivity) to share in the general growth of the economy is to raise cab fares. Undersecretary Feldt in the Finance Ministry said to me: "The only way to equalize incomes between low-productivity industries and high-productivity industries is to accept inflation. I don't see any other way to do it." (It may be pointed out that the Swedes would never accept a system such as the American so-called guidelines wage policy, which aims to fix a ceiling on wage increases in accordance with actual increases in the general prosperity but does nothing in the way of a floor to assure any part of the benefits of prosperity to those unlucky enough to be nonunionized or in inefficient industries.) Inflation is sometimes also praised for its help in keeping the economy puffing along at top speed, in much the same way that an automobile can cover ground when driven to the maximum, even though it develops rattles and strains in the process. In commenting on the many faces of inflation, economist Lars Lindberger said: "It is conceivable that a favorable view [of inflation] is so widespread that we will very likely continue to have a rising price level for some time to come."

But even the Swedes can see that inflation has its ultimate drawbacks. For one thing, polls show that the average man, who is not equipped to analyze all the intricacies of the advantages, is dead set against it. More importantly, it can affect the foreign trade balance if the ever more costly Swedish goods are unable to compete with their foreign rivals, whether on the export market or at home. For many years Sweden had no problems of this type, but in 1965 she experienced a yawning $280,000,000 payments deficit (on current account—currency losses were avoided because of short-term capital imports). It cannot be definitely shown that inflation was to blame for this, but it helped persuade the government it should attempt a stronger stand against price rises. As noted, inflation has continued, albeit at a slowing pace; but the concern is real.

Nevertheless, it is difficult to believe that the Swedes will willingly abandon their full employment policy to fight inflation. At it happens, they may not have to. Since the mid-fifties there has been under construction a potentially gigantic anti-inflationary weapon which, though less neat than the dramatic innovations of the thirties, is unquestionably an equally powerful economic instrument. This is the active labor market program, which helps workers hurt by plant closings, technological obsolescence, mergers, or other difficulties and which is a welfare measure, as well as an economic instrument.

This clever program, administered by the Labor Market Board (*Arbetsmarknadsstyrelsen*), offers to help those stranded in depressed areas or poor industries through free vocational guidance, free retraining, relocation assistance, and assistance in finding jobs. (The latter is carried out through a nationwide network of employment agencies. Private agencies are prohibited. When I asked Bertil Olsson, head of the Labor Market Board, why, he replied, "We don't believe they serve any useful function"—a sentiment anyone who has ever been at the mercy of the rapacious New York City employment agencies can heartily agree with.) In 1966, the program processed about 1,100,000 jobs (many temporary) and filled about 80 percent. It gave vocational training (in courses of two weeks to two years, during which trainees receive wages) to 40,000 persons, issued 33,000 travel grants, 7,000 family travel allowances, and 23,000 start-up grants.

One of the functions performed by the program is to reduce the dependence on orthodox economic management techniques. Unemployment is usually combated through measures that stimulate the entire economy, but such action is of little purpose if the unemployed are, because of geography or lack of skills, not in a position to accept the employment. The active labor market program thus makes it possible to pinpoint the areas where help is needed, with a precision and selectivity beside which the normal methods appear clumsy and old-fashioned.

The theory is that now that the program has been slowly built up to its present massive dimensions, it may be possible to refrain from keeping the economy in a constant state of overexcitement. As explained by the Labor Market Board theoreticians, the aim need not be "no percent unemployment," but perhaps 2 or 3 percent unemployment, with the active programs attacking the problems of those 2 or 3 percent. Thus, the economy can theoretically (though it has not yet) be kept cooled down from the red-hot tempo of the past. "I don't want to exaggerate the importance of the program," observed Olsson of the Labor Market Board, "but it does definitely create more flexibility in economic policy."

In addition to its value as a short-term policy instrument, the program aids in the long-term overhaul of the economy—the structural rationalization that is intended to procure more strength and efficiency. It has won praise in this endeavor from, among others, the OECD, which remarked after a study of the program: "The result has been a greater willingness ... to support technological and economic changes which will benefit the national economy."

Almost everyone familiar with the program is full of praise for it. The economist Erik Lundberg, who tends to be critical of many of the Social Democrats' economic ideas, said: "The Labor Market Board is not very impressive—it has no majestic building with Roman columns—but it is much more important to the economy than the Riksbank."

Another similar tool (similar in that it is selective) was added in 1965: an industrial location program designed to give loans and outright grants to companies establishing plants in depressed areas, particularly in the north, where structural rationalization in the forest industries is constantly destroying jobs. Though the program has been a decided help to the north, it has been sharply criticized by both management and labor representatives for distorting market forces. An LO economist explained to me: "We object to the establishment of low-wage industries in the north under this policy. It's an example of the conflict between planning and the free market. There's always a temptation to think you can do everything through planning." Bertil Olsson remarked of this type of policy: "In theory it's wrong, but I'm a practical man. I ask the critics how they would solve the problems up north. They tell me that's my job."

One of the most admired and most imitated Swedish inventions in the economic-management field has been the idea of investment reserve funds through which the economy can be stimulated at critical points.

The funds counter the regrettable (though understandable) tendency of business to invest in new plant and equipment during boom times and to hold back during weak periods, which is just when such action would be most helpful to the economy. Under this program, a company can set aside up to 40 percent of its pretax profits in a special reserve earmarked for capital spending. When the government detects a weakening in the economy, it announces that the funds thus accumulated can be used on approved capital projects (in practice, all projects have been approved). Companies that take advantage of the opportunity write off the costs immediately, and the funds escape taxation. Companies are even offered as a reward a small extra benefit, amounting to an extra depreciation charge of 10 percent of the total (which means an extra tax deduction of that amount).

The program is completely voluntary. But from a practical point of view there are good reasons to participate. The company must deposit 46 percent of the reserves with the Riksbank and may keep the other 54 percent. But if it chooses to let the money run through to its net income instead of siphoning it off into the investment reserve, it will have to pay out about half in taxes; so, from an immediate cash point of view, it is a little better off to build up a reserve than not to. If the company gets tired of waiting for the government to signal a release, it can pay the taxes and transfer the money out of the reserve. (Under certain conditions it must also pay a nominal penalty.)

This ingenious idea not only helps smooth out the rough spots in the business cycle, but in addition gives business an incentive to invest in new facilities (which also helps the economy) and helps business profits. It is customary for governments to fight recessionary tendencies through increasing government spending, but the investment funds let the same purpose be served by private business—an example of the Social Democrats' willingness to let business cooperate in government tasks, the important point being that the job gets done.

Folke Lindberg, head of the Association of Family-Owned Companies, who is generally critical of government policies, said of these funds: "The idea is so well arranged that you deduct even though you think you may never want to use the money."

Despite the few unique ancillary features, the actual management of the economy is carried out in a basically capitalistic framework. Much of the special Swedish flavor in economic management is, in fact, aimed at preserving and more efficiently exploiting the vitality of capitalism.

Where, then, does the Socialism come in? The answer is that in the *production* of the country's wealth, it doesn't. Though there are perhaps a few more government controls than in some countries (the government exercises tight control over the capital market, for example), they don't significantly alter the basically capitalist structure.

But the *distribution* of the economic resources thus produced does bear a strong Socialist stamp. The idea, in line with the Social Democratic Party's egalitarian ideals, is to attain as equal a distribution of the wealth as possible. The state is not, of course, able to confiscate property from the wealthy and hand it over to the poor, nor can it exercise any appreciable direct control over incomes. Its influence, with the help of the labor movement's dynamic wage demands for workers, has been felt in flattening out income differences, though there are no precise measurements on this extent. Most experts feel that a distinct leveling out in incomes took place in the period from the 1920's to about 1950 and that there has been little change since. One comparison shows that the income of a Stockholm city councillor, which was ten times that of an industrial worker in 1920, dropped to seven times in 1950 and that of a government agency head dropped from eight times to four times in the same period.

Exact comparisons with salaries of higher-level personnel in private industry are difficult to come by, but the trend has been similar. Eli Heckscher, prominent Swedish economic historian, wrote: "Since 1915, labor has received the major share of the increased national income." The Social Democrats are distressed that the movement toward equality has hardly budged in the last couple of decades, but in some degree they are to blame, their constant stimulation of the economy having created a great need for upper-echelon employees, with consequent steady rises in their salaries.

The tax system, combined with the social benefit system, has also been used to bring about a more even distribution of income, since the steep progressivity of the tax burden ensures that higher income groups will pay more into the system than they can get out of it. But the leveling-out process has slowed down here, too. Direct (*i.e.*, income) taxes rose so high that the government became reluctant to push them up further, and tax increases since 1960 have taken the decidedly un-Socialist form of higher indirect levies, notably a general sales tax, which at this moment stands at 11 percent—a technique that hits low-income groups especially hard.

But as the trend toward one Socialistic goal—*i.e.*, the even redistribution of income—has slowed down, another element generally favored by Socialists—the dominance of the government over the economy—may be said to have taken its place. The public sector (*i.e.*, government spending) has expanded from 17 percent in 1946 to well over 30 percent at present and is still growing. Individual real after-tax incomes have nevertheless also risen, and it can be persuasively argued that the economy can well afford heavy expenditures for collective needs. Dieter Strand, a highly intelligent Social Democratic theoretician, who helps run one of the party's newspapers, explained to me that needs were still great. "There are disastrous gaps," he said, "mental health services, dental care, more schools, more retraining for adults." But the planners sometimes seem to have become so accustomed to arranging new spending programs that they have become irritated at the inefficiency with which the average man carries out his spending activities and are selflessly offering to take over these burdens. This can be easily interpreted as a disadvantage of the Swedes' possession of great organizational talents. Strand told me: "People who were getting more and more money and who saw how much was being taken in taxes began to see how much could be done with the money publicly—a more efficient way of organizing things. In the fifties and sixties we have gradually got people to understand that certain things have to be organized centrally."

For whatever combination of reasons—wise policies perhaps, plus the good fortune to have missed two world wars—the Swedes have registered startling gains in wealth. Just sixty years ago a parliamentary commission was pondering the worrisome phenomenon of massive emigration as Swedes fled their impoverished homeland. As this is being written, there is agitation for another, similar parliamentary investigation—but this time into the problems caused by the floods of impoverished foreigners who are drawn to Sweden by a desire to share in the country's impressive wealth. In the period following World War II, growth has been especially rapid. Gross national product grew at an annual rate of 3.2 percent in the 1950–55 period, 3.5 percent in 1955–60, and 5.1 percent in 1960–65. Historian Åke Elmér has written: "In 1910, Sweden was one of Europe's poorest countries and even in the thirties was well behind, for example, Great Britain. But during the postwar period, our country has come to the forefront in Europe and probably now stands in third place in the world after the U.S. and Canada."

At the present time Sweden is among the world's most prosperous countries. In 1965 gross national product per capita came to $2,490, which compared with $3,560 for the United States and $1,810 for Great Britain. Comparisons of the wealth of various countries are difficult, but here are some indications: the Swedes' per capita consumption, unadjusted for differing price levels was, in 1960, 54.5 percent of the U.S. figure (Britain at 49.9 percent); a method devised by American economist Colin Clark indicated that the Swedes' consumption was 58.9 percent (Britain, 63.1 percent) of the United States; and studies of the German Statistical Bureau showed Swedish consumption at 67 percent of the United States (Britain, 78.7 percent).

The Swedes often do not accept such figures. Gunnar Myrdal has written, for example: "Ordinary Swedes are now as well off as ordinary Americans—perhaps a little better off." It depends, of course, on the exact meaning of the comparisons. With the combination of varied welfare benefits, widespread unionization (with solidarity as a key feature), and the full employment policy, there is almost no real poverty in Sweden, certainly not in the sense of the oppressive, degrading variety that exists among substantial groups in the United States. Because of these factors, plus tough coercive measures against negligent landlords, there are no slums in Sweden, and even ancient or poorly equipped residences are generally maintained in a good state of repair.

But if the lower levels of society are higher in Sweden, so the upper levels are lower. The Swedish ideals of egalitarianism have had a strong impact. Salaries for top executives in major corporations are a fraction of those in the United States, and $8,000 is considered a princely income. Anyone earning $10,000—which included just 1 percent of all income earners in 1965 (as against 15 percent in the United States)—is considered one of society's elites. Family incomes above $10,000 are registered by 3 percent of Swedish families (23 percent in the United States). Moreover, the tax system acts as a powerful hindrance to the accumulation of wealth.

But it is not accurate to say that the ordinary Swede is as prosperous as his American cousin. The vastly more numerous rich in America serve to raise U.S. average figures, but even the ordinary worker tends to earn more. Figures compiled by the Swedish Employers' Confederation put hourly wages in U.S. manufacturing in 1964 at $2.51, compared with $1.45 in Sweden. Strict comparisons in money terms actually probably overstate Swedish incomes owing to differences in price levels, which are generally higher in Sweden than in the United States, the only important exceptions being rentals on most apartments, which are subsidized and rent-controlled. These being left out of account, price levels in Sweden are considerably higher than in the United States, as anyone who has lived in both countries will recognize. Measured in terms of possession of various material goods, Swedish standards again show up less favorably. Less than 25 percent of the urban population lives in one-family houses (compared with 75 percent in the United States), and the Swedish houses tend to be on the small side, generally with four rooms or less. Most of the population lives in apartments, and these are, as noted previously, rather small and still poorly equipped by U.S. standards. All city dwelling units taken together, 29 percent of them consisted in 1960 of two rooms or less (against 7 percent in the United

States), and 38 percent lacked a private bathroom (against 4 percent in the United States). In terms of ownership of autos (363 per 1,000 inhabitants in the United States in 1963 vs. 205 in Sweden), TV sets (327 vs. 239), and the other signs of prosperity, the Swede is well behind the American and roughly on a par with the Canadian, though well ahead of other Europeans.

All this is not, of course, meant to imply that the United States is better than Sweden or that the American is happier than the Swede. The advantages of living in an efficiently organized society with a high degree of personal security and desirable nonmonetary benefits, such as the statutory four-week vacation, can have considerable value. But judged strictly on the ground of *material* welfare, the Swedes are decidedly in a worse position than the Americans.

The Swedes have not always been as careful with the facts when publicizing their country as one might wish, and I believe that an accurate understanding of the resources they have to work with is important. Americans frequently underestimate the accomplishments of the Swedes (which I believe have been considerable) through a failure to consider the results in relation to the resources (which are meager in comparison with the wealth of America).

The major criticism lodged against Swedish economic policies has been the indifference to the inflationary effects of the relentless pursuit of growth and full employment, but it must be noted that whatever the theoretical values in the argument, the Cassandras predicting impending disaster have been invariably proved wrong in practice. In a way, the development has been a kind of *Perils of Pauline*, in which certain disaster has at frequent intervals seemed unavoidable, only to be handily averted for reasons that are not quite clear. At this moment (late 1967) the forebodings of doom (the balance-of-payments deficit in 1965 and 1966, which was widely expected to undergo only gradual improvement during a five-year period) have suddenly and inexplicably greatly improved, as exports have boomed and imports have been held to a nominal gain. Perhaps only minimum credit for this achievement can be accorded the government's economic thinkers, who are fully as surprised as anyone else. But it does suggest that the bold and risky policies that have been pursued had their merits after all.

X

The Businessmen and the Socialists

It should be remembered that however great the skill with which economic development is guided, goaded, and relied on by the government, an indispensable element in the process is the cooperation of the primary custodians of the economic resources on which the system is built. In Sweden this means private businessmen, who, like businessmen elsewhere, are not noted for their sympathy for Socialist political parties, and the retention of the goodwill of this group is obvious. Said one business leader to me: "They realize we're all in the same boat. If private business fails, what happens to the social welfare programs then?"

The government must therefore enlist the cooperation of businessmen without allowing them to take over the system but also without inspiring them to grasp the opportunities for sabotage or other obstructive practices which are available. That this delicate trick has been pulled off is surely one of the marvels of the Swedish system. Businessmen supply assistance to the government in many ways, yet are kept firmly under control of the government. On its side the government displays a knowledgeable sympathy for the aims and needs of business.

To say that businessmen as a group are enchanted to have the Socialists in power would be going too far. On the contrary, they would doubtless gladly see the Social Democrats removed as soon as feasible. Some government policies cause businessmen intense irritation, and they would make numerous changes if they had the chance. But these are for the most part minor disagreements rather than major conflicts. Basically, businessmen accept the system. As a journalist specializing in business and economic matters, I have spoken with scores of Swedish businessmen, ranging from presidents of large banks and corporations to minor executives and small entrepreneurs, and have found very few who have any appreciable bone to pick with the Social Democrats.

The wide-ranging system of welfare benefits, for example, is rarely attacked by businessmen. Jonas Nordenson, head of the General Export Association, gave me his interpretation of businessmen's views on the welfare system: "I think there is basically a strong acceptance of it, though it's a question of at what rate and *how* things should be done. We have differences of opinion (we definitely oppose the housing policy), but I think we do combine a vigorous private enterprise economy with social welfare." One section of the welfare system that businessmen are particularly fond of is the active labor market program, which means that help stands ready at all times to ease any social difficulties caused by plant shutdowns or other business decisions. Curt Nicolin, president of ASEA, remarked to me: "I am in favor of welfare for everybody," but added pointedly, "when it is based on sound economic principles." As for its long-term value, he takes a coolly rational view: "The concept of the welfare state has been around for a long time, but in its highly developed form it is actually quite new. To judge from the first few years' experience that it is an impossible way to organize society is not justified."

An oft-cited example of the government's basically friendly attitude to business is the corporate tax setup, which is regarded as among the most liberal in the world (even if businessmen frequently complain about the steeply progressive personal income tax). Tore Browaldh, chairman of Svenska Handelsbanken (Sweden's largest commercial bank), said, "We have the best corporate tax system of any country in Europe."

Actually, the corporate income tax rate is not especially low; national and local taxes total about 50 percent. But a string of provisions relating to reserves tends to cut taxable profits sharply and makes the actual effective tax rate considerably lower than in most countries. As profits are siphoned off into one or another of the available reserves, the amount coming down to the point where the tax is figured—and thus the tax itself—can be quite freely raised or lowered (mostly the latter, of course).

A case in point is the network of rules on depreciation. As the reader may know, when a company buys a new machine, it does not list the cost as a business expense during the year of purchase. Whether the actual cash paid comes from borrowings or from the company's own savings is of no interest to the profit-and-loss statement. As far as the books are concerned, the cost is split up into small pieces which are deducted from income gradually over a period of years, as the machine is used. These deductions are the depreciation charges and are deducted from income even though they are expenses only on paper. Obviously, the larger the depreciation charges, the smaller the total income subject to the tax collector's attacks. Many companies therefore feel it is advantageous to shrink the period of time over which the machine is depreciated, thus increasing the size of depreciation charges and lowering the *taxable* income (and income tax), but actually raising the amount of money the company has to work with, during the years in question.

It is just this that the Swedish rules permit. All capital goods (except buildings) may be written off at any desired rate, up to a maximum of 20 percent of cost annually or 30 percent of book value (*i.e.*, the value of the item in question after previous depreciation charges), and a company is free to shift from one method to another from year to year, depending on which is momentarily more convenient. In effect, this means that capital goods can be written off in a minimum of about four and a half years, compared with an average of approximately twelve to fourteen years in the United States.

Another similar provision is the rule on inventory reserves. Inventories may be carried on the books at anywhere from 40 percent of value to 100 percent, at the option of the company. This seemingly innocent rule can have a powerful effect on the profits a company reports and thus on its taxes. If it appears that profits are going to be especially high one year, meaning an extra burdensome tax load, the company can simply whisk the money into an inventory reserve and adjust the percentage at which inventories are carried on the balance sheet, and the difficulty is taken care of.

The most ingenious of the special reserves is the investment reserve idea, described in a previous chapter, which permits a business to stash away—tax-free—a large chunk of profits in a special fund earmarked for later investment.

Because of the numerous possibilities of shuffling profits from one reserve to another, most corporations report for tax purposes only the income it is advantageous to report—often just enough to cover dividends. A visitor may erroneously assume he is being kidded when a financial executive blandly explains: "First, we find out how much in dividends our shareholders want. Then we work backward through the books to come out with just that amount."

But these favorable tax rules are not an across-the-board gesture of kindness to business. As it works out, they are of special benefit only for growing companies, and the faster a company grows, the more it is able to benefit. Businessmen often grumble about this necessity to keep growing and about the fact that when growth begins to level off, taxes tend to jump sharply. But spurring growth is, of course, one of the government's fondest aims.

As could be expected, there is a certain amount of regulation of business practices in Sweden. But this regulation, though effective, often has almost a casual character. There is a distinct reluctance to establish formal controls over business when it can be avoided.

For some time there was much discussion and an official investigation of the business of charter-plane package tours. This sort of travel is enormously popular (most of it is to Mediterranean beach resorts) among the sun-loving Swedes. The number of such trips sold in 1966 has been estimated at 400,000. The business has attracted a large group of entrepreneurs, ranging from large respectable companies to more shaky firms. The investigation was called when a number of the smaller operators were unable to provide the transportation promised, leaving their customers stranded at the airport. Every effort was made to solve the problem without legislation. Trade Minister Gunnar Lange told me: "We would rather that tourists looked after themselves. The travel agencies themselves have tried to organize their business properly. If that doesn't work, we might have to have more laws, but I have always been against more legislation if it can be avoided." The situation eventually deteriorated to a point where a guarantee of financial stability was required, but only as a last resort.

The precise dividing line between strict government controls and voluntary self-regulation by business itself is sometimes difficult to discern. For example, there is something called the Council on Business Practices (*Näringslivets Opinionsnämnd*), whose principal function is to act as a complaint department for advertising.

Sten Tengelin, head of the council, emphasizes that the

council is "purely private." Well, yes. It is supported by twenty-six large organizations, for the most part prominent business groups, but also including the Consumer Cooperative Society and the three major union organizations, some of which have more or less close ties with the government, as well as the government's Consumer Council.

The council does not initiate objections, but processes those that are submitted by others. When a complaint is received, it is relayed back to the advertiser for his comments, then to the complainant, and so on back and forth a few times. "It's rather inefficient in a way," said a staff member. "You can't really count on a decision in less than six months or so. But you've got to let both sides express their views. If the advertising in question violates accepted business ethics, we ask the defendant not to repeat it and to confirm his willingness to abide by our decision in writing."

How often does he agree? "Almost always. We have no real power. We can't make him stop. But it very seldom happens that a company ignores our advice."

A typical case brought to the council concerned one of the numerous charter-travel tour companies. A dissatisfied traveler had complained that, among other things, the company had promised in its advertising that it could assign firm hotel room numbers at the time they first made their arrangements in Sweden and that a free champagne party would be thrown for all members of the group once they were in Majorca. However, according to the traveler, he failed to receive any advance hotel room number, and there was no champagne served at the champagne ball. The company defended itself by pointing out that it never claimed it assigned advance room numbers to *all* customers, but since it booked entire blocks of rooms for whole seasons at a time, it was in a position to do so in some cases and that inasmuch as it was the only company in Sweden that did this, it didn't see why it shouldn't boast of the fact in its advertising. As for the champagne ball, it went on, there had never been any claim that authentic French champagne would be served, but every guest did receive—as promised—a bottle of Spanish bubbly that differed from the genuine article only in name.

In its decision the council suggested that if the company was not prepared to give fixed room numbers to all its customers in advance, it should clearly say so in its advertising. On the other hand, it allowed that it was perfectly plausible to stage a champagne ball without genuine champagne. The company then agreed to modify its statements about advance firm room numbers and presumably continued to advertise its parties as champagne balls.

Though Tengelin believes the council's powers might well be enlarged to allow it to initiate complaints, as well as to process those submitted by others, he believes the council should continue to be private, not governmental. "We already have as much effect as very strict legislation would have. We don't usually act as fast as we would like, but we still act faster than government bodies usually do."

To an outsider it seems improbable that such a group as this could have any effectiveness. But a close look at its operations suggests that its decisions really do carry weight. Tengelin pointed to one obvious factor: "There is always the threat of stricter legislation." This is clearly reflected in the operations of two committees related to the council: one regulates liquor advertising, the other proprietary drug advertising. They carry out prepublication checks of all advertising in these fields and can forbid publication of anything that violates the rules. But both committees are sponsored by business. They originated from suggestions by the government to prohibit all advertising in these fields because of abuses that had occurred; the government agreed that self-regulation be given a try and has been apparently satisfied with the results.

But beyond the threat of stricter legislation, there is the peculiar Swedish atmosphere. Said Tengelin: "You have to understand that there is a fairly unanimous outlook on business ethics here. We haven't that gap between the interests of business and the interests of society as a whole that exists in some countries. These social facts make it much easier for us to be effective."

Very much the same sort of attitude prevails in Sweden's antitrust administration. The similarity in approach exists despite the fact that the antitrust machinery is not private, but governmental. But voluntary compliance and negotiation are the bases for its functioning.

For many years after it was set up (in 1953, with modifications in 1955), this unusual regulatory body worked marvelously well, even though the anticompetitive practices it was dealing with were neither prohibited nor punishable by law. Furthermore, these practices are hardly even mentioned in the law that set up the antitrust bodies. An outstanding feature of the legislation is its vagueness, being mainly an announcement that efforts will be made "through negotiation to eliminate the harmful effects of restraints on competition. . . ." Early in 1966 the legislation was revised (much to everyone's regret) and became slightly tougher. But the idea that disputes are best settled through discussion rather than coercion remains a basic tenet.

The antitrust facilities are divided into three parts: an investigative arm, a kind of public prosecutor, and a final court. What makes the apparatus odd is that for the most part none of the three arms has the power to do anything beyond publish findings and make recommendations.

Helmer Olsson, head of the investigative part, the Price and Cartel Board (*Statens Pris- och Kartellnämnd*) pointed out that the only practices flatly outlawed are vertical price-fixing ("fair trade") and collusion among companies bidding on the same contracts. "Other types of restraint of trade, such as cartels, monopolies, and mergers among major companies, are considered generally to be injurious but aren't prohibited. All restraints on competition can be investigated, and if the investigation shows that an agreement is contrary to the public interest, certain measures can be taken: not by force, however—only by discussion and negotiation."

The Price and Cartel Board only ferrets out facts, never expresses an opinion about whether a practice is or is not against the public interest. One of its more curious chores is compiling the data that go into Sweden's *Cartel Register*, a directory listing intercompany "agreements to restrain competition," with the names of the companies involved and details of the agreements, which might cover production, sales practices, or prices. All the data are from the companies themselves, which must supply all the facts when the board asks. The *Register* currently lists something over 2,000 agreements, in fields ranging from steel to beauty parlors.

The next phase of the antitrust mechanism is the Commissioner for Freedom of Commerce (*Näringsfrihetsombudsmannen*), who, with a staff of twelve assistants, ponders the socioeconomic consequences of restrictive business practices and decides if they are against the public interest. If he concludes they are, he tries to persuade the enterprises involved to modify or abandon the agreements. Attention can be focused on an area by material turned up in the Price and Cartel Board's investigations (some of which are undertaken at the commissioner's request), queries from businessmen, or angry letters from consumers. "Anyone, in fact, is free to complain and to have his complaint looked into," said Åke Sundquist, present commissioner.

But the legislation is extremely flexible, and there is no obligation to attack any particular practice. Said Sundquist: "We have monopolies in certain industries—containers and cement, for instance—but our investigations have not shown that these monopoly enterprises have had unjustifiably high prices. In cement we found prices in 1962 were about the same as in 1951, despite considerable inflation in most areas. This shows there's nothing for us to worry about."

It might be assumed that since the commissioner has no power to apply penalties, his decisions are largely academic.

But it doesn't work out that way. "We get about 175 to 200 cases a year, of which about 80 or 90 are complaints from other businessmen," he said. "Usually, all but 3 or 4 a year are settled here." About a third of the cases are simply dropped, because the practices in question are not judged objectionable. "On the whole," Sundquist averred, "we've been very successful. When it's decided a practice is harmful, the entrepreneurs usually respect this opinion. But we can't issue injunctions. We have no sanctions. We rely mainly on negotiation and publicity for our success."

For those few cases which cannot be settled by the essentially powerless Commissioner for Freedom of Commerce, the next stage is the nine-member Freedom of Commerce Board (Näringsfrihetsrådet), which has the last word and until recently was also essentially powerless.

At this final stage, when a recommendation is made by the board and the company refuses to modify or abandon the practice, the board can suggest to the government that it take action: adjust duties to facilitate the entry of foreign competitors, establish state-owned enterprises, or push new and harsher legislation. For many years the force of these implicit threats worked well.

In 1965, however, a furniture manufacturer refused to supply his merchandise to a discount house, claiming that the latter specialized in goods of inferior quality and that he didn't want the public to identify him with such products. Impervious to cajolery, persuasion, and negotiation—plus fervent pleas from other businessmen—the manufacturer refused to budge. A group of business associations issued a stern statement in which it "strongly emphasizes the importance of enterprises faithfully respecting the decisions of the Freedom of Commerce Board." The furniture manufacturer stubbornly insisted to the last that he could not afford to sell to the low-price firm.

The board didn't see it that way, and neither did the government, which called for new legislation allowing the board to levy fines when refusals to deliver were found to be unjustified. The new legislation went into effect early in 1966, though without upsetting the basic reliance on negotiation and discussion, which still dominate the work of the antitrust machinery.

It is a bit surprising to see a business association angrily countenancing businessmen to comply with the requests of a Socialist government, as if it were only a question of an innocent admonition to look both ways before crossing the street or to watch out for forest fires. I asked Axel Iveroth, president of the Federation of Swedish Industries, about this. He seemed surprised that anyone would think it unusual. "But the law is set up to promote competition," he replied, "and since we believe in competition, we believe the law should be respected. Besides, we have our own representative on the Freedom of Commerce Board, and our opinions are very often the ones that are applied."

It turns out, in fact, that one of the nine members of the Freedom of Commerce Board is a representative of industry (other groups, such as farmers, consumers, and labor, are also represented), who happens to be a vice-president of the Federation of Swedish Industries. Behind him stands a group (sponsored by the federation and four other business associations) called the Industry Council for the Promotion of Competition (*Näringslivetskonkurrensnämnd*). Lennart Körner, head of this group, said: "I meet very often with the commissioner to see what new cases are coming up. When it appears, in the light of my knowledge of the subject, that the companies will eventually be forced to comply with the opinion of the commissioner, I try to make this clear to them. Many companies feel it is better to get a solution through discussion and negotiation if they can be shown they will probably lose anyway."

Körner spends much of his time, understandably, defending the business viewpoint and often carries his point, perhaps proving that it is better to cooperate on the cases that are hopeless anyway in return for being able to swing opinion over in the borderline instances. A few years ago a large stylish shoe store was unable to get delivery from a certain shoe manu-facturer. The manufacturer defended himself with the argu-ment that he practiced "selective selling," meaning that he attempted to maintain an aura of prestige around its brand by restricting the number of outlets. The commissioner didn't accept this argument, but Körner thought it was defensible in this particular case. The case went to the board, which decided against the commissioner and in favor of the shoe manufacturer.

Nevertheless, relations between Commissioner Sundquist and Körner are quite good. "These organizations have done very, very much for us," said Sundquist. "Just now Mr. Körner is working on a case where about twenty manufacturers of ladies' dresses refuse to deliver their merchandise to a big discount store in the south. He is trying to persuade some of them to change their minds. We will be very happy if he succeeds."

Thus does a government activity become interlocked with the organizations. Körner said: "One can say that we have the same purpose as a governmental body. We don't try to defend business at all costs. But it's often easier for us to come to a solution with companies than for the commissioner. That is, it's less painful if it comes from another businessman."

Considering its low-pressure nature, the antitrust adminis-tration has been remarkably successful in helping abolish in Sweden the heavy dependence on cartels that has long existed in European countries. Sundquist said: "Before 1953 we had many cartels with fixed prices." But most have been dissolved or modified, either voluntarily or in negotiations with the authorities. "Investigations have been made of prices before and after, and I can assure you that in most cases we have had lower prices and harder competition than we otherwise would have had." But this revolution was carried out without resort to force or harsh measures likely to generate bitter antago-nisms among businessmen. Today, except in export fields, where the relatively small Swedish companies must band together to survive in international competition, cartels are of minor importance.

The willingness of business to cooperate is also shown in its attitude to the government's industrial location policy, a system of subsidies designed to aid depressed areas in the north. Business groups bitterly opposed the scheme. Iveroth, president of the Federation of Swedish Industries, said: "We opposed it because it's a distortion of market forces. It doesn't use resources in the most efficient way."

But far from continuing to fight the program after it went into effect in an attempt to cripple it and show how wrong it was, industry is cooperating in its administration. Business representatives serve on the boards that decide which proposals from companies should be accepted. Iveroth calmly explained: "We are just trying to see that the subsidies do as little harm as possible. It's better to be in touch with the government so that you can influence them than to isolate yourself and not be able to influence policy at all."

Iveroth, despite some fairly critical opinions of the Socialist government, believes that the businessman in Sweden has some advantages over his counterparts in other countries: "In many respects there are more risks for government action against private enterprise in many other countries than in Sweden. We have here a theoretical background that we are familiar with. In the U.S. the government can strike very hard and erratically." He cited, for example, sudden attacks by the antitrust authorities and interference by Presidents in business pricing policies. "Here, we negotiate with the government all the time, and our opinions are respected. We know where we are."

Some individuals in the business community have exceptionally warm feelings for the government. Tore Browaldh, the bank president, said: "A more positive attitude toward business would be hard to imagine." Browaldh pointed to the great flexibility of business regulation as a prime example. During one of the recurrent flurries of anxiety regarding inflation in 1965, price controls were loudly proclaimed in some quarters as being the only possible answer. A government committee set up to study the question coldly turned thumbs down on the notion. Said Browaldh: "They have broken with the old

Socialist traditions"—that is, the idea that the government should attempt to control everything.

But even businessmen who are firmly opposed to the government are not particularly acid in their opinions. Per Eriksson, sales manager of Volvo, said: "Relations between the big industries and government are on a much more personal level than in other countries. We are very friendly to the government, and the government is very often receptive to Volvo's viewpoints." He added, however: "I still feel that if we had had a government on the other side, business would have been better off."

Johan Paues, president of Dynäs, a small forest-products company, favors the basic welfare system but is critical of the government: "Incentives are severely curtailed by the tax system, which has as its aim the redistribution of wealth. Eventually, it will make it more difficult to find people to tackle the really tough jobs that require intellectual ability and a willingness to work hard. As time goes on, this will probably curb the rate of economic growth." Paues thinks this is a mistake: "For stimulating progress, there's nothing like letting a man earn a lot of money and keep it."

Nevertheless, Paues, who has been a top executive in the very free economy of Brazil, takes a realistic view on the organization of the economy: "I've lived in a completely free enterprise society, and I think I did reasonably well there. But I don't think the system would work in Sweden or in the United States. It has been decisive in the initial growth stages of industrial societies, but after a certain stage the system has to adapt to new conditions. This doesn't mean I don't believe in the principle, but the idea of going back to unrestrained free enterprise is simply wishful thinking."

An essential part, I believe, of the business-government harmony is a relatively close agreement on the workings of the economy. Both business and government agree that efforts should be made to assure industry of the capital it needs for expansion, and both sides have felt in recent years that consumer spending must be held down in order to do this, usually by raising taxes, though they can and do bicker about the extent and the priorities involved. Policy disagreements occur, in fact, on almost every major issue, but there is a broad range of accepted economic principles: there does not exist in Sweden a left-wing economics and a right-wing economics, and much of the solemn nonsense that goes under the guise of economic discussion in the United States would be no more than an object of amusement in Sweden. The general level of economic sophistication is unusually high in Sweden. Even small businessmen and middle-level executives often display a surprisingly thorough understanding of economic principles.

This understanding arises at least in part from economists' active participation in the country's life. Already early in this century, Gustav Cassel, one of the most notable Swedish economists, began a series of almost weekly articles in a prominent newspaper. The articles, written in easily understandable terms, continued for forty years and helped accustom the public to discussion of economic questions on a professional level. In 1939 the American economist Richard A. Lester was awed by the prestige accorded to members of his profession: "In Sweden, academic economists probably enjoy more respect and influence with the people and the government than anywhere else in the world. A number of Swedish economists write regularly for the newspapers and periodicals; some of them are members of parliament...." This high prestige of economists still exists. Their opinions are regularly reported in the press and are often given extensive treatment, even by the normally lowbrow papers. News coverage of economic events, such as presentation of the budget, adjustment of the discount rate, and proposals affecting economic policy, is on a very sophisticated level—on the whole, a much higher level than in America (despite the disappointing overall quality of the Swedish press).

Some insight into this problem was given to me by Torsten Carlsson, chief economist of the Skandinaviska Banken, in an explanation of opinion on deficit financing. Since World War II, Sweden has been able to run the economy at top speed without, on the whole, resorting to deficit financing, at least partly because of her booming foreign trade. Despite occasional small deficits, the total budget has been in balance or close to it most of the time, and if only the current budget is considered—*i.e.*, leaving aside the capital budget—it has run at a steady surplus. I asked Carlsson what would happen if conditions made continuous and heavy deficit financing desirable. Would an outcry be raised? "We have nothing of the opposition against the idea you have in the U.S. It's surprising that that exists there, despite very advanced economic teaching in America and some very good economists. The question of balance in the formal sense is not so important, because you can sometimes have that and an imbalance in other areas. I don't know exactly how deep understanding of this goes here but certainly those in opinion-influencing positions—even conservatives—would not hold the ideas of American businessmen. I don't think a businessman here would dare to make parallels between a private individual's economy and a state's economy. He would be criticized and even laughed at. Even if there were some opposition, communication is so close here between businessmen and the various organizations that responsible economic opinion would soon be spread among businessmen in general. The type of primitive reaction that is so common in the States wouldn't last long."

As indicated earlier, Swedish businessmen are by no means unanimously delighted with the Social Democrats and their ideas of how a government should be run. Some observers believe that businessmen are willing to cooperate on a practical level in order to win small concessions and freedom from government interference, but that this surface amiability masks deep underlying suspicion and hostility on both sides. Erik Lundberg, the economist, remarked: "They cooperate on the short range, but over the long term they know the government is after them." When I asked one top executive in a leading company why industry representatives were so willing to cooperate with government when they clearly didn't go along with the Socialists' thinking on many subjects, I got this reply: "After this has been going on for so many years, it becomes extremely tough to break the pattern. And the longer it continues, the more difficult it gets. Everything is so well organized and runs so smoothly; it would take a great deal of courage to be the one to cry stop."

XI

The Swedish Woman

Judging from available accounts, nearly everyone who has visited Sweden any time during the past several hundred years has found the Swedish woman to be one of nature's truly impressive achievements. Samuel Kitchel, a German, wrote in 1586: "Swedish women are naturally beautiful, finely shaped, pale-skinned, neatly dressed, charming, and stately." In 1804 the Englishman J. Carr noted: "The Swedish ladies are in general remarkably well shaped and have a fair transparent delicacy of complexion. . . ." Albert Vandal, a Frenchman, exclaimed in 1876: "The beauty of Swedish women is proverbial."

Any contemporary visitor of average perceptivity can easily confirm the justice of such observations, but no Swedish woman, at least none of those who speak or presume to speak for their sisters, will willingly allow him to conclude that such truths exhaust or even make a good beginning on the real state of the Swedish female. Speaking of foreign observations, they would likely prefer one of Mary Wollstonecraft Godwin, who in 1796 spoke of Swedish women as "these poor drudges" and concluded: "The men stand up for the dignity of man, by oppressing the women."

Many women feel that although the rest of society has been thoroughly modernized in the past few decades, the renovation process has been carried out primarily to suit the men and that women should now claim their share of justice.

Actually, the facts show Swedish women do not have it all that bad. In 1858 they were given the right to claim all legal rights at the age of twenty-five. In 1864 they got the right to go into business. In 1918 they obtained full suffrage. In 1921 they were given full equality in marriage. The first woman member of parliament was elected in 1921, and today there are 46 women members (out of 384). In 1925 women were given the same rights in civil service as men. In 1959 the last formal barrier (except the prohibition against female accession to the throne) was removed when women were admitted to the priesthood, although this is still much resisted by male priests. In the thirties, women were given protection against dismissal from employment on grounds of engagement, marriage, or pregnancy. More recently, separate male and female wage scales have been abolished by labor-management agreement.

Moreover, the opportunity for women to lead independent lives is large in Sweden, possibly greater than in any other country. The most unperceptive visitor cannot fail to notice the independence with which women freely go out alone in the evening or in other ways assert their nonreliance on the opposite sex. A foreigner who encounters numerous women taxi chauffeurs, bus drivers, and barbers and who notices that Swedish women lawyers, economists, and members of other professions carry their responsibilities with an unusual seriousness of purpose (while, remarkably, retaining their femininity) may be very slightly puzzled to learn that a great struggle for women's rights is going on.

Yet it is frequently stated that women are the Negroes of Sweden, and they are no more moved by the argument that they are better off than the women of Turkey or Portugal than discontented blacks in South Africa are moved by statements

that their material welfare is better than that of the citizens of
Chad or Upper Volta.

Indeed the position of women has in recent years become one
of the hottest subjects of controversy, as such things go in tranquil Sweden. Although the woman question has been a more or
less live topic for many decades, the discussion received substantial fresh impetus with the appearance of two books, which
illuminated different aspects of the question and which were
published, by coincidence, almost simultaneously in 1962–63.

One of these was *Kvinnors Liv och Arbete* (Woman's Life and
Work), a rather scholarly collection of essays by economists, psychologists, and sociologists on different aspects of the woman's
position in the employment market. The book concludes that
the barriers to (1) the entry by women into fields traditionally
dominated by men and (2) their slow progress in the professions
they are allowed to enter derive from purely emotional, groundless prejudices. It includes extensive quotations from business
executives who were asked to defend their strong, but often
irrational and contradictory, feelings against hiring women or
against hiring them for any but the lowest, worst-paid, traditionally feminine jobs. The book argues persuasively that higher
absenteeism and other seemingly unfavorable signs of women's
job performance may be traced to such facts as the lower average
age of women workers (because they are not encouraged to stay
on the job) and the discouragement that results from being
given lower-grade, monotonous positions. The book pleads for a
better break for women already employed and a removal of the
bars to traditional masculine occupations.

The other book was a polemic, by essayist Eva Moberg, entitled *Kvinnor och Människor* (Women and Human Beings).
This was, in a way, a reworking of the familiar argument that
woman, in addition to her biological duties, should be encouraged to develop other talents and interests. However, a new
twist was added; Miss Moberg emphasized that the woman's
role can never be straightened out until something is also done
about the man's role. It is hardly fair, she declared, for the

woman to be urged to acquire a schizophrenic view of her mission in life while the man is allowed serenely to concentrate all his energies on his work. The job is not only to get the woman into the factory but also to get the man into the home. Housework, cooking, cleaning, and taking care of the children are chores that should be split down the middle. This might well result in the introduction of part-time work for both partners, so the home can be properly managed.

The impact of these two books has been enormous. The first one, a 500-page-plus volume written partly in dull academic prose and partly in Norwegian, sold out the first printing of 3,000 copies in five months—an extraordinary achievement in a country of Sweden's size. A later condensed version sold 7,000 additional copies. But it was probably Eva Moberg's book that had the greater influence. At first her views were vigorously attacked—in great part, oddly enough, by women. But her arguments gained adherents, and three years later they enjoyed the support of virtually all influential opinion in Sweden. All previous thinking on the subject was turned upside down. Mrs. Annika Baude, who helped in the research for *Kvinnors Liv och Arbete* (Woman's Life and Work), spoke to me of the impact of Miss Moberg's ideas: "It was the first time responsibility for the problem was put on the man. One can no longer talk about the question without talking about the problems of the man."

One reason for the books' success was that their viewpoints happily coincided with problems of labor shortage being dealt with by officialdom. Per Holmberg, an economist with the Labor Market Board, told me: "Consciousness of the problem is very high. Dissatisfaction among women, but also among men, is increasing rapidly." Holmberg noted the economic waste involved: "It's been accepted for housewives who hold a degree not to use it, despite the fact that they often have too little to do. It's a form of unemployment. They are in effect being retired at a very early age." Holmberg estimated that the gross national product could be upped by 25 to 30 percent if all the potential women workers could be given employment.

Mrs. Baude remarked to me: "Our full employment is a fake.

The reserve of women who would be available for work if it were conveniently available are not registered among the unemployed." She cited the case of a community of 4,000 whose official figures showed no unemployment, yet when a new plant was established in the town, the company was able to recruit 300 women workers almost immediately. She put the total amount of this "hidden unemployment" at 100,000, which she said is a "conservative" estimate.

The underutilization of highly trained women is especially painful. One study in 1966 showed only 83 percent of women dentists to be employed, 85 percent of lawyers, 83 percent of economists, 75 percent of agricultural and forestry experts, and 87 percent of engineers. Marianne Höök, a gossipy newspaper columnist, commenting on the importing of badly needed nurses from Korea and the Philippines, which requires investment in language training, housing, and other assistance, asked, "Why can't such money be spent on some of the eleven thousand trained unemployed (i.e., married) Swedish nurses we already have? They already have homes, and they can speak Swedish."

At least one part of the problem is the tax question. Tax rates are already high, and a married woman's income is added to her husband's, thus pushing them up into a higher bracket. Per Holmberg mentioned an additional obstacle: "Having a wife who sits at home has become a status symbol in the same way as ownership of a Mercedes or membership in the Rotary Club." A third problem is the dire shortage of day nurseries where working mothers may leave their children. In Stockholm there is room for only 4,500 children in such nurseries—and a waiting list of 3,000.

The day-nursery shortage is critical, since a main goal is to get away from the idea that it is only middle-aged women with no small children who should hold jobs. Mrs. Baude pointed out that many women with children under seven are already working but that prejudices block further progress: "Few people like to talk about this because it's considered to be immoral to leave a child during the day." Mirjam Israel, well-known child psychologist, asserted: "That children need an intimate, friendly contact with the adult world seems to be beyond question. But there is nothing that says (and hardly any modern researcher who says) that (1) it must be the mother or (2) it must be only one person." Thus, the emphasis is on getting the father to share in taking care of the baby—up to a point, anyway ("Nature itself seems to oppose a division of the responsibility," grumbled one publicist for the cause)—and expanding the number of day nurseries for children of working mothers. Eva Moberg, who started the agitation, replied recently to a query on the most urgently needed reform: "Point one: a strong expansion of day nurseries."

The school system is helping out in the effort to eliminate, or at least blur, the distinction between masculine and feminine roles. Handicraft classes are no longer divided according to sex: boys study sewing and girls study carpentry. Anna-Lisa Lagby, head of the joint management-labor Woman's Labor Council (*Arbetsmarknadens Kvinnonämnd*), told me: "We must begin in the schools." This council commissioned a study of social-study textbooks which sharply criticized the authors' perpetuation of traditional ideas. Sample: "Näslund swarms with sex-role prejudices. 'Boys like to go in for woodwork and to repair things. Girls like to use a needle and thread.' 'A girl is considered to be more suited than a boy to take care of the home and children.' " One book is castigated for showing Father reading the paper while Mother feeds the baby; another for showing only men in such occupations as electricians and firemen, and women as telephone operators and nurses. Mrs. Lagby said the response was encouraging. "Many textbook writers contacted us to discuss revisions, and later editions have been changed. Some authors were quite interested. They said they had never thought of it that way before."

This council also encourages girls to seek advanced training and not only in traditional feminine fields. One booklet points out: "The choice of a career is just as important for a girl as for a boy. Nowadays every healthy person must be prepared to provide for himself or herself.... Not all girls are attracted to housework (although perhaps most are), and many girls, given proper encouragement, can make a valuable contribution in technical occupations...."

The Labor Market Board actively drums up job interest among women, principally through propagandizing for its free vocational training courses. All these courses are growing at a rapid clip, but the participation of women is growing even faster: they made up about 11 percent of the 10,000 persons trained in fiscal 1959–60, but about half the 55,000 trained in 1966–67. A distinct effort has been made to infiltrate women in the courses in traditional masculine fields, but this turned out to be difficult. Mrs. Ingeborg Jönsson of the Labor Market Board said: "So far we have not been particularly successful in our efforts to interest women in training in the so-called male occupations, and therefore, in spite of theoretical objections, we have been obliged to experiment with special women's courses in the traditionally male sectors."

What effect has all this agitation had?

Separate pay scales for men and women (once felt to be justifiable because of higher absenteeism among women and other such factors) were abolished, beginning around 1960. The process was completed by 1966, and Arne Geijer, head of LO, was able to note: "During the past five years an improvement has occurred; women's salaries now average 77 percent of men's, compared with 70 percent in 1960." But he added: "This means that we have only come partway." Women do not occupy the better jobs, of course (one study showed that 73 percent of all women employees were stuck in eighteen low-paying categories, while only 12 percent of the men were in such positions), and for this reason their earnings still don't measure up to the men's.

The number of women holding jobs has been rising markedly. The percentage of married women gainfully employed has climbed from 14 percent in 1940 to about 30 percent at present. Fully four-fifths of the entire growth in the labor force in the 1950–64 period was due to the entry of married women into the labor force, and they had a significant impact on the economy. Ingvar Svennilson, leading economist, explained the greater than expected economic growth in the early 1960's: "Married women rushed out on the labor market at a much more rapid pace than we had counted on." It is believed or hoped that the trend will continue. One study estimated that the percentage of working wives in the twenty to forty-four age group, 45 percent in 1961, would climb to 50 percent by 1970. Interest in continuing to exploit this rich vein of hidden talent is keen, since it is calculated that the very slight population increase over the years to 1980 will be offset, as far as the labor force is concerned, by decreases in working hours and increases in the number of people going to universities. Curbs placed on immigration in 1967 leave women as virtually the only hope over the years ahead.

Some change has been noted in women's interest in aiming for higher positions. The number of women in institutions of higher education has been rising rapidly for some decades; the proportion of women among young people passing the *studenten* (which qualifies them for pursuing advanced education) stood at only 33 percent in 1941 but had risen to about 50 percent by 1960. The big campaign of the last few years has had a perceptible effect in decategorizing professions by sex. The proportion of women among those choosing scientific-technical specialities in secondary schools rose from 34 percent in 1960 to 42 percent in 1965, and the proportion of women in technical training in Gymnasiums (roughly corresponding to junior colleges in the United States) rose from 4 percent to 9 percent. A sharply rising trend is shown in the female percentage of those just beginning training in the upper-level "male" professions, when compared with the percentage of females actually engaged in those professions. The logical conclusion is that women are more aggressively attacking the male vocations today than they were in the past. For example, in 1965, 9 percent of all those practicing law were women, but 19 percent of the new law students were women; in medicine the figures were 14 percent and 21 percent, and in engineering 2 percent and 5 percent. Per Holmberg of the Labor Market Board concluded: "It's not a very rapid development, but it is a development. The problem is to get women into traditional men's courses. People think that women are not gifted in technical matters. But our tests show that there is no important difference."

Many labor-short corporations have willingly accepted the women's rights arguments and have made special efforts to enlist women in "masculine" jobs. Volvo is one such company, and visitors to its factories are treated to the sight of numbers of Swedish girls rubbing their attractive elbows with the men on the assembly line. Volvo is well satisfied with the results and notes that although "absenteeism of women is approximately twice that of the men," this "is outweighed by the fact that the turnover among the women is only half." It also solemnly records a shift in mood since the girls were added: "The general atmosphere on the assembly line has improved."

Some progress is being achieved in the much discussed area of day nurseries. Following a long period of inactivity, the authorities in Stockholm (where the shortage is most keenly felt) began a program in 1965 to accommodate 500 additional children annually during the 1966–75 decade, meaning a doubling of the number of places.

But most of the people engaged in the campaign are distinctly dissatisfied with the progress. On being asked if there was much response among younger girls exhorted to take more care with their careers, Mrs. Baude said sadly: "No, nothing. They don't take advantage of their opportunities; they feel they can be supported all their lives. It's the American influence; it appeals to the laziness that is in us. We're making some progress, but it's slow." Perhaps the biggest disappointment has been the failure of men to insist on their right to do housework, despite the campaigners' insistence on this as a key element in the drive. Marianne Höök remarked: "There is much latent, unarticulated discontent among men with the negative aspects of the man's role." Per Holmberg said: "The women must give up their monopoly of housework!" To help get the point across, newspapers have frequently pictured Cabinet ministers and other celebrities happily washing the dishes or vacuuming the rugs. But a survey in 1966 showed that the average working wife spent two and three-quarter hours a day on housework, while the average husband spent fifteen minutes. Another frustration has been the poor results of the heavy doses of equalized craft courses and other propaganda aimed at children. One survey of preferred vocations among schoolchildren showed that boys were still most enchanted by the prospects of being auto mechanics and electronics technicians, while the girls wanted to be child nurses and beauticians.

One occasionally receives the impression that for some of the women involved, this hot discussion has a strong element of a puritanical antisex crusade. The accusation is frequently made that one of the men's most effective methods of oppressing women is by emphasizing their sexual role. Rita Liljeström, a newspaper writer, remarked bitterly: "Television stars, conference hostesses, and girl guides at fairs constitute a Swedish version of the Japanese geisha." Margareta Ekström, a literary critic, complained of the French new wave films that "the main female character is hardly more than a model for the man's daydreams." Marianne Höök noted approvingly a report that François Truffaut had said he was tired of sex (in films at least) and had glowingly praised Soviet women, after a trip to a Yalta beach resort, on their indifference to being sexually attractive (they have broken through the "sex wall," she happily reported).

I have been assured, however, that the campaign is not at all antisex in character. A prim young mother, who has been actively involved in the women's rights struggle, explained to me why she thought the idea of, for example, attractive waitresses in Playboy Clubs was dreadfully disgusting, said, "It's not an objection to sex, but only to women going around being beautiful and nothing else."

Allowing men to gawk at half-naked girls does put women in a special position, but some observers argue that the proper way to equality is, not to persuade men to be less interested in the sexual attributes of women, but to get women more interested in the sexual attributes of men. Joachim Israel, a sociologist who has written endlessly on the question, told me: "If you had men going around in bathing suits serving drinks to women, that would be fine. But why must it always be the other way around?" Another crusader for equality of this type is a young lady named Nina Estin, who in 1966 launched a "pornographic magazine for women," containing photos of handsome nude men, called *Expedition 66*. She explained. "The magazine can be seen partly as a reaction against the vogue for ordinary pornography, which is directed only to men. . . . The man's anatomy offers just as much stimulation to a woman's erotic thoughts. . . ." (But when the magazine came out, Marianne Höök, for one, didn't think the "Playboy mentality" any more suitable for women than for men.)

There are, indeed, a good number of women campaigning for a woman's right to have as much right as a man to a free and untrammeled sex life and to be able to take the initiative in sexual advances without risking social opprobrium. Gunnel Thörnander, an attractive young woman who works for Swedish Radio, explained to me that sexual freedom was a new idea in the emancipation efforts: "But it's just as important as jobs and careers. You can't just be partly free; you must be wholly free, in every area." In 1963, Kristina Ahlmark-Michanek gained a certain amount of notoriety by writing a book, called *Jungfrutro och Dubbelmoral* (Belief in Virginity and the Double Standard), in which she advocated undertaking sexual relations "for friendship's sake." Since then a number of others have added their voices to the cry. One has been Barbro Backberger, who has aggressively attacked the assertion among authors of books for teen-agers that "boys have a stronger and more distinct sexual drive than girls." She said: "I myself had my teen-age love experiences damaged and dirtied by such mercilessly distorted sexual views."

Miss Thörnander is just as discouraged about the progress in women's sexual freedom as the job-equality crusaders are about their progress: "It's very hard to change attitudes in this area. It is probably accepted by intellectual and artistic people." But she conceded it could be worse: "It's much better in Sweden than in most countries."

It may be useful to digress briefly for a glance at the much discussed subject of sex in Sweden. The question must be approached with trepidation, for on no other subject are the Swedes so sensitive to the real or imagined criticism of outsiders. Swedish sex has been often discussed abroad with more imagination than objectivity (though not nearly so often as Swedes believe). As a result, many Swedes assume that visitors are mainly interested in tracking down evidence of licentious behavior. A foreign keynote speaker at a business conference in 1964 won approving headlines when he avowed that he did not intend to spread stories back home about the Swedes' sexual practices. For my part, I have become accustomed to being asked, when I inform a Swede that I am a journalist, "Oh, you're one of those who write about sex."

One consequence of this is a strong defense against foreign opinions. Prince Bertil, when asked by a reporter in Canberra about sex in Sweden, piously replied, "As far as sexual freedom is concerned, I wouldn't say there is such a great difference between Sweden and other countries." When a group of businessmen went to America in 1965 to drum up trade, they were given a selection of prepared statements that might come in handy in discussions of various subjects. One of the subjects was "Sin in Sweden." The suggested statement was: "Scientific studies made in the U.S. and Sweden indicate that there are no significant differences between the two countries regarding sexual behavior." A handbook prepared by the Swedish-American Foundation for students and others planning to visit the United States cautions: "American sexual morality is considerably stricter than it is in Sweden. This is a condition that one ought to respect. If you personally should share today's so-called 'liberated' views, you do neither yourself nor your country a service by more or less openly declaring the fact." Although Swedes often justifiably boast of their relative lack of hypocrisy in sexual matters on the domestic plane, they sometimes reserve a separate attitude for export.

The truth of the matter is that the sex life of the Swedes is not nearly so exciting as some foreign press reports indicate, but neither is it so prim as many Swedes would have you believe. One can say that, on the whole, the same sensible, practical approach is taken in the sexual realm as is applied to any other area, and it is surprising that so many Swedes want to conceal this fact to foreigners. Since the sexual instinct appears to be ineradicable, the Swedes reason that the problem is, not how to suppress it, but how to organize it as efficiently as possible.

One element that tends to confuse the issue and that sometimes shocks foreigners is the acceptance of the fact that unmarried people sometimes go to bed with each other. That no attempt is made to segregate Swedish university dormitories by sex, that municipal camping facilities can be freely used by couples whether or not they are married, that unmarried couples frequently sign up (as unmarried couples) with travel agents for group tours abroad—such phenomena can hardly be taken to mean that unmarried Swedish university students, campers, and tourists have sex lives, while those in other countries do not. One would have to be incredibly naïve to believe that a rule barring men students from women's dormitories in an American university means that there are no sexual encounters between the men and women students.

Frankness is not, of course, the only factor. Openness is possible, indeed, only because a large part of the population accepts sexual intercourse between unmarried couples as a natural and unspectacular phenomenon. Various authorities with whom I have spoken, including conservative moralists strongly opposed to the "new" morality, put the percentage of couples indulging in premarital sexual intercourse at upwards of 80 percent. Parents frequently arrange a guest room for their child and future marriage partner when the latter stays overnight, and the parents' premarital gift of a trip to Paris or other exotic spot is by no means uncommon. A textbook called *Vägen till Mognad* (The Road to Maturity), by Lis Asklund and Torsten Wickbom, prepared for use by students of fourteen to seventeen in connection with a TV series for schools, asserts: "Here in Sweden the opinion has become more and more general that the woman and the man have the same right to sexual experience before marriage."

Mrs. Asklund, a former social worker, who now gives advice on emotional, sexual, and marital problems on the radio, explained to me: "Some people claim we say people *should* live together before marriage. That's not what we say. But we accept it. We accept it absolutely. If you take engaged people in Sweden today, I think ninety-five percent of them are sleeping with their partners. Naturally, we are very much troubled with young people having children they can't take care of and venereal disease. But if two sixteen-year-olds who are in love and have been going together have sexual relations, I don't think that hurts them, as long as they use contraceptives. I think most people in Sweden accept premarital intercourse between two people who are in love." There is very little prostitution in Sweden (although it is not forbidden), and Mrs. Asklund remarked on this subject: "We don't need prostitution. We would think it terrible that a man should have to go to a prostitute while his fiancée sits home." Margareta Vestin, mother of four daughters and an official in the National Board of Education, part of whose job is to spread the word among teachers on the women's rights question, gave me her attitude: "I don't think it's good for a couple not to go to bed before they are married. I have one girl who is fourteen. She is a virgin now, but at sixteen probably not. I like innocence as long as you can have it—but not too long. I feel that if a girl really likes a boy, she should go to bed with him."

There are no sex-behavior studies of the Kinsey type in Sweden (although one was commissioned in late 1966), but a few small surveys have been taken. Typical of these was a 1965 study made by Georg Karlsson, a professor at Uppsala, among students in six different schools with an average age of 22.4

for the males and 21.0 for females. The study showed that the proportion of those who had had sexual experience ranged among the different schools from 62 percent to 86 percent. The median age for first intercourse was 17.0 for men and 17.6 for women. Another study was carried out in Örebro by Bengt Rundberg and Hans Linderoth, child psychologists, among 500 young people, average age 18. About half said they had had intercourse—57 percent of the boys and 46 percent of the girls.

Some observers believe the changes in Swedish society over the past few decades have brought a great change in sexual behavior. Professor W. E. Mann, a Canadian sociologist who visited Sweden in 1965 as part of an international study of sex patterns, gave me his theory. "It is partly because of Protestantism," he said, "which allows more intellectual freedom. This country has had almost no Roman Catholic development. Furthermore, there was no Puritan revival, as with Wesley in Britain. Moreover, the domination by a state church has meant that the church's influence has waned; there are no lay organizations, little contact with the people, few collections. The church is not dependent on the people. Into this religious vacuum came the Social Democratic Party, and women became emancipated relatively early, because of this movement."

No doubt such influences are important for some layers of society, but increasing democratization has also played a role. Lis Asklund pointed out: "Thirty years ago the working class behaved much the same as everyone does now. Psychologists and sociologists have talked about the great changes that have taken place, but this is because they themselves are mostly from the upper classes." A certain casualness in sexual behavior has prevailed among some social groups for a good many years. Having children out of wedlock was common for many years in certain parts of the country, and marriage was often delayed until the first child was on the way or already born. Too, some villages were so isolated during the long winters that the couple could not make their way to a church until spring to formalize a marriage that had long been consummated.

It is nothing new for foreigners to be shocked by the Swedes.

Mary Wollstonecraft Godwin complained about "the total want of chastity in the lower class of women" in 1796, and George Matthew Jones, an English traveler of 1829, noted stiffly that Stockholm "by no means" was "the purest capital in Europe," a circumstance he traced to the influence of the art-loving, well-traveled king of the eighteenth century: "It would have been well for Sweden, if Gustavus III had never visited Italy, he having brought back with him the seeds of a demoralisation, for which the specimens of the fine arts which accompanied them will never be able to compensate."

It is not surprising that, in a country where everything is organized, there is an organization for sexual matters: the National Association for Sex Information (*Riksförbundet för Sexuell Upplysning*), usually known by its initials, RFSU. This group was founded on a national basis in 1934, with the sponsorship of unions and other organizations. Its stated goals are "harmonious sexual relations and planned parenthood; more candor and increased knowledge in sexual matters; more research and broader information about biological, psychological, social, and cultural aspects of sex life; improved conditions for families and single parents; and increased Swedish contributions to international family planning."

RFSU operates a string of thirty-two shops which sell contraceptives, other articles of personal hygiene, and books on sex. It also sells condoms through the mail and in automatic vending machines. Its posters reminding the public to buy contraceptives—with such slogans as: "Honestly now: Can she trust you?"—have gained international recognition. (In line with the equality-for-women campaign, one newspaper complained: "Why does RFSU speak only to the man?" RFSU indignantly replied by referring to another poster reading: "Both of you have responsibility.") Its sales are about $1,200,000 a year, and it is believed to be the country's largest merchandiser of contraceptives, a rising proportion of which are sold through vending machines on main thoroughfares. Because RFSU is an idealistic nonprofit association, it has trouble competing with other companies. "Our price level is about sixty to seventy percent of that of our competitors," said Lennart Ajax, its president. "We have had certain problems with our vending machines. Owing to our lower prices, we can't pay high rents and in some cases have had to take down machines because of better bids from the competition."

The profits of the business side, which now run about $70,000 a year, are turned over to what Ajax called "our idea people." This part of the association operates clinics, to fit diaphragms, makes pregnancy tests, prescribes oral contraceptives, and sells uterine devices (plastic spirals). "But it's more than just technical things," said Ajax. "We also answer questions on sex problems in general: impotence, frigidity, pregnancy. We give contraceptive advice free by letter or in person." No moral position is taken, and anyone over fifteen years of age (sexual relations under that age are forbidden in Sweden), whatever his or her marital status, is given whatever help and advice is within the association's powers. "If a woman comes to our clinic to get advice about contraceptives, she should of course be helped," said Ajax. "If people come to us for advice, they must get it. If a homosexual comes to us with a problem, our psychologist tries to find out what his problem is. But if he wants to be a homosexual, it's not our job to cure him."

One of RFSU's most important tasks is helping improve Sweden's system of compulsory sex education in the schools, which despite its fame abroad, is frequently and severely criticized and is now being thoroughly restudied by a government commission. Kjell Hansson, an official of RFSU, explained to me: "Sex instruction is compulsory for the pupils, but not for the teacher. It's very difficult for them to talk about it when they have never learned anything themselves." RFSU, therefore, organizes lectures for schoolteachers, tries to publicize a more factual approach to sex problems, and occasionally ventures into the schools themselves with special lecture material to demonstrate different birth-control devices.

It should be emphasized that RFSU, despite its rather unusual character, is an organization of the highest respectability, and it is invariably recommended as a reliable source of information on sexual matters by other authorities in Sweden. It has no doctrinaire ideology. It does sponsor the publication of a few books (sex manuals, scholarly and sociological studies) and sells others (defending homosexuality and other forms of deviancy). Kjell Hansson explained: "We don't agree with all the books, but they serve a good purpose, because they stimulate discussion. We have a mission in that people—even young people—have a right to get information about contraceptives and sex functions. Sex is a natural part of every human being. Knowledge doesn't solve everything, but we are better off if we know more."

It might be well to make clear there are numerous shades of opinion on sexual matters. Even those appealing for more tolerance quarrel bitterly with one another. Carl-Gustaf Boëthius, a religious writer who has been attacked for his suggestion that the church modify its strictures against premarital sex, has in turn attacked Lis Asklund for her too permissive attitude. And Lis Asklund says she has been called a "Victorian puritan" by Joachim Israel. Similarly, Maj-Britt Walan, a government official concerned with sex education, suggested establishment of an institute to make pornography more freely available to those who can benefit from it. But because she cautioned that this service should be restricted to married couples, she was called a bigot by Lars Ullerstam, author of *The Erotic Minorities*.

Although the heavy discussion of sexual freedom—such as proposals that state bordellos be established, that teen-age couples should be encouraged to set up housekeeping to gain experience, or that newspapers should inaugurate special classified ad departments for sex deviants in search of partners—can be interesting, it is apparent that a great deal of the talk is just talk. Swedes also have their reticences. They are often shocked at the goings-on in the Reeperbahn in Hamburg or Pigalle in Paris, and the rare striptease spectacles offered in Stockholm (mainly for the tourist trade) are almost invariably staffed by foreign artists. Some of these find the Swedish attitude not at all what they expected. Rita Renoir, a French nude dancer, has been quoted as saying: "The Swedes are thought to be quite free: that's not true. When I went to Sweden, I said to myself: 'The Swedes are used to total nudity, so in order to thaw them out, I'll have to go all the way.' Well! They were very shocked."

Moreover, there are a good many people who are much against current ideas of sexual liberty, and ringing protests against these ideas are common. Some years ago a group of 140 doctors gained some fame through a sharp criticism of prevailing standards of sexual behavior. In 1965 there occurred a figurative "moral march"—a protest petition, signed by 100,000 indignant women, which was stimulated by one of Sweden's slightly lewd films. The petition, presented (with no discernible effect) to the Minister for Ecclesiastical Affairs and Education, pointed out: "History shows that people whose morals have sunk too low have often gone under as a nation and become an easy prey for foreign conquerers." One public opinion poll showed that the majority of people over fifty thought Swedish morality (it was strongly implied that it was primarily a question of sexual morality) was too low.

But the typical Swedish sexual behavior, though decidedly more liberal than that accepted in America, is not considered by most Swedes to be a question of morality at all. (In most respects, in fact, Swedes are appreciably and unmistakably more moral and more honest than the inhabitants of most countries.) Moreover, in a country where so much effort is devoted to the deadly serious pursuit of efficiency, there would seem to be more to admire than to condemn in Swedish society's relatively casual acceptance of intimate relations between unmarried couples.

Some of the more radical agitators want to go beyond ideas about sex and to abolish the family. Probably only in liberal-minded Sweden could a leading newspaper present, on Christmas Eve in 1965, an article entitled "The Holy Family," a sarcastic polemic by Barbro Backberger on the unwillingness of social thinkers to attack an institution that had outlived its value. Another woman journalist wrote: "There is today no reason for young people to marry. The man can protect his children in other ways. The woman has the opportunity to support herself."

The thought is a logical one. Women have a great deal of freedom to enjoy an independent sexual and social life with little of the subtle pressures that exist in other countries, to receive the full protection of the welfare state regardless of marital status, and (despite the complaints of the equal-right campaigners) rather good economic opportunities. One might naturally assume that an increasing number of women would choose an independent life. But it hasn't turned out that way. The marriage rate is still below that of the United States (6.9 marriages per 1,000 population in 1963 vs. 8.8), but the proportion of married people in the entire population rose from 48 percent in 1930 to slightly over 60 percent in 1960. Per Holmberg, the Labor Market Board economist, said: "Barbro Backberger is wrong. The family is of greater importance for the individual today than ever before, because of urbanized society and greater individual isolation. Most people have a need for a stable emotional relationship with a person of the opposite sex." It can be added that although Sweden's divorce rate is high compared to those of other European countries, it is lower than that in the United States, and it appears especially low when one considers the ease with which a divorce can be obtained. It is granted if there is evidence of a "deep and lasting division" between the two parties, and it is considered sufficient proof that such a division exists if they say it does. After a one-year separation the divorce is granted almost automatically and at little cost. If one party resists, it becomes more difficult, but the divorce is generally obtained anyway.

There are a good many women in Sweden who establish a family without the benefit of marriage, though only rarely with the clear intention of doing just that, and they often find it a perfectly practical way of life. About a sixth of all children born in Sweden are out of wedlock. (It is not common for

Swedish women who become unexpectedly pregnant to seek an abortion. Abortions are allowed, but only under very special conditions. Every year hundreds of foreign women, unaware of the rules, come to Sweden expecting to obtain an abortion, but almost all are turned down. Many Swedish women who want abortions go to Poland. There is some demand for liberalizing the current law, and a government investigation is now looking into the matter. Ironically, just as the law was being bitterly attacked in Sweden in 1965, it was praised as a model for American legislation in a New York *Times* editorial.)

Largely because of special welfare benefits, the position of the unmarried mother is considerably better in Sweden than in most countries. She gets the same free medical assistance, prenatal care, and cash payment at birth as the married woman. She is entitled to the low-interest home-furnishing loan (maximum $1,000) available to newlyweds and she receives the usual $175-a-year child contribution.

In addition, she is assigned a child welfare officer (*barnavårdsman*). According to Inga Johansson, head of the Stockholm Child Welfare Board: "He is supposed to think of everything for the child. In a way, he fulfills the position of a father. The mother has someone to discuss the child's problems with." The child welfare officer, a function created in 1918, advises the mother and assists her in housing, education, and other problems. He is assigned to her before the birth of the child and stays with her until she marries or the child reaches the age of sixteen. She gets a child welfare officer whether she likes it or not.

A problem often faced by the unmarried mother is that of earning enough money to support herself and her child. Therefore, she can get free aptitude testing, vocational counseling, and, if necessary, retraining. While in training, she receives a basic monthly stipend of $80, money for her rent, about $10 to $35 for someone to take care of her child during the day, transportation money (about $8 in Stockholm), and a $3 clothing allowance, plus, of course, the regular child contribution, which works out to $15 a month. In addition, she receives from the father of the child a regular allowance, depending on his ability to pay but a minimum of $22 monthly. If the father is unwilling or unable to pay this amount or if he cannot be located, it is paid by the Child Welfare Board.

The welfare people help persuade the father to affirm his paternity and agree to make support payments. Most often the father signs a statement, and that's that. Sometimes a court must decide, on the basis of blood tests, anatomical investigations, and such, who the correct father is—a procedure that is necessary in about a sixth of cases. Mrs. Karin Danielsson of the Child Welfare Board told me that reluctant fathers are most often found among foreigners in Sweden. "If I ask a Swede to come and see me," she said, "he comes. But foreigners often won't. They feel that the Swedish state arranges everything. 'What do I have to do with it?' they ask."

According to Mrs. Johansson, the program has been a success, in the technical sense of both helping women who need it and helping change society's opinions toward unmarried mothers. "I have worked here for forty years," she said, "and things have changed very much during that time. An unmarried mother can be a teacher, a nurse, or in any other profession. Many years ago if a single teacher, for example, had a child, people would talk rather much. Now it doesn't matter. Some feel it is even better to be unmarried, partly because taxes are lower."

One of the few Swedish women who felt the unmarried mother's position was sufficiently favorable that she willingly, even deliberately, achieved that position is an attractive thirty-four-year-old lady named Siv Wilén, who lives on the outskirts of Stockholm with her seven-year-old son, Peter.

"I had met his father two years earlier here in Stockholm; he was an American soldier stationed in Paris at the time. I don't know why, but the first time I saw him, I made up my mind he was to be the father of my child. During the next two years I think we saw each other four times, but we corresponded the whole time." Why did it take so long? "I couldn't convince him. I brought up the subject, but he said he didn't want a child. He wasn't the marrying kind, you see. I told him I didn't want him to marry me; but I don't think any man would believe that, and he didn't. I finally went to Paris over Easter of 1959. But I didn't convince him. I sort of fooled him. I just wanted that child so much I didn't care what I did. Now I can't even remember what I told him." What was his reaction? "When he found out, he tried through a mutual friend to convince me I shouldn't have the child. I wrote to her and told her in a nice way it was none of her business and to tell the man to drop dead: I had what I wanted, and that was that."

Miss Wilén's sense of independence was so strong that when the father avowed his paternity, she instructed him to cross out the part on the form where fathers must agree to pay support (even though his foreign residence would have permitted him to forgo making any actual payments), depriving her of a monthly state allowance. "The law was changed in 1964," she said, "so even those as silly as I was now get the money." When I spoke to her, she had not seen the father again, although he had written to her at one point. "He wrote and tried to be nice," she said, "and said he had been a skunk, but perhaps I was nasty to him. I now wish he would at least send a birthday card to Peter."

She said she had found her situation "about what I thought it would be" and has been able to manage (she is employed as a secretary), even though she has had to devote a great deal of time to her sick parents. Has she had any regrets? "Never." How is it to do without marriage? "I can only speak for myself, but I have not had any difficulties at all. I don't know what people say behind my back, but as far as I know, nobody minds that I have a child and am not married. I wouldn't mind getting married now, but I'm too old, too used to being by myself. Anyway, I don't feel the lack of anything by not being married."

I happened to mention to Mrs. Johansson of the Child Welfare Board that in some tax-supported housing projects in the United States certain discriminatory rules are sometimes applied against unmarried mothers. "We do it in another way," she said. "Here they are the first to be taken care of."

There are, on the indisputably sound theory that unmarried mothers' needs are greater than most, a small number of apartment houses constructed especially for them.

I visited one of these—a bright new structure in one of Stockholm's neat suburbs, containing two-room-plus-kitchen apartments for twenty-eight mothers and their children, as well as a day nursery. On a visit to the establishment, I approached the day nursery, where a boy about four years old ran up to me and asked, "Are you my father?" Birgit Rönnblad, manager of the nursery, explained when I spoke to her: "Whenever a man comes here, the children always hang onto him, so I believe the father is important. Even with all the advantages unmarried mothers have here, it's still quite a struggle. As soon as they get ill or the child gets ill, they have difficulties. And they have nobody to discuss problems of the children with. They can get advice here and from Mr. Anderson [who is in charge of the house], but it's hardly the same." Nevertheless, Mrs. Rönnblad emphasized that the unwed mother's lot had vastly improved over the years: "It's not a shame any longer to be an unmarried mother."

Gösta Anderson, a young serious gentleman and a child welfare officer by profession, agreed: "It's much easier to be an independent mother now than twenty years ago." But he did not overestimate the value of a house full of nothing but unmarried mothers (if they marry, they must move). "It's something of an emergency solution," he said. "It's not ideal. It would be much better to have an apartment in an ordinary house. But they are all happy here."

The mothers, who pay rents of just over $50 a month for their apartments, seem to agree. Furthermore, when I asked some of them about the social problems of an unmarried mother, they couldn't think of any. Birgitta Eilander said: "The hardest thing is that you can't get a flat. I didn't want to marry the father because I thought he didn't really want to marry me, and I didn't want to force him. I see it like this. If the father had married me, we both would still have to work. Taxes would be much higher. And in getting a place in a day nursery, unmarried mothers come first. If the child is sick, I can call a social worker to come watch her during the day—that costs about $2 a day—and even though they have many children to look after, they have to go to unmarried mothers first. People at work think I'm very clever to work and keep house, but if I were married I might have to do all that and wash my husband's shirts, too."

Connie Hulterstedt, who gave birth at the age of nineteen, was married at twenty, and was divorced at twenty-two, told me: "The only problem I have had is to get a flat. I was never worried about being an unmarried mother. It's so usual in Sweden. I think it's easier to live alone here than in other countries." Anita Danielsson, who became pregnant in California, said that even though she decided not to marry the father of her child, "I believe in marriage." She was, in fact, planning to marry when I spoke to her. But she didn't feel it was particularly difficult to be an unmarried mother: "People don't look down on you in Sweden." When I asked her how her family reacted when she wrote them from California that she was pregnant, she replied, "At first my mother was a little bit shocked, but that was because she was afraid I would stay in America."

The battle for women's rights is evidently destined to rage for some time, and no doubt more victories will be won by the crusaders. Some observers may watch with regret an evolution that threatens to bring about fundamental changes in the superbly feminine and widely admired Swedish woman. Foreigners often have the distinct impression that the women in Sweden lack much of the coldness and stiffness of the men; if this is because the men are conscious of their status and the women, having no status to speak of, are not, then one can at least have mixed emotions about the value of the reforms being fought for.

In the heat of the discussion some seemingly odd ideas are produced. Some people may have thought it a triumph for women's rights that the father of an illegitimate child could be forced to make support payments. But one of the debaters, Inger Becker, threatens to come full circle in holding that this only encourages the maintenance of inequality. A woman should have as much responsibility as a man for using contraceptives, and if she fails in her duty, possibly because she is trying to trick him into marrying her, she should be penalized and the man not be compelled to pay. "Perhaps then," Miss Becker concluded, "the woman will be less inclined to be careless about contraceptives. . . ."

Perhaps the oddest proposal of all was made by a lady named Anna-Carin Andersson: "The women's organizations defend their existence by working for the abolition of roles identified with sex, but through their mere existence they are conserving these roles. . . . The women's organizations' greatest triumph would be to abolish themselves. . . ."

XII

The Artistic Life

Can the arts receive sustaining nourishment in a hyperorganized country where a primary emphasis is on economic efficiency? J. T. James, English traveler, noting a certain lack of artistic ferment along with a grim state of poverty, approvingly reported in 1819 that the Swedes had "wisely turned their attention to those matters of political economy, which ought, in the course of nature, at all times to precede the development of taste in the arts." Joseph Marshall, a tourist of the eighteenth century, also opined that Sweden was by no means "a kingdom to which any person would resort to be entertained by the arts," but allowed that the natives were "in general a very patient and industrious people, and capable, with proper encouragement from the government, of making a great progress in the arts...."

That a claim can yet be made for the "great progress" is not certain, but it is clear that now that the "matters of political economy" have been well taken care of, the Swedes are being given "proper encouragement from the government." There is, of course, disagreement about the ultimate value of state interference in the arts. Despite the rather positive examples of, say, the plays of Molière (who was an employee of Louis XIV's), the Taj Mahal (built by edict of the Shah Jehan), or the Parthenon (constructed partly as an antiunemployment measure in the slump following the Persian Wars), the possibility has often been denied, and state support for the arts has been frequently denounced as unsound, improper, and uneconomic.

But the Swedes are giving it a good try, and government support for the arts has undergone a considerable boom in recent years. Central government spending specifically on art, literature, music, and so on climbed from about $6,000,000 in fiscal 1961–62 to about $14,000,000 in 1966–67, an increase of 130 percent. This is still not much, but it is, relative to population, roughly fifty times as much as the U.S. National Foundation on the Arts and Humanities had at its disposal in 1966–67. Moreover, the figures do not include spending on libraries, museums, and artistic education, nor do they include the considerable amounts spent by the municipalities on their own initiative.

The new spirit in this field was touched off by, among other rumblings of discontent, May Day demonstrations in 1960, in which prominent artists protested against their subordinate position in society. K. G. Hultén, head of Stockholm's Museum of Modern Art, remarked to me: "We were starting to get an intellectual proletariat or even an intellectual lumpenproletariat."

Quite quickly, there developed a whole new government attitude and a whole new government program. Roland Pålsson, an official in the Ministry of Ecclesiastical Affairs and Education who is in charge of both, explained to me: "Formerly, the arts were considered a luxury that could be indulged in after all other demands had been met. But now there is a willingness to meet the need for art exactly as in other sectors."

Meddling in the arts was not a new activity, of course. Pålsson pointed out: "We are still subsidizing the royal opera in exactly the same way as Gustav III did in the eighteenth century." Among the major elements in the state's traditional support to the arts are the main Opera in Stockholm, another opera house in Göteborg; partial subsidies of three large and three small symphony orchestras; and the famed Royal Dramatic

Theater, which, in addition to operating its two Stockholm theaters, conducts numerous tours of the provinces with major dramatic productions. Stockholm also has two city-supported theaters, and many of the other towns in Sweden, even those with populations of under 100,000, have their own theaters with first-class productions of dramatic works of high literary quality.

In the present expansion of state subsidies a number of new twists have been added. One of the more interesting is a system of life pensions created for Sweden's most outstanding artists. The pensions are, in effect, guarantees that the recipients will always have an annual income of at least about $5,500 (inflation-protected), but nothing is paid unless the pensioner's own income falls below about $6,000. Since many of the approximately 100 leading creative figures who have been awarded these pensions—e.g., Ingmar Bergman, Pär Lagerqvist, and Birgit Nilsson—have not the slightest need for the money and will probably never draw one red öre from it, the idea has been severely criticized. Olof Lagercrantz, a frequently querulous cultural commentator, called the pensions "a swindle, which makes it possible for the government to appear simultaneously as a generous Maecenas and as a frugal pinchpenny." A few artists who were picked for the honor even rejected it. Lars Forsell, a poet, playwright, novelist, and film maker, who has been awarded one of the pensions, said to me: "I had the feeling they picked only the popular figures in Swedish art; perhaps they felt the taxpayer would react negatively if he saw unfamiliar names on the list. I'm exactly the kind of person they shouldn't give it to. But one day I might be very happy to have it—you never know." On the criticisms of the pensions, Pålsson said: "There has been much misunderstanding. But the purpose is that the pensions should go to the elite of the artists. We can't accept the idea that someone who has made great creative contributions should be let down when he is old. With these pensions, of course, he doesn't have to wait until he's old; he gets it whenever he needs it."

A more flexible element of support was a rapid expansion of temporary grants. These grants have grown from $85,000 divided among 30 artists in 1961–62 to $500,000 parceled out to 153 artists (37 writers, 48 painters, 15 composers, and 53 "others") in 1966–67. They range up to $2,400 a year and are dealt out for up to three years. Because the grants, though they carry far less prestige than the life pensions, pay out hard cash regardless of the recipients' other income, they are often more highly esteemed than the pensions. One artist told me that he received a telephone call from a civil servant wanting to congratulate him on his imminent receipt of a life pension, and he exclaimed: "For God's sake, see if you can get them to change their minds and give me a simple little grant instead!" He got his way.

Not all the new ideas have been successful. One piece of legislation provided that apartment-house builders could obtain low-interest government loans, in proportion to the total cost of construction, to provide sculptures, paintings, or other ornamental art. It was calculated that if the builders accepted his option about $8,000,000 worth of art, which in practice is usually monumental sculpture, would be bought for these purposes each year. But there was little actual subsidy involved, and few builders did. Pålsson conceded that the plan was a failure: "Perhaps in the future we can find builders more interested in art. But so far it hasn't been of any importance." But he did not regard this failure as especially serious, since there probably aren't enough good sculptors in Sweden to produce $8,000,000 worth of additional works each year, though he added: "The artists don't agree, of course."

A new activity of a very different type is the so-called Experimental National Concerts, patterned somewhat after the touring theater companies of the Royal Dramatic Theater. The program was begun in 1963 on a trial basis and was concentrated in four of Sweden's twenty-four counties.

Two types of concert are given: school concerts and regular evening programs. All the programs are worked out with local committees, who choose only the artists and types of music they want from those available. Nils Wallin, head of the program, said to me: "I try to create ideas for the local groups. I try to persuade them to accept new music. We act, not just as agents, but as a kind of pressure group." The central organization pays all travel and expenses for the musicians (to put all areas, wherever located, on an equal basis), plus a quarter of their fees, and provides printed programs, posters, and publicity helps. "We feel it is very important that the people pay something," said Wallin. "People must learn that culture costs something." Concerts for all shades of musical taste, including the Stockholm Philharmonic, chamber music, preclassical music, are offered. The organization also produces its own phonograph records and sells them at cost.

In explaining his philosophy, Wallin touched on part of the reasoning underlying the whole art-subsidy program: "You can't force culture on people, but we can't accept the argument that people have the chance to choose freely under present conditions. They do in theory, of course, but they are handicapped by their background, thoughts of status—a lot of barriers. They get pressure from commercial culture and pop music. I'm not opposed to pop, but I want people to be aware of another culture as well. So we are trying to give real culture an equal chance to compete."

One characteristic of the art-subsidy program is the warm embrace it accords to the most varied types of art. One of the oddest recipients of the state's largesse is an organization known as the Fylkingen. This organization, founded in the thirties, concentrates on music "nobody thought worth doing at the time," according to its present head, Knut Wiggen, a dazzlingly original pianist and thinker. It has thus successively concentrated on (and abandoned after its example began to be emulated by others) chamber music, post-Romantic music, and preclassical music. It is now rather heavily involved in electronic music. In 1966 the state was annually contributing roughly $16,000 to it, and the city of Stockholm $24,000. Wiggen pointed out that in 1960 the city's contribution was only $2,000, and the state's nothing at all. "It is beginning to be something," he said, "but when you compare it with the opera [which receives more than $3,000,000 annually] it's ridiculously little." This is particularly true when one considers that in Wiggen's view, the traditional opera, like most other traditional forms, is now obsolete. There is, claimed Wiggen, "a strong wish among composers to stop playing instrumental music." It is not entirely clear what might replace these outdated forms, but Wiggen spoke enthusiastically about combining various art forms. When I spoke to him, we were interrupted briefly by a visitor, prompting Wiggen to remark: "That fellow at the door —he's a composer and film producer, who is making a film combining electronic music and picture fantasies." Wiggen is also interested in combining art and technology. "It's not difficult to see what's wrong with the world," he said. "We should stop killing each other, stop having so many babies. The aims are not difficult, and the technology is not difficult. Only one thing is difficult: why we don't do it? They have many possibilities here in Sweden to make a happy life. They don't use them." Wiggen emphasized that most current thinking about art is wrong: "To understand art as a manifestation of life, that's something. But to understand the difference between one note and another, that's not worth much." Wiggen grumbled about the mania for conventional concerts: "The trouble is that our esthetic view is from the last century, and we are living in the present century. The reality for us is the electronic machine." In 1962, Wiggen built a "music machine" which could play for many hours automatically and without repeating itself. He sent one of the machine's "compositions," a program piece in fourteen movements, six hours for each movement, to the Norwegian authority in charge of performing rights (Wiggen is Norwegian-born). "I didn't get a single öre," he said, moaning. Nevertheless, the machine gave him the idea for an electronic-music studio, which at this writing is nearing completion. Swedish Radio is subsidizing the studio, which he claimed will be the world's largest. He is heavily involved in attempts to promote cooperation between artists and technologists and in 1966 held a series of conferences at which representatives of both could discuss their mutual interests (not entirely successful owing to disagreements with some Americans who had been supposed to help sponsor the plan). In explaining all these ideas, Wiggen concluded: "I think we are going away from making pieces of art and going into making life happier." When I asked Wiggen if it disturbed him to know that I understood very little of what he was saying, he cheerfully replied, "No, I find it quite natural."

In any case, nobody tells Wiggen what to do. Said he: "We have one rule: we must give ten concerts a year. Both the government and the city of Stockholm are unusual in that they give us money without saying anything about how we should use it. Most people who want to do unusual things have no money, and those who have the money want to do only conventional things."

A central role in Sweden's cultural life is played by Swedish Radio, which runs the television and radio operation and which, though a creature of the government, enjoys an independent position. Actual ownership is held by the press (two-fifths), various large nonprofit organizations (two-fifths), and commercial interests, primarily those in the communications field (one-fifth). The government names ten members and the chairman of the twenty-one-member board. No commercials are permitted, and so vigorously is this rule observed that in consumer education programs, trademarks on products are turned away from the audience unless there is some strong reason for showing them. Financial support (except for school programs and overseas broadcasts, which are financed by tax revenues) is provided by license fees (now $7 a year for a radio license and $20 for a TV license). The fees bring in $60,000,000 a year, of which about $35,000,000 goes for programming activities on three radio networks and one TV network (which offers forty-two hours of broadcasting a week).

The more important of the branches is television, which occupies an enormous position in Swedish life. The merits of various programs and the timing of the second TV network, which is now promised for the end of 1969, are discussed endlessly in the press, and controversies over programs become front-page news. In 1966 a newspaper poll to determine the best-known personage in the country was easily won by a TV personality. Some programs are watched by virtually the entire population. Sven Delblanc, a young novelist, remarked to me: "TV has changed everything. On Christmas Eve, we have always traditionally eaten our roast ham, but now 60 percent of the people are sitting in front of the TV when they are supposed to be eating their ham. Last winter a television series was based on one of Strindberg's novels, after which it sold 250,000 copies in a few months; before that, in all the fifty years of its existence, it had sold only 1,500,000." There is little opposition to TV from intellectual quarters. Indeed, the head of the television part of the operation, Nils-Erik Baehrendtz, is a professor of literature. Of the constant controversy around his job, he said: "We don't discuss politics in this country, so television is a popular topic."

On the whole, television tends to be heavy and boring. About 20 percent of the time is spent on extremely ancient (and usually low-quality) movies, 15 percent is taken up by an announcer's reading the news to the audience, and around 18 percent by solemn, heavy-handed talks and discussions. About 40 percent of the programs are imported; for some years these were concentrated largely on U.S. offerings (usually the dreariest situation comedies), but as European quality has improved, U.S. representation has declined.

On the positive side, however, TV has some worthy achievements to its credit. "Our drama department is really our strong suit," said Baehrendtz. "We produce forty or fifty original dramas a year. As a result, we have created an enormous new audience for drama." Maintaining a balance between giving the listeners (and various pressure groups, who insist that more time be given to discussing their points of view) what they want and consciously striving for high-quality programs pose problems, and Baehrendtz candidly admitted: "We have far from succeeded in making good programs of real cultural value." In some areas, however, a certain quality has been reached. "We

make many rather expensive documentaries," explained Baehrendtz. "Every Saturday night we have a half-hour documentary.
There was a great deal of resistance at first, but now it's one
of our most popular features. We had a three-program series
on Crete, several on art, one on Trinidad. Next week there is
one on Dahomey." Because of such documentaries and the high
proportion of imported programs, Baehrendtz believes TV has
had a strong impact on increasing the Swedes' understanding of
the world outside Sweden.

Swedish Radio's high cultural ambitions are well illustrated
by the music department. I remarked to Magnus Enhörning, co-
chief (with Karl-Birger Blomdahl, Sweden's leading composer)
of the serious music department, that radio stations in New
York were much more music-oriented than Swedish Radio. "In
some ways, that may be true," he conceded, "but American
radio is not really taking part in the musical life of the country,
as we are." He was right. Although SR's resources are limited, it
probably takes more initiative of its own in music than any
radio or television station or network in the United States, even
though there are many U.S. stations that play more music (recorded). Nearly half of SR's 2,300 hours per year of serious
music are live. SR has its own symphony orchestra (the largest
in Sweden—104 men), its own string quartet, and its own choir,
plus two outside choirs, used more or less regularly on a fee
basis. It subsidizes an excellent annual concert series featuring
outstanding guest artists from abroad and another series concentrating on contemporary music (in connection with which a
first-rate magazine on the arts is published). SR commissions
some original works, for which it pays $2,400, plus the regular
fees for performing rights. It also operates its own music school
and provides a considerable amount of miscellaneous free-lance
work—special programs, talks, reports on festivals. ("The radio
is the biggest consumer of music in Sweden," said one composer.
"Almost everyone in music does something for the radio.") In
1968 the radio plans to launch a "music conservatory of the air,"

involving thoroughly serious lectures on music theory, and the publication of a number of textbooks.

SR is enthusiastic about promoting modern music. "We think that's very advisable," said Enhörning, "both for people to know what's going on and so that young composers can be heard." But the radio is rigorously eclectic. Enhörning explained: "If you are sitting in my position in a monopoly station, you are not allowed to have any opinions. We play music in every field, from the Middle Ages to the present. You could say we have no policy of our own."

One of the Swedish state's attempts to support cultural activity—its support of the church—must in the most charitable view of things be scored a failure.

Since the sixteenth century, when Gustav Vasa confiscated the property of the Catholic church and deprived it of its power, Sweden has been officially Lutheran. The church is supported by the state, and members of the hierarchy are appointed and paid by the government. Technically, Sweden is firmly religious. Religious studies are mandatory in the schools. Prayers are regularly broadcast on the radio. On certain religious holidays all places of amusement are closed. Since exit from the church, meaning an escape from the miniscule church tax, was made possible in 1952, less than 1 percent of the citizenry has resigned. About 95 percent of the people marry and about 90 percent are confirmed in the church. A 1957 poll showed that if church and state were separated, 72 percent would apply for membership anyway; a similar poll in 1965 showed 60 percent would do so. A poll in 1955–56 suggested that although only slightly more than half the people pronounced themselves Christians, fully 84 percent definitely believed in God, and only 6 percent definitely did not.

Yet there is little expression of religious interest. Each Sunday, approximately 3 percent of the population can be found in the state churches, and about $2\frac{1}{2}$ percent in the so-called free churches (which have far fewer, but much more diligent, members). Only about one Swede in five goes to church as often as once a month. Antireligious views are often expressed in the press, frequently with considerable vitriol. A popular newspaper whose inquiring photographer had asked his subjects if atheism should be given equal time on the radio received four out of five positives and was able to publish the results without arousing indignation or probably even much interest among the readers.

Carl-Gustaf Boëthius, former teacher of history and philosophy and editor of the state church's magazine *Vår Kyrka* (Our Church), explained to me that the split between the church and the people derives from the development of the workers' movement at the end of the last century. The pillars of the church, who were identified with the upper classes, were horrified by the movement and threw their influence against it. Said Boëthius: "The workers' movement was not antireligious—until the workers found out the pastors were against them." Boëthius also traces a vein of radicalism in literature which began about 1880, with the early works of August Strindberg and others. Said Boëthius: "They said that the church wanted to hold men in slavery, that the church is an illusion, and so on. From that time there has been a strong hatred between educated people and the church. Many of the most influential papers have fought against religion." Boëthius dryly summed up: "So in defense the pastors said, 'Good-bye, world. God has given us our work. We will do our own work and forget about these people.' "

Boëthius says this estrangement is perpetuated by the pastors' refusal to modernize their thinking. He believes the church should adopt more up-to-date ideas, along the lines of those advocated by the new theologians in Great Britain. "I went on TV in 1964," he told me, "and said it was silly to maintain that all premarital sexual intercourse is immoral. We know that at least 80 percent of all people who marry in Sweden have had sexual intercourse with each other. Every one of you, I said, know people who are living together without being married and who are good people. It is positively immoral to say that they are not. Well, 744 pastors [out of a total of about 2,600] signed a petition saying that this immoral person should be relieved of his position. The board of the church said that Mr. Boëthius has a wrong opinion, but we want there to be free speech; it is good to have discussion."

Actually, the twentieth-century ecumenical movement owes a great deal to the Swede Nathan Söderblom, a pastor who died in 1931, and a liberal movement has existed since his day. Boëthius argues that the church has not responded. "What has been the church's answer?" he asked. "The clergy has become more and more reactionary."

A typical controversy is that over women pastors. Women were allowed to become pastors in 1959, and there are now a little more than a dozen; but many conservative pastors oppose them. Boëthius said: "Women pastors are almost totally isolated from other pastors."

The situation is the more painful to Boëthius because he believes Swedes have a deep need for religion. "I don't think the people of Sweden are a happy people," he said. "They have it very good materially, but a high proportion of them have great anxieties. There are so many frustrations, difficulties, and these difficulties are signs of the emptiness of life in the welfare state. It leads directly into a religious need—if there were a church that could help, but there isn't."

Olle Gnospelius, assistant pastor of the Stockholm Cathedral, has a more conservative view of things (he is, in fact, a Conservative member of parliament), but he candidly concedes the mistake of the church in opposing the workers' movement: "The church believed the movement was antichurch, which it wasn't. Many labor leaders were very good Christians. They prayed during strikes, for example, but the church didn't understand. About 1910 the church tried to reestablish contact with the workers, but the damage had been done."

However, he parts company with Boëthius over the way to heal the division. He said: "The liberals believe the Bible can be interpreted as a historical book; you find the word of God in it, and it is the business of the pastor to translate this word of God into terms of modern man. For me, the Bible does not *contain* the word of God; it *is* the word of God. I must let my wish to interpret be subordinated. An example is the debate about women pastors. I am very good friends with three women pastors in this diocese. We work together. But I don't recognize their pastorship because the word of God does not permit it."

What remedy does he propose? "I think the church must be very faithful to the word of God. Faith comes from preaching. That means we have to get more substance in our sermons. Also, pastors should become more friendly; this is a way to come into contact with the people. There is a growing need for personal contact and personal confession." Needless to say, he takes issue with Boëthius' opinions on sex but emphasizes the importance of providing help. "If an unmarried couple comes to me for help and the girl is pregnant, I help them. I don't scold them, but I don't tell them it's right, either. It is probably true that more than 80 percent of couples have premarital sex relations. But many of them come to regret it."

There is no present indication of a revival of interest in the church in Sweden. Attendance figures at state churches stopped dropping in 1955 (those of the free churches have continued to decline) but have not turned upward. Many observers believe that ending state support for the church, which is favored by almost everyone and will most certainly come about in a few years, may provide the renewal of energies the church has been needing.

Another state-created—but independently operated—cultural entity is the Film Institute. The Swedish film—associated with such world-renowned names as Ingmar Bergman, Alf Sjöberg, Vilgot Sjöman, and Bo Widerberg—would hardly seem to be in need of assistance. But following the arrival of TV, attendance in motion-picture theaters declined as it has in most countries. Film production itself normally runs at a loss in Sweden. It is possible at all only because the production companies, which also own the theaters, feel it helps stimulate interest in films. Under the impact of TV the situation worsened, and progressive reductions in the entertainment tax, combined with small government subsidies, were of little help.

In 1963, therefore, the Film Institute was established, and the entire remaining theater tax (then running at about $2,300,000 annually) was diverted to its exclusive use in this way: the theater owners agreed to turn over the equivalent of the tax receipts directly to the Film Institute. It was made independent of the government, which, however, appoints four members of the eight-member board, plus the chairman, who votes in case of a tie. "This may suggest that the government controls the institute," said Harry Schein, who is executive member of the board and operating head of the institute, "but that's not true —first, because the members are appointed for three years and the government has no control over their votes, and, second, the chairman's vote has never been used."

The institute's major—or at least most noticed—activity is to distribute grants to the producers of quality films. The grants, which have ranged between $20,000 and $60,000, are calculated according to a complicated voting procedure by expert juries (membership on which is constantly rotated and on which the government is not represented), with a bonus for films which are of high quality but lose money. Among its other activities, the institute operates a school for film makers, supervises a film archive, and runs a traveling series of quality films to small towns where such productions are rarely shown.

Schein, the guiding spirit behind the creation of the institute, is Austrian-born, became wealthy through his business, and retired at an early age to devote himself to his artistic interests, one of which is the film. I asked Schein why they didn't hand out the money before the movies were made. "I'm quite sure it would lead to bad movies. Anyone who came with a proposal to make a film on Dag Hammarskjöld with Max von Sydow playing the lead [this, translated to American terms, would be something like a life of Abraham Lincoln starring, say, Marlon Brando], would most certainly get a lot of money, and you can be sure it would be a lousy film."

What results has the institute had? Schein said: "No one can imagine what the film industry would be without it. Now, about twenty-five Swedish films a year are produced. In the year before the reform there were twelve. Last year about ten or twelve new young directors were given the chance to make films. A few years ago this would have been unthinkable. In the beginning the scramble for new directors was rather comical; almost anyone with a beard was offered the chance to make a film." Schein, around whose personality a certain amount of controversy has arisen because of his aggressive efforts to promote Swedish films (he has been accused of being a dictator), explained: "When the reform was made, everybody was happy. Now everybody is dissatisfied. 'Where are all the new masterpieces?' they ask. But all the reform was intended to do was to create an atmosphere. What people forget is that good films are not produced by political reforms but by good artists."

Not surprisingly, artists of all kinds are organized, not in loose social groupings, but in societies which have all the characteristics of labor unions, plus political pressure groups. There are sixteen such groups in all, ranging from dance teachers to pop music composers, and they are combined into a top organization called the Artistic and Literary Professionals' Organization (*Konstnärliga och Literära Yrkesarbetares Samorganisation*). Stellan Arvidsson, a poet, novelist, and high school principal who is head of this body, explained to me that it was formed at the end of the 1950's and that it was largely due to its agitation that the government's new artistic interests became aroused. "All these organizations worked out a twenty-four-point proposal, which we handed over to the government. To a great extent, the government has been working along the lines of our program."

One idea the group was not responsible for but helped improve is the system of library royalties to writers. This was begun in the mid-fifties with a payment of 3 öre (6 cents) per loan. The royalty has been gradually raised to 6 öre (1.2 cents), of which 2 go directly to the writer and 4 to a writers' fund, administered by the writers themselves, which helps older writers and gives travel grants and five-year grants of about $2,000 a year. (Eventually, ten new such grants will be handed out each year.) Arvidsson gave me an example of a more direct attack: "One of our member organizations had a strike with Swedish Radio in 1964, and we called a sympathy strike for our other groups. They couldn't have any lectures, for example, by science writers; composers wouldn't work for them. It lasted a couple of months, and the salaries were raised by about 50 percent." He noted with satisfaction: "We have very strong solidarity."

Jan Gehlin, who, in addition to his work as a novelist, poet, playwright, and judge, is head of the Society of Authors (*Författareföreningen*), told me of an even more peculiar artists' strike which occurred in the early fifties: "Our material is used in schoolbooks. We said we wanted royalties of 3.50 kronor per page per thousand copies. They offered us 1.75 kronor. We found that most of the people who made up these books were teachers and professors, so we asked them in effect to strike against the publishers, and they did. The whole business was absolutely paralyzed. They tried to deal with the authors on an individual basis, but we refused. Finally, the National Board of Education said they didn't have any books. We said that was too bad. We got 2.85 kronor. We consider that we won: we went down 26 percent and they went up 50 percent. This was the first time we acted like a real workers' organization."

There is some feeling that the organizations, membership in which carries a certain amount of prestige, constitute a kind of elite who deal out all the benefits to themselves and oppress those outside. This feeling is doubtless strongest among painters and sculptors, partly because there are so many of them and partly because the power and prestige of the National Artists' Organization (*Konstnärernas Riksorganisation*) can be important when public commissions (the major source of employment for painters and sculptors) are handed out. The organization keeps a central file, for example, of members' work, which prospective awarders of commissions may examine. Carl E. Wahl, administrative secretary of this group, told me: "We open our membership lists twice a year. Last April we had 125 applicants for membership, and we took 52. We have a jury of 4 painters, 2 sculptors, and a graphic artist who examine the works. Any style of art can be accepted." The organization has a certain amount of humility, however: "It's a hard job for the jury to select. We know there is a possibility of making mistakes, but we don't want to keep anyone out who is a good quality painter." But he would admit that nonmembers had a pretty hard time? He sighed. "All artists have a hard time."

In any system of government support to the arts, there exist obvious dangers: art will become subordinate to the state; only certain types of art will be favored; dependence will hurt the artists' vitality; only certain cliques will be favored. It is true that the organizations are heavily represented on the committees that decide on grants. But Roland Pålsson of the Ministry of Ecclesiastical Affairs and Education said: "The committees work in full view of public opinion, and the membership is changed every few years. It never has happened that anyone complained he was neglected because he wasn't a member of the organization." K. G. Hultén of the Museum of Modern Art, speaking of artists who might be excluded because they were not members of the Establishment, said he did not personally know of any, but: "I fear there are such cases. I hope there are not many." However, he told me that several artists who were fond of the bottle or who had other antisocial habits had nevertheless received honors, and he mentioned in particular one prominent painter, whom he described as "very nasty," but who nevertheless was given a life pension.

Understandably enough, most artists in general are in favor of the government support, even though many have serious misgivings. Sven-Erik Bäck, one of Sweden's most talented modern composers and head of Swedish Radio's music school, who has received a life pension, told me: "I believe too much security is unhealthy. I'm convinced of that. That's the way an artist should feel. His only security should be in his work. But I have a family, and they have to live. I cry for security." There is little or no feeling that dependence on the state is unhealthy. Jan Gehlin, head of the Author's Society, said: "I haven't met anyone who feels he has to be too careful of what he writes because he is dependent on the state." Gunnar Bucht, head of the Composers' Society and a leading composer (his first opera was premiered at the Stockholm Opera in 1966), would be only too happy for composers to be more deeply involved in society: "What is going to happen to the artist? Perhaps something will be demanded from him. I say, 'Why not?' We should have a function in society. You might say our deepest aim is to have a function in society." Jacob Branting, a poet and editor of a Stockholm newspaper's cultural page, said to me: "When people receive these grants, they don't feel any obligation to be positive about anything or feel themselves to be servants of the state." I asked Hultén if he thought artists might become more dependent on the government, and he replied: "Yes, but the government will be more dependent on the artists, too." Artur Lundkvist, a novelist, poet, and critic, is often severely critical of the government, yet when I asked him if he considered the subsidies to be harmful, he replied: "No, just the opposite. The more an artist feels he is paid by the state, the more he will oppose it. Those grants go mostly to the very rebellious writers. The more you attack the state in this country, the more you get out of it." Most artists agree with Svante Foerster, a young novelist, who told me: "They are on the right track. Now we are beginning to get as good conditions as a metalworker."

If the opinions of the artists are clearly favorable, the reactions of the people at large are much more obscure. There is some pride in the fact that politicians have not attempted to interfere in the administration of the programs. "That wouldn't be ethical," remarked Hultén when I asked him about this. Gehlin said: "I have often talked about the Danish government figure who declared he was against support to the arts because 'the most beautiful poetry, painting, and music has always been produced by artists who were starving to death.'" Nothing like this, or like the arguments over the Arts Council in Great Britain or demands in the French parliament that support be withdrawn from the subsidized theater's presentations of plays by Peter Weiss and Jean Genet, occurs in Sweden.

It is possible that this is a healthy sign. But it is also possible that it reflects, not acceptance, but merely indifference. In a poll conducted in 1961, when the new programs were just getting under way, 52 percent of the people pronounced themselves against regular subsidies to artists, and it may be presumed that this somewhat unsympathetic attitude persists. Yet never has there been any important protest against the programs. Nils Wallin, head of the Experimental National Concerts, said: "Many people have no opinion but are arranging the concerts because they are told to. Many of them are convinced of the quality if it comes from Stockholm. The local groups are terribly angry if the printed programs or posters arrive late. But I very seldom hear anything about the music."

The unquestioning attitude is often noted by foreigners. American-born Dave Kushner, TV film director, translator of Ingmar Bergman, and Stockholm businessman, said: "When it comes to culture, the Swedes are completely passive." Another American resident, who has been in a position to observe the cultural life closely and over a long period, told me: "I think the mass of people here are willing to delegate opinion-making decisions to authoritative persons. The people have great respect for authority. In some ways it is a very admirable thing. People behave responsibly. They are very law-abiding. But in the artistic area it builds up a passive kind of museum-type culture. You don't get the feedback that is necessary for a creative artist. They are taught at an early age not to respond. I believe this hurts creativity." (This nonresponse is often evident, but it should not be assumed that Swedes never show enthusiasm. Anyone who has seen the proper and dignified Swedes clapping, shouting, and stamping their feet following a concert by, say, David Oistrakh, can easily conclude that if there is anything capable of forcing a response from a Swede, it is a satisfying artistic experience.)

Pålsson of the Ministry of Ecclesiastical Affairs and Education is under no illusions about the people's reactions to art:

"The whole top side of society is convinced our program is right, and that art enriches life. Well, that's enough to keep this department going, but it is not really enough. In our cultural policy we have to create new demands. To the majority of the people, we have to introduce forms of culture they have never had contact with before. Of course, a demand exists from some people, who want a greater output of theater, music, and art, because they have more spare time. But there is also a view that society must see to it that output creates a demand. Both are right." Artur Lundkvist echoes a common view—common among artists, that is—that the people are in need of more art: "The development in Sweden is more and more to the materialistic—and vulgarly materialistic—aspects of life. People are dissatisfied but can't say what about. They feel life is empty but can't say why."

In many ways the artistic sophistication of Sweden seems clearly to have increased over the years. If the advances made in the Swedish system have, by making people more materialistically minded, reduced their feelings for art, this influence has been at least partly offset by factors that have worked in the opposite direction: more leisure time, more widespread educational opportunities, and more financial resources. "In the nineteenth century," Hultén said, "Sweden didn't even have a culture." As recently as the 1930's Artur Lundkvist's enthusiastic efforts to introduce such exotic names as Rimbaud, Eliot, and Breton into Sweden met considerable indifference. His attempt to persuade a publisher to issue a Faulkner novel was indignantly rebuffed. Today important works by British, American, and French writers are reviewed in Sweden when published in their home countries, and well-informed Swedes are as familiar with the names of Pinter, Beckett, Le Clezio, and Bellow as they are with their own writers. Sven Delblanc, the novelist, said: "We have many more books published now than fifteen years ago, more serious music, more theaters. There is three times as much poetry produced and read now than fifteen years ago." Knut Wiggen said: "Before we were introducing music that was already well known abroad. But by 1960 we caught up with international standards, and we began to produce our own Swedish music that was new by international standards."

Such evidence of progress is apparent primarily among intellectual leaders. The gap between the artists (and those involved in the effort to bring art to the masses) and the masses themselves seems large. An active interest in artistic matters is not commonly found among, say, well-educated middle-class Swedes, even though it is easy to be impressed with the intelligence of such people. It is not unusual to meet Swedes who can read five languages with ease but who have little interest in reading literary works in any of the five. A typical reflection of Swedish interests can be seen in guidebooks to other countries. In Berlin, for example, many people might consider the Dahlem Museum—with its stunning collection of German, Flemish, and Dutch painting, not to speak of the "Queen Nefertiti" from Egypt—a major attraction, and the *Guide Michelin* to Germany devotes a half page to this institution. Yet a 134-page Swedish guide to Berlin alone finds room for only eight lines. Again, a lengthy newspaper article on the Museum of Modern Art in Vienna soberly examined the reasons for this establishment's lack of popularity (it pinpointed the absence of well-organized activities for children) without mentioning a single painter represented. In early 1967 a hopeful sign appeared in the form of a magazine directed to the general reader and devoted to literature called *Böckernas Värld* (The World of Books), which must be one of the few literary journals anywhere with no book reviews (it specializes in folksy articles about writers, illustrated with pictures of their children); it has not been successful, and at this moment the publishers are reported to be considering measures to give it a more popular appeal.

Attempts by aggressive and imaginative private culture promoters do not in general seem to stimulate much response. A case in point is the theater situation in the capital. Stockholm is extremely fortunate to possess, not only the two theaters of the Royal Dramatic Theater, but two theaters run by the city as well—not to mention the Royal Opera. All these establish-

ments are imaginative, resourceful, and constantly on the alert
for foreign plays of merit (though the country's greatest literary
figure was a dramatist, Swedish literary artists do not usually
choose dramatic forms of expression). And they all run at fat
losses. There are also four or five privately operated theaters,
but they concentrate almost exclusively on musical revues and
the most dismal commercial Broadway comedies. One of them,
in the spring of 1967, made a daring effort to break out of this
deadly pattern. It began with Peter Weiss' unconventional,
striking, controversial drama about Salazar (which received ful-
some praise in, among other places, the New York *Times*). But
the public reception was disappointing, and the play was closed
down. It was replaced by another imaginative, unorthodox, and
well-received drama—this one by Boris Vian. That was also
unsuccessful, and the theater had to end its season considerably
sooner than planned because of its losses.

While the government's high-powered campaign for the arts
may be slowly bringing about changes in the public's indifference which will eventually become noticeable, it is already
having a significant impact on the situation of artists. Public
commissions, grants, and other forms of largesse are of considerable importance to artists, and it is surprisingly possible
for artists to support themselves from their work. This is probably most apparent in the case of writers. It is, of course, impossible for a writer in Sweden to approach the vast financial
success of the top American writers who benefit from fat long-
term contracts, sales to motion pictures, and high fees from
name-hungry magazines (one novelist asked me with undis-
guised and justified envy: "How much does Norman Mailer get
paid for an article in *Esquire?*"). Nevertheless, what with numerous outlets for literary journalism, the state and city grants,
and book and library royalties, it is possible for even young,
little-known writers to live by free-lance writing. Such a thing
is, of course, almost unheard of in the United States.

But, embarrassingly enough for the arts campaign, a sizable
number of well-known and admired literary figures not only
have not been encouraged to scale new heights of creativity by

the improved position of artists, but also have all but abandoned literature altogether—a phenomenon that has taken place
coincident with the campaign's sharpest growth. Such respected
younger writers as Sara Lidman, Per Wästberg, Göran Palm,
and Folke Isakson have cut their literary activity sharply and
increasingly devoted their energies to more practical—and therefore presumably more socially useful—tasks as explaining the
evils of *apartheid*, imperialism, and militarism. This trend is all
in one direction—to the left—and has become ever stronger in recent years. Writers who do not join in this movement are often
bitterly attacked. It has prompted Fred Fleisher, American
journalist and longtime Stockholm resident, to write: "Swedish
cultural life seems marked by an increasing acceptance of
narrow-minded intolerance. . . . Personally, I find this tendency
frightening."

One problem the campaign has not solved (it in fact works
against it) is the lack of a well-developed private market for
painters and sculptors, who at present are overwhelmingly dependent on large public commissions. Öyvind Fahlström, a
painter and poet, who is perhaps Sweden's best-known artist and
who lives mostly in New York, remarked to me: "It's not easy
for a painter to exist in Sweden. There are people who buy art,
but not a steady stream. There are good galleries here, and
sometimes you can have a successful show; but then nothing
happens for a year. Nobody seems to be interested." Nor is
private subsidization of artistic activity encouraged through tax
deductions. I asked Roland Pålsson about this. "It's not popular among artists," he said. "They don't want to be in the hands
of private donors. They would regard it as a kind of eighteenth-
century patronage. The artists' organizations would immediately turn against it." Some artists, who apparently are no more
eager to be in the hands of the state than in the hands of
private donors, expressed themselves in favor of such a system
in conversation with me, but the picture will probably not
change soon. When I asked K. G. Hultén of the Stockholm
Museum of Modern Art if he thought a private market for
art might develop, he said: "Not a chance."

A different type of problem which the campaign can probably do nothing about, but which is doubtless even more irritating to many artists, is the failure of Swedish art to penetrate the rest of the world. Although Sweden is justly famous for its world leadership in design (glass, ceramics, jewelry, and furniture) probably the only Swedish artistic figures known abroad are from the film. It would seem undeniable that Sweden's literature deserves to be more widely known. Such worthwhile older living writers as Eyvind Johnson, Gunnar Ekelöf, Artur Lundkvist, and Harry Martinson, not to mention the many fascinating names of more recent years—*e.g.,* Pär Rådström, Per Olof Sundman, Birgitta Trotzig, and Per Olov Enquist—are hardly known outside Sweden.

Perhaps it is not possible for any such campaign to make any appreciable impact on the public's appreciation for the arts. Some of the promoters involved have a tendency to talk about culture distribution as if it were a question of so many smallpox vaccinations to be carried out; one somehow feels this is the wrong attitude.

But no definitive judgment on the drive can be made for quite some time. It is still in its early stages and was not intended to produce instant culture. At the least it must be recognized as one of the most heartening signs of improvement in Sweden's sometimes drab landscape. In fact, its true significance may be said to lie in the willingness of the government, which has previously given the heavy emphasis to hard, materialistic progress, to give high priority to the promotion of spiritual values. Too, it must be recognized that the power of the state to grind out masterpieces is limited.

Wilhelm Moberg, one of Sweden's most popular novelists, said: "You can't produce a genius with money; all you can do is help a genius, when you find him, to pay his rent." Harry Schein of the Film Institute declared: "If the theory is that when you put people in touch with culture, it will immediately improve them, then I don't believe a word of it. All you can do is change the atmosphere." Prime Minister Tage Erlander, in referring to the reasons for the present program, said in 1966: "Economic progress did not produce the harmony that the pioneers dreamed of." He went on: "We hope for a democratic culture that can reach everyone. But we have a long way to go before we can reach that point."

XIII

Is Sweden Boring?

The center of town is suffused with a penetrating calm. Here and there, a group of laughing teen-agers moves through the crisp fall air. The public square outside the concert house has shaken off its daytime bustling energy and now sleeps peacefully. Clusters of neon signs atop the buildings blink excitedly down at the nearly deserted streets. In brightly lighted Hötorg City—a maze of shops, banks, restaurants—the silence is eerie. A thin, but steady, stream of traffic flows through the quiet streets, a monotony broken only by the occasional unmuffled roar of a teen-age tough's jazzed-up auto. At seven o'clock, before the first of the two motion-picture showings, a stir of activity around the movie houses quickly arose and quickly died; the same will happen again at nine and eleven. A few restaurants, so few the casual passerby can miss them entirely. No cafés, no bars, no pubs. A handful of dreary, cheap cafeterias and tearooms, for the most part half- or more than half-empty: a few teen-age couples bent in quiet conversation, groups of Greek or Italian workers huddled together. Almost all of these will close in a couple of hours. It is now eight o'clock. This is Stockholm at night.

Is Sweden boring? Many non-Swedes think so. A typical comment, by a Frenchman who lived for three years in Göteborg: "Sweden is all right, especially for children, but it's so dreadfully boring. It's like a pepper steak without the pepper."

Surely no more devastating criticism could be made against the Swedish system than that, in the blind pursuit of economic efficiency, the pleasure has been taken out of life. As LO points out: "Regard to physical and mental health and well-being... must be given priority over more crude economic values...."

It should be stressed that although some Swedes agree that Sweden is dull, most (I believe) react negatively to the suggestion. Sven Delblanc, the novelist, said to me: "I have never found Sweden boring. I find it impossible even to discuss it." Lars Gustafsson, novelist and critic, commented: "I have not succeeded in finding out what these critics mean. If you try to force them to explain themselves, they refer as a rule to our lack of nightclubs and the long, dark winter."

It is no doubt just, as Gustafsson says, that the charge lacks precision. But Sweden's excruciating dullness includes a good deal more than the winters and the nightclub shortage, and an examination of some of the ingredients may be of interest.

The most commonly voiced type of complaint stems from the incredible emptiness of its cities in the evenings, which gives the country an eerie quality of deadness. Even in central Stockholm the streets are generally bare, and it is nearly impossible to find a stir of life or facilities offering so much as a cup of coffee or a glass of beer after a movie or concert; in the suburbs and many smaller towns it is not possible at all—hence descriptions, such as that of Mme. Menie Grégoire, who made a goodwill lecture tour through Sweden in 1961 and later bemoaned the country's unsettling *tristesse,* which she noted in numerous connections, not least the "sadness of a country which contains not one public place, not a café, not a bistro...."

It may seem trivial, but it is nonetheless true that much talk of this kind (and there has been much of it)—the empty streets, the nervous hurry of citizens home immediately after work, the peculiar stillness of the cities, the lack of not only nightclubs as Gustafsson mentioned (Swedes tend to think any establishment serving alcohol in the evening is a nightclub) but also of restaurants, bars, pubs, cafés, beer gardens, tavernas, or other pleasure palaces—is intimately connected with the question of alcohol. And the many hindrances on the sale of alcohol in Sweden effectively block the establishment of any appreciable number of such above-mentioned watering places.

The fact is that a good part of the puritanism, hypocrisy, and tabu that in many countries is concentrated in the sexual area has in Sweden become firmly attached to alcohol. Although agitation for more tolerance for sex deviants is common, hardly ever does one run across a plea for a better break for the drinker. It is easy to develop a drinking problem in Sweden; the problem is simply getting something to drink. This is especially odd, considering that the Swedes have always been rather sturdy absorbers of alcohol. Matthew Consett, an English sightseer of 1789, noted uncomfortably that the first course at dinner was invariably accompanied "in both sexes by a bumper of brandy" and complained that "the custom of drinking spirits prevails rather too much." Another tourist around the same time observed: "It is said no man comes to Sweden without learning to drink snaps and wear galoshes." In the latter part of the nineteenth century, tippling was double the present rate, but it is still high. One seventeen-country comparison shows the Swede's average annual consumption of hard spirits 1959–62 (4.8 liters) second only to Yugoslavia (5.7 liters) and ahead of the United States (4.5 liters), and studies show that about 90 percent of the people are occasional or habitual drinkers.

Toward the end of the nineteenth century a strong temperance movement arose. Some employers were using alcohol as a means of keeping the workers docile—by allowing liberal credit in taverns, for example, against the eventual paycheck.

When the Socialists began to agitate, they quickly perceived that to get the worker to fight for economic justice, they would first have to sober him up. The fight against alcohol was therefore closely identified with the Social Democrats. The free church (evangelical) movements, closely identified with the Liberal Party, also joined the temperance crusade.

Antialcohol sentiment rose steadily, and in 1914 the state set up a liquor monopoly. All who wanted (except those who had been blacklisted for alcoholic excesses) were issued ration books and assigned quotas of up to 3 liters a month. Married women got no ration cards at all, and only those unmarried women of some position got them. No beer stronger than 2.8 percent alcohol was allowed. Bars were prohibited; liquor licenses in restaurants were strictly limited, consumption was restricted to 15 centiliters (about two to three drinks) per restaurant visit, and none was allowed without food. Moreover, in 1922 the temperance groups forced a referendum on prohibition, which was defeated by less than 1 percent.

But the system was not as effective as it was irritating, since anyone who had used up his ration could always borrow. There are many jokes about the uneaten dust-covered sandwiches that were carried in and out of restaurant kitchens (and paid for over and over again) as necessities for drinkers. One Swede has assured me that he once saw a wooden sandwich. Restaurant guests who actually intended to eat the food were wise to specify the fact when ordering.

The temperance people were also dissatisfied. They suspected the rationing encouraged people to use up their quotas and thought that drinking would drop if it were abolished.

Therefore, in 1956 the ration cards were done away with, strong (4.5 percent) beer was permitted, and restrictions on restaurants were eased. But there is still a phenomenal amount of red tape. There are only 275 liquor shops, run by the beloved state-owned Systemet, in all Sweden. (Grocery stores may sell the 2.8 beer plus an in-between—3.6—beer added in 1965.) In sparsely settled areas the purchase of a bottle may mean a drive of several hours. The Systemet still has its blacklist, and at certain times all customers are required to produce identification, which is checked against the list. The food requirement in restaurants has been abolished in some cities, although in one remote area I found a fat charge for a full meal added to the price of a drink, even though the restaurant flatly refused to produce the meal. (It is still forbidden to serve snaps without food, so that you can order an ordinary martini freely, but not a vodka martini—vodka is classed as snaps.) But many restaurants have established their own food requirement. Liquor is mercilessly taxed. The portion of tax in the retail price is 90 percent for *renat* (plain potato snaps), the most popular drink (which costs $5.50 a fifth), 79 percent for Scotch ($10), 49 percent for red wine ($1 and up). In a bar a glass of whiskey usually costs $2 to $2.50, and a glass of beer $1 to $1.25.

If rationing did not work, neither did its abolition (sales of liquor rose sharply), and the authorities had another idea, which also did not work: they began actively promoting wine and, with it, more moderate drinking habits. The liquor monopoly now carries a huge line of wines from France, Germany, Italy, and other countries. It propagandizes heavily to educate the public about wine and to remove the upper-class stigma, and it operates a telephone service that gives free, courteous, expert advice on the selection and serving of wine. (The Systemet also propagandizes against alcohol generally and must be the world's only corporation that spends considerable sums of money advertising against its only product.) But although wine consumption per capita rose by 115 percent in 1956–65, consumption of hard liquor dropped only negligibly.

Perhaps the most interesting aspect of the antiliquor feeling is the heavy punishment that awaits drinking drivers. Automobiles are frequently stopped for spot checks, and the police occasionally block every road in an area and stop every car. Suspected drinkers are given a blood test (maximum 0.05 percent of alcohol, equivalent to two weak beers), and those who fail are given stiff prison sentences (up to six months.) The roadblocks, when normally thousands of cars are checked, rarely turn up more than a dozen or so drinkers. Most Swedes abstain altogether from drinking while they drive, and guests at a party often take cabs home and return next day for their autos.

These burdensome liquor controls can be partly explained by the nature of the temperance movement. As noted, the movement's alliance with political movements has always been strong, and today, although the membership of the temperance groups is only 3 percent of the population, more than a third of the members of the Riksdag belong.

Swedes love traveling to Majorca, Rhodes, and the Canary Islands, where they can drink cheaply and in great quantity, and one might conclude that the controls show the grave dangers of "government through organization," wherein a tiny group of militants is able to impose its will on the majority. But evidently, even though the Swedes don't like the system, they do not want to get rid of it. In 1961 there was a proposal that the permitted allowance of alcohol in the blood should be reduced to zero for drivers, and a poll showed 80 percent of the people in favor. In 1963 another poll indicated that only 13 percent thought liquor prices should come down. A 1963 poll showed that fully two-thirds of the people had distinct admiration for teetotalers (only 3 percent found such characters annoying).

The strict attitudes have had a clearly depressive impact on Stockholm's night life. Lars Bremberg, head of the Temperance Board in Stockholm, remarked to me: "About sixty years ago we had quite a lot of cafés and bars, but they disappeared with the reform." The figure is now down close to zero; 94 percent of the liquor sold is consumed in the home.

At the present time there are in all Sweden approximately 1,700 restaurants which serve some sort of alcoholic beverages above the level of 3.6 percent beer—just under 1,000 of the fully licensed, the remainder concentrating on wine and beer only. In Stockholm there are roughly 120 establishments selling wine and beer and 110 fully licensed restaurants.

The number is, predictably, held down by the licensing procedure. Bremberg explained to me what happens when an application is received by the Systemet: "The *Systemet* goes to the City Council, which asks the Temperance Board for an opinion; then it goes back to the council, which votes on the question, then back to the Systemet, which then asks the police about the applicant, and they ask the governor of Stockholm, but before it goes to the governor, it goes to a special commission which deals only with restaurant licenses." The applicant can be tripped up at any of these stages. Once a license is granted, it is good until the next quadrennial renewal time (the last was in 1965), when all restaurants holding licenses and wanting to renew them or to gain promotion into a higher class must reapply. Most of the renewal applications are granted, and most of the applications for promotion are rejected. In 1965 9 wine-and-beer restaurants applied for full rights, and 7 were rejected; 11 restaurants serving only weak beer asked for wine-and-strong-beer rights; 5 were rejected completely or partly. But they all can apply again in 1969.

The categories are based on the peculiar Swedish idea of the function of a restaurant. Bremberg said: "First and foremost, the restaurant must have a certain standard of decoration. It is usually obvious which restaurants belong in which category."

The fully licensed restaurant, which is usually what is meant by the slightly sinful word "restaurant" (people who advertise for future marriage partners often note their virtues by disdaining an interest in "restaurant life"), is generally expensive and lavishly, though often tastelessly, decorated and offers indifferent food and wretched service. But this is not as objectionable as it sounds, because Swedes rarely go to restaurants, and when they do, it is because they have to for some reason, not because they expect to have a good time. Apart from tourists, the backbone of the clientele is businessmen entertaining (if that's the right word) other businessmen, and they invariably choose the expensive spots. They do not mind the restaurants' drawbacks. Bremberg said: "The idea has been that restaurant life should be expensive and not too much fun." He added: "The prices are almost always higher in a fully licensed restaurant, but you can usually get a better meal in a wine restaurant." But if a businessman were taken to a wine restaurant that offered better food, as well as better service, he would probably be offended.

Eating can sometimes be pleasurable experience in the wine (*i.e.,* no liquor) restaurants, which are patronized mainly by the small numbers of young people who have become attracted to such non-Swedish habits. One of these is Le Gourmet, an attractively decorated place with a pleasant atmosphere, and I asked Bremberg why it had been denied a hard-liquor permit in 1965. "That was possibly a borderline case," he said. "But it would be unusual for a restaurant like that to have a full license—a small place serving French food. If we gave them a license, it would probably change to the style of the ordinary fully licensed restaurant, and the customers would suffer."

It is interesting that Swedes, when they discuss this question, should often do so in terms of nightclubs, as seen in the earlier quotation from Lars Gustafsson. For many years no nightclubs were permitted. When, primarily in the interest of tourist promotion, nine such establishments were opened in 1956 and permitted to stay open until 3 A.M. (summer only), they turned out to be large, sumptuous, expensive—and deadly boring. There are no casual bars or cafés in Stockholm. There are two or three restaurants that attempt to appeal to genteel drinkers but for the most part maintain an upper-class stiffness that is unpleasant if one wants a less formal atmosphere. But because they are so few, they are always jammed, making them even less pleasant. In addition, there is a handful of bars in the large hotels, largely for the benefit of tourists, which are roughly as casual as, say, the Bank of England. Ed Maze, an American who lives in and enjoys Stockholm, writes of "an uncanny, almost church-like silence" in the typical restaurant or bar. Anyone who wants to relax with a quiet drink and perhaps strike up an idle conversation (as is possible in the neighborhood bars of New York, the pubs of England, or the cafés of Paris) is simply out of luck. Most of the simpler restaurants will not even serve you a glass of wine or beer without a food purchase or will do it in a sufficiently insulting way that you will not ask again. A popular workingman's resort used to be the beer café, a simply decorated, somewhat gloomy establishment selling primarily weak beer, coffee, and sandwiches. But such places, which are heavily discriminated against (they must close at 8 P.M.; they cannot serve strong beer; they must not have drawn curtains) are rapidly being closed down; the number in Stockholm has dropped from about 500 at the turn of the century to about 75 currently. It is somewhat odd to see the pressure put on this workingman's institution (one newspaper called it "the most innocent of pleasures") by a Socialist government.

A discussion of restaurants is incomplete without a small digression into the general subject of Swedish food. Sweden has never been famous for its food, partly because there has never been very much of it. The thin rocky soil and harsh climate do not favor a robust agricultural base, such as exists in neighboring Denmark. For centuries it was customary during years of poor harvests to make bread from the bark of trees, but according to foreign travelers of earlier centuries, there was not so much difference between this and the ordinary black bread, which was normally baked in large quantities once or twice a year. The English traveler J. T. James noted in 1819 that the people in the countryside were so used to a poor diet that "many do not survive their first visit to Stockholm." He told of an event which he said occurred in 1788: "The Jämtland regiment of militia was ordered to do duty in the capital," where the soldiers immediately began to die in large numbers because even "wheaten bread and a little meat" were "too strong and nutritious to stomachs accustomed to other fare, and a coarser ailment in consequence prescribed. An inferior bread was then baked for the regiment, adulterated to the requisite degree of meagerness and indigestibility, and a strict attention forced to the poverty of the rest of their diet." James maintained that the health of the regiment immediately improved.

Today the situation is better, but only somewhat. Restaurant food is normally unimaginative, monotonous, and bland. More-

over, the differences between the prestigious fully licensed establishment and the local cafeteria (leaving a few of the wine
restaurants out) are minuscule, except in decor and prices. The
typical meal is a small, thin, linoleumlike piece of meat, accompanied by a tired leaf of lettuce and a mound of doughy fried
potatoes. Subtle sauces are almost unknown, and spices are used,
if at all, with powerful restraint. Some of the Swedish specialties
are particularly unappetizing: the famous meatballs (a mixture
of hamburger and pork plus bread crumbs and chopped onions), blood pudding (a breadlike concoction of animal blood
and meal which is fried), pea soup with pork (mashed peas
mixed with cheap pork slivers), *pölsa* (shredded lung mixed with
fat and meal), Jansson's Temptation (a casserole dish composed
largely of chopped onions and chopped potatoes). Most Swedish
dishes consist of chopped onions and chopped potatoes (with
chopped beef, chopped veal, or chopped pork mixed in), and
the peculiarly sour smell of these familiar ingredients gets to
be a recognizable presence in residential areas.

It should be noted that numerous other countries rank low
in cooking skills, and one of them is the United States. But one
advantage of eating in America is that it is not necessary to eat
American food, whereas foreign restaurants are almost non-
existent in Sweden. I believe it is fair to say that no other country of comparable economic advancement has progressed so little gastronomically. Upon meeting a Swedish business executive
who had lived and worked for two years in Paris, I asked him
what he thought about Swedish food, compared with French
food. We were at that moment sitting in Ambassadeur, one
of the more pretentious Stockholm eateries, to which we had
been mutually invited by another businessman, and were gnaw-
ing on rubbery chunks of meat accompanied by a large trayful
of pulpy fried potatoes half-drowned in a pool of grease. "Oh,"
he said, shrugging his shoulders, "it's just the same. No difference." Cooking in homes can be better than that in the restaurants (I personally know some extremely good Swedish
cooks), but even here one may be shocked. On one occasion I
was invited to a relatively lavish dinner in a private home for

about twenty persons: expensive liquors were offered, and the finest wines were served in exquisite crystal glassware. In most respects it was an excessively elaborate spread, but the main course was meat loaf. One may easily get the impression that the Swedes have no interest in food. A Swedish acquaintance of mine, who is a professional gourmet and has written extensively on the subject, assures me this is wrong: "They are very interested in food. It's just that they have no taste."

In any case, as the Swedes' economic resources have expanded, they have chosen to channel them primarily into the ownership of tangible goods rather than items of mere enjoyment, such as food. In the 1934–38 period the Swede consumed an average of 49 kilograms of meat a year, roughly on a par with the Frenchman's 55. By 1960–61 the Frenchman, whose financial resources had risen in the meantime much less than those of the Swede, had increased his meat consumption to 74 kilos, a gain of 35 percent, while the Swede's consumption inched up only to 52 kilos, 6 percent above the 1934–38 level.

And roughly 60 percent of the meat, I am told by Mrs. Pernilla Thunberger, a woman's page editor at a Stockholm newspaper, is *korv,* a kind of frankfurter made mostly of fat. It comes in different shapes, but in the form of *falukorv,* a long fat sausage, it has been called the national dish. It is used in different ways. It is an all-purpose delicacy—*korv* and eggs, *korv Stroganoff, korv Bourguignonne.* When one first eats this blandtasting *korv,* one may think he has been served up a helping of another famous Swedish product—paper pulp.

A man who has made an effort to raise Swedish taste in food is Tore Wretman, operator of three of Stockholm's most expensive restaurants, including the famous Operakällaren in the Opera Building, surely one of the world's most elegantly decorated dining spots. It is usually rated as Sweden's top restaurant. It probably is; at its best, the food is on the level of a medium-grade French establishment, and it offers many dishes which involve a succulent sauce—a great rarity in Sweden. It is said that hardly anyone in the country knew what garlic was before Wretman used it. Wretman is an urbane, sophisticated gentleman (he owns what he believes is the world's largest private collection of antique cookbooks), and he has no illusions about the food habits of the average Swede. When I suggested to him that it was in search of good food that so many Swedes traveled abroad, he said: "They go abroad *in spite* of the differences, not because of them. They come home from Paris longing for Swedish cooking." But even in Wretman's restaurants, the chances of having a truly enjoyable eating experience are small. Usually, the maître d' is not available to show you to a table, the waiters are sullen and rude, and the service is agonizingly slow. I once waited in vain for an hour and five minutes to be served in one of the Wretman establishments, and when I left, the headwaiter was deeply offended by my ungracious behavior. I do not believe that Swedish restaurateurs understand that eating should or could be an enjoyable experience, in which the surroundings, the service, the food, and the general ambience combine to give pleasure. In Wretman's Operakällaren one may be impressed by the seventy-five-year-old-building, awed by the thirty-foot ceilings, dazzled by the stunning view (it sits opposite the harbor from the Royal Palace), astonished by the fulgent masses of greenery—and depressed with the overall experience. An effort has been made to persuade the *Guide Michelin* people to come survey the restaurants in Sweden. Fortunately, the effort has so far been unsuccessful. One of the elements in the *Michelin*'s rating system is the *accueil* (the gracious welcome the prospective diner expects to receive from the host), and on that score I do not believe a single Swedish restaurant would pass.

But things are getting better. Bremberg of the Temperance Board told me: "They're unbuttoning now. It is changing—slowly—but it is changing. Ten years ago Prinsen [one of the few semibohemian places in Stockholm] was alone; now there are plenty of places where you can see these bearded types. In another ten years Stockholm will be completely changed." K. G. Hultén of the Museum of Modern Art remarked to me: "The foreigners who have come to Sweden have helped. The food may not be very good now, but it's much improved since the war. It used to be hardly better than baby food—all those chopped-up things." An investigation into the liquor business is now under way, and one of the members of the committee caused a sensation in 1966, when he suggested the Systemet be abolished and the other rules loosened. The Swedes' travels to foreign lands have also helped accustom them to new tastes, and some of the younger people are no longer satisfied with the bland Swedish diet. A small number of foreign-style restaurants have opened in Stockholm in recent years, and unusual imported foods are increasingly making their appearance on the grocery stores' shelves.

Swedish cities tend to seem even duller than they really are because of the methods of city planning, which, like many other things in Sweden, is competent, thorough, scientifically organized—and somewhat arid. Unfortunately, a strong influence on Swedish city planning is a deep and widely shared dislike for cities. Many Swedes have positively poisonous opinions of cities, and rarely will you see a Swede so aroused as when he tells you how much he detests city life. A poll in 1956 showed that only 19 percent of the people favored city living. Professor Sune Carlson remarked to me: "We're just a bunch of farmers. We really don't know how to live in cities."

Planning is facilitated by the government's great power. Göran Sidenbladh, chief of city planning for Stockholm, said: "Landowners in Sweden do not have a very strong voice in the possession of their land. The government on all levels interferes with conditions under which a landowner may use his land; this is a tradition that stretches back two hundred or two hundred and fifty years." The result: "Almost all cities have a plan." In addition, some larger areas have regional plans, which take precedence over the city plans.

The end products are cities which do not look like cities. Planning since the war has affected Stockholm, for example, in two principal ways: (1) Numbers of dwellings have been torn down in the center of town and replaced with primarily a huge complex of office buildings, public squares, and pedestrian malls, which have produced a certain sterility in the center of town; and (2) virtually all new residential construction is concentrated in more distant areas, especially into vast, thoroughly planned, rather monotonous developments, which have produced a certain sterility in the suburbs.

These suburban communities are planned all at once, with apartment houses, shopping centers, schools, transportation connections, churches, and other conveniences—all scientifically laid out years before the first tenant moves in. All these suburbs look more or less alike, not only around Stockholm, but also from one end of the country to the other, with a central shopping center hooked into the subway station surrounded by gaunt apartment houses stuck amid fields of green. When one-family houses occur (this is not often), they are closely grouped in regular clumps of look-alike boxes. Nothing could be better planned. Everything is designed in the best of taste. Nothing is neglected. And nothing could be more tedious. Admiring foreign experts constantly gush over all this neat, shiny perfection, but they do not have to live in the midst of it. The cities are not much better than the suburbs. Most of Stockholm is simply suburban monotony set down close to the center of town.

The placid Swedes do not become overly agitated by such matters, and what criticism there is exists, as one architect sadly remarked, "mostly among other architects." John Magnus Lindberg, head of a small but serious-minded citizens' committee called the City Environment Group (which has helped preserve some of the more interesting older parts of the city), noted: "We haven't succeeded in raising much of a discussion in Stockholm."

It is probably unfair to judge the city center plan, which is not yet finished and won't be until approximately 1980, but the pallid results so far do not augur well for the rest of the project. It seems possessed of a ghostly dreariness. Said Erik Stark, an architect who has been severely critical of the planners: "Sidenbladh doesn't want any dwellings in the center. The whole area is completely dead after six o'clock." In defense of the project, planning chief Sidenbladh pointed out that even those parts of the city that now stimulate nostalgic thoughts were once new. "Similarly," he said, "the areas around Sergelgatan will be a precious memory to those who are now growing up." Anyone who walks through these vast deserts in the evening, far removed from residences or other signs of life, may have difficulty swallowing this.

Much attention has also centered on the suburban developments. John Lindberg of the City Environment Group said: "If you make a list of Sidenbladh and the others who plan these suburbs and take a map and locate their own residences, you will get a striking impression of how these environments stand in the eyes of those who build them. You don't find them in these bedroom cities." But Sidenbladh, who lives in an ancient one-family house in one of the most charming old areas of central Stockholm, noted some of the difficulties: "People say the democratic process should play a role. I don't see how that is possible. It takes four years from the time you start construction on a project to the time people will live there. Even if you could find the people who were going to live there four years ahead and asked them what they wanted, they probably wouldn't be able to tell you. When Vällingby [the first huge self-contained suburban project, built just after the war] was started, nobody had seen such a thing, so it was not possible to ask people what they wanted. And Farsta [the second such project] had to be started before Vällingby was finished."

Swedish city planning has attracted great interest and even admiration abroad, not usually, however, for its esthetic qualities, but for its thoroughness. Hans Erland Heineman, a Swedish architect, answered the critics who complained of the drabness of the results: "They demand a Brasilia, a Marina City, a Sydney Opera House, and this is a field in which our country has perhaps not been able to supply the big sensations. In many ways, the Swedish architects of today seem to take a more analytical view of the planning of towns and buildings than their colleagues in other countries. This analytical view has given Sweden a body of architecture possessing unexampled consistency of quality. . . ." Or, as some might put it, tiresome sameness. One reason for the unimaginative approach was given by C. F. Ahlberg, head of regional planning for Stockholm: "If we didn't have a housing shortage"—which diverts attention away from esthetic qualities and toward more efficient methods of building—"I think we would have more experimentation."

But attacking the problem is not easy. Architect Mårten Larsson, who occupies a number of important positions in Sweden's design world, said: "How much does the environment mean to most people? When you ask people what means most to them in an apartment, the environment outside comes very low down on the list."

One of the planners, John M. Stäck, an articulate architect in the city planning organization, *does* live in one of the newer suburbs. He was working on the plans for Skärholmen, the latest area, when I spoke to him. He explained that some lessons had been learned in the earlier developments: "One thing you can do is build a little more densely—not so many parks, which are nice in the summer but not so pleasant in the cold dark winter. So we try to plan a little more densely." But Stäck emphasized that such minor improvements cannot solve the basic problem. "We get complaints about dullness. But it's impossible for a plan to fill the streets in a suburb full of life and gaiety in the evening. The people must fill it with life themselves." Speaking of the shopping areas that are the center of the new areas, he said: "We do not build anything. We have nothing but a pencil and paper. Why doesn't someone build a Tennstopet [an unusual and popular downtown restaurant]? It's not forbidden. Our policy is to let everyone build what he wants. I'm not religious, but I want to help the churches build; it adds something to the environment. One reason we like to have a school near the center is so there will be a room available in case a string quartet needs a place to play. We plan the street network so that if someone wants to establish a small bar, it can be done." But he is realistic: "People's habits are still from when they lived on farms."

But the situation seems to be improving—slightly. Each new suburban development is a little less monotonous than the one before, and some younger people are beginning to have a different attitude toward cities. In 1965 a trio of architectural students staged in the Museum of Modern Art a dazzlingly eccentric exhibition in which several slide projectors flashed quick-changing pictures on a number of screens simultaneously. The show was supposed to suggest something of the variety and excitement of a large metropolis. Mårten Larsson said: "When most people here talk about the city, it's as a devil. But these people love the city, and that's what the exhibition tried to show." Even Erik Stark, the highly critical architect, told me: "The young architects are going to change the whole pattern of town planning in Sweden. I hope so, anyway."

The average Swede, of course, does not consider his hostility to city life as a source of boredom, because his greatest pleasure is recreation, especially outdoor recreation and most particularly outdoor recreation in wild and deserted environments. For the Swede it is far less important to have a neighborhood bar down the block than to be able to step outside the door onto a ski trail (about 400 miles of which are maintained in the Stockholm area alone).

Gustav Sundbärg, the critically perceptive observer of his countrymen, wrote in 1911: "The characteristic of the Swedish people that is most deeply rooted, and that forms the key, as it were, to the whole, is their intense love of nature. . . . In no other country do you see such a need during the summer to flee the suffocation of the city to spend as much time as possible in the tranquil lap of nature." Today, despite the pernicious influence of automobiles, TV, and other inducements to listlessness, astonishingly high percentages of the Swedish people still maintain contact with nature. A survey in 1964 showed no less than 79 percent of the people (including 65 percent of those fifty-six to sixty-five years old) indulged to some extent in "nature walks, berry picking, or mushroom picking" (a similar survey in the United States showed 15 percent interested in such activities), 26 percent go bicycling (9 percent in the United States), 19 percent go camping (8 percent in the United States), and 65 percent swim. (Actually, U.S. activity is overstated, because the Swedish survey covered only those between eighteen and sixty-five, whereas the U.S. survey started at age twelve.) Interest in calisthenics is widespread, and thousands of people attend regular calisthenics sessions, including many specializing in housewives' exercises. Tens of thousands of Swedes swarm up into the mountains each summer to hike along the many trails. Hundreds of vast recreation parks, with facilities for swimming, hiking, skiing, and camping, dot the countryside. The city of Stockholm alone operates fifteen near the city, and numerous others are run by nearby suburban communities. A 1966 survey showed that fully half the adult population below age sixty-seven indulged in some form of regular exercise. In the summer the Swedes rush every weekend to their country cottages. Claes-Eric Norrbom, an official in the Ministry of Agriculture, estimated there were 375,000 to 400,000 cottages in existence in 1966 and expected the figure to rise to 600,000 by 1970. He explained to me: "Life in an urbanized society creates the feeling that we must get away from the urban environment." The Swedes have the time, too: they get thirteen or more holidays and vacations of four weeks and up (higher executives and government officials often get two to three months). Historian Åke Elmér remarked: "If you ask the average Swede what he considers the most valuable of all the recent social changes, he will surely answer: more leisure time."

The government has been devoting particular attention to nature, and spending on conservation jumped from less than $50,000 a year before 1962 to more than $2,000,000 in 1966. Lars-Erik Esping, head of the Conservation Board (*Statens Naturvård*), said the new interest came "from a feeling that the state must do more to conserve nature" for the people. He told me: "You understand that Swedes don't think living in towns is the real way to live." In other words, the Swede who finds his cities boring does not think in terms of livening them up, but of escaping them. Halvar Sehlin, head of the Swedish Touring Club (*Svenska Turistföreningen*), a 225,000-member group which promotes mountain hiking, remarked to me: "People are very aware of their dull lives; they feel they should have more open-air life."

But all this calm and peaceful orderliness that is so apparent in Sweden is only a surface indication of the calm and peaceful orderliness that lies beneath.

As mentioned previously, the practical Swedes find so little difficulty agreeing on most matters that they do not go in much for controversy, nor are they given to fierce intellectual questionings. This tendency may be seen in the general shortage of stimulating conversation. It may also be seen in the panel discussions which occupy such a large position in Swedish TV. So harmonious and so unwilling to engage in controversy are the Swedes that these programs are invariably punctuated by long silences and often seem to be on the point of running down altogether.

Considering the Swedes' background, this is perhaps explicable. Traditionally, the most gifted people have chosen professions in which the search for precise certainty is more central than a more speculative pursuit of knowledge. And possibly because of the Swedes' firmly ingrained habits of concentrating on practical matters, the exercise of a lively intellectual curiosity is neither widely indulged in nor especially admired. One public opinion poll recording the Swedes' feelings about various personal character traits showed that 39 percent had decided objections to people who "like to discuss everything."

The same tendency away from the speculative and toward the practical appears in education. Chris Ottander, a lecturer in philosophy, said: "The general problems of theoretical philosophy . . . are more and more being replaced by specific questions dealing with the assumptions and methods of the investigations and conclusions of natural science. . . ." Similarly, students of foreign languages and literatures tend to stick closely to the former and neglect the latter. Alvar Ellegård, a professor of English, noted the dominance of language studies in secondary schools, and added: "On the postgraduate level the emphasis on the language side is even more marked. Over the last generation a large majority of the doctoral dissertations issued from the modern language departments . . . have been on linguistic topics. . . . The chairs in Scandinavian languages are also held by language men."

A manifestation of the previously mentioned passion for education is the popularity of adult courses, most of which are managed by thirteen independent, but state-subsidized, organizations. About a million registrations are recorded each year (naturally, some people register more than once). The overwhelming majority of the courses are in clearly practical subjects (principally foreign languages), as well as child-raising, crafts, and other such subjects. (Music is also popular, but the bulk of the music courses are guitar lessons for Beatles-struck young people.) Having become accustomed to the high popularity of literature courses in similar institutions in New York, I was surprised that such courses were so few in Sweden, and these few on a rather elementary level. I asked an official of the largest adult education group, ABF, if he knew why this category accounted for only one-fourth of 1 percent of the total number of courses. The courses are set up on the basis of demand, and he couldn't say why demand in this area was so low, but he ventured: "People like to read, but they don't like to discuss." History is another subject that falls flat (history and geography together—largely films and lectures about regions of Sweden or tourist spots abroad—are even less popular than literature at ABF). Sven-Arne Stahre, an other ABF official, commented: "Just why this subject should rank so low in appeal is something which defies ready explanation. One reason, perhaps, is that Sweden lives on the periphery of world events, by virtue of noninvolvement in war and political conflicts, plus the accident of geography, which may account for a widespread provincial or isolationist attitude. In any event, attempts to make history more attractive in study materials have so far met with little success...."

In many respects the typical Swedish calm is reflected in the country's press. The Swedes are among the world's most voracious consumers of newspapers—in 1963, 534 copies per 1,000 inhabitants, compared with 476 in Great Britain and 319 in the United States.

But the quality of this popular item of consumption leaves much to be desired. In line with Sweden's political and geographical isolation and the low level of interest among Swedes in events outside Sweden, the papers concentrate almost exclusively on the local scene. Anders Yngve Pers, a member of a distinguished newspaper family, has observed: "Readers interested in international problems—among them many newspapermen—have long deplored the scant interest of the Swedish press in events of real importance outside the borders of the country." In the leading newspapers many important events abroad are either skipped entirely or reported in only a fragmentary and badly mangled fashion. In the small-town prints, only foreign events of truly gigantic proportion get even a mention.

But even domestic reporting is of poor quality. Articles are often verbose, rambling, poorly organized, and heavily larded with the journalist's personal opinions. Moreover, the virtues of a clear headline and a concise lead have yet to penetrate Swedish newspaper writing.

The main interest in Swedish newspapers does not lie in their news pages, however, but in their cultural articles. Because there are few intelligent general magazines in Sweden (a handful of excellent literary and artistic journals and a huge mass of lowbrow weeklies, but nothing in between), the newspapers take over some of the tasks handled by magazines in other countries. They customarily have the *kulturella sidan* (cultural page), which in practice is very often several pages

and which defines "culture" quite broadly. The range of subjects can be astonishing—literature, economics, art, science,
film, philosophy, architecture, and travel pieces. Some of the articles are by staff writers, but all the large papers keep on re-
tainer a stable of writers who contribute more or less regularly,
and complete outsiders are also used. Even all the evening tabloid papers—in most ways so vulgar as to make some of the
cheaper papers of New York, Paris, or London seem positively
prim by comparison—have serious, well-respected staff writers
and free-lancers contributing to their cultural pages. On these
pages are conducted the debates the Swedes are so fond of. This
means that either the newspapers argue with one another (most
of them run a regular feature quoting editorial opinions from
other papers, either to quarrel or to agree) or that different
contributors attack one another in the same paper—and occasionally both occur.

Almost every well-known person in Sweden (and a great
many obscure ones) finds it worthwhile to write for these pages.
Lars Gyllensten, a medical school professor, novelist, and member of the Swedish Academy, explained to me that although
the articles have a short life, an advantage is that reader reaction is expressed almost immediately. "It depends on the in-
flammability," he said. Having just written some articles attacking Christianity for a Stockholm paper, he said, "From that
point of view, these articles were very successful. Most people
thought I should be damned."

Although these pages thus sometimes give an impression of
great controversy, on topics of any importance (religion is not
considered important) the cultural pages more or less openly
push a single viewpoint; this makes the whole business considerably less stimulating than it might be. In the much discussed women's rights question, for example, all the debaters
have agreed that women should be allowed to pursue careers,
and all urge more day nurseries, retraining programs, and enthusiasm for housework among men. I asked a woman literary
critic who had been with one of the large papers if it wouldn't

be an idea to try to dig up a contributor on the other side, if only to liven the debate. Although admitting the theoretical merits of the argument, she replied, "Oh, no, you simply couldn't do that. Everyone would object."

In large part, this is merely a reflection of the conformist intellectual temper prevailing in Sweden. Once a position on an important question has been taken, great amounts of argument are not necessary. In many ways, in fact, the newspapers appear to be enthusiastically participating in the creation of a Babbitt spirit in Sweden's cultural life, which, like the original Babbitt, complacently accepts a conformist view of society and the world, a smug chauvinism, and a passive unconcern for questioning the current *idées reçues,* though without, needless to say, the original Babbitt's bombast or tastelessness. The papers are full of references to the superiority of Swedish quality, the great respect in which Swedish UN representatives are held, and other evidences of their readers' superiority. Feature articles on foreign countries are often devoted to poor lands, such as Spain, Greece, or Turkey, in which the writer contentedly boasts of the ways in which Sweden outpaces the subject at hand. The United States presents a special problem because of its obvious great wealth, but the newspapers get around the difficulty by concentrating to the maximum on race problems and poverty or—if it becomes necessary to mention some evidence of wealth—to point out that there are many poor people. Some of the writings could easily, with the change of a few words, read as a parody of the stereotype American tourist following his first trip to Europe. In 1967, Oskar Lindkvist, a member of the Swedish parliament, visited Los Angeles and stayed a few weeks. Because he spoke no English, the only job he could find was as a dishwasher. One could assume that a tourist speaking no English and spending most of his time washing dishes might find it difficult to probe deeply into American social conditions. But Lindkvist found it possible to become an authority on the race problem and on housing and on his return was solemnly and repeatedly interviewed at length by the newspapers for his insights into these questions. A novelist named Bosse Gustafson who traveled through America in search of, among other things, products to import into Sweden happily reported in *Aftonbladet* (the major Social Democratic organ), that there was nothing to be found: "Here, there is not one worthwhile idea to steal, not one thing that isn't better and more attractive at home.... Everything produced is clumsy, poor quality, unimaginative, from silverware to architecture."

Lars-Olof Franzén, cultural editor of *Dagens Nyheter*, the country's largest morning daily, reported on a *Partisan Review* survey of American intellectuals' opinions on America's future. Neglecting to cite the more optimistic views, Franzén quoted the poisonously pessimistic views of such writers as Susan Sontag, Michael Harrington, and Robert Lowell and smugly concluded that in America "there is little hope."

But if there is a large element of Babbittry in Swedish life, where are the native Sinclair Lewises and the H. L. Menckens to chronicle their stupidities? The newspapers frequently quarrel with one another, true, but invariably without disturbing the basic conformity of viewpoint. *Aftonbladet's* exposé of the poor quality of American manufactures was ridiculed by the other Stockholm evening tabloid, *Expressen*, but many of the opinions expressed in the latter are, on the whole, not appreciably more intelligent.

Thoroughgoing social criticism is not often found anywhere in Sweden. The debates take place within limits tacitly agreed on, and extensions of the limits are not permitted. In the women's rights question nobody defends the right of a woman to concentrate on home and family instead of pursuing a career. In discussions of aiding underdeveloped countries nobody argues against such aid. Often, when I have inquired about the absence of social criticism in Sweden, I have been referred to a couple of books, published in 1966 and 1967, which criticized the shortcomings of the welfare system. But if it is acceptable to attack the inadequate doctor supply and other defects of the system (such criticisms are quite common), it is unheard of to attack the whole idea of free medical care, or free schooling, or subsidies to families.

It should be emphasized that when I say certain criticisms are "not permitted," I mean they are not permitted by the prevailing atmosphere. There is not, so far as I have been able to learn, any significant effort to suppress dissenting views. Quite the contrary, the record shows that only a minimum of aggressiveness is required to gain attention for such opinions. As related earlier, Eva Moberg's novel position on the women's rights question was initially attacked, but in the end she won virtually unanimous support for her viewpoint. If there is widespread conformity in Sweden, it is because there is a will to conform, not because of pressure. I have been struck by this fact many times. Sven-Ivar Ivarsson, in eight years as president of the moderately powerful Taxpayers' Association, had been severely critical of the state administrative apparatus for, among other things, its inefficiency, wastefulness, and failure to take advantage of modern accounting methods. So impressed was the government with the perspicacity of the criticism that in 1963 it set up a special department for program budgeting and hired as head of the new body . . . Sven-Ivar Ivarsson. Another critic, after he had attacked the quality of weekly magazines, was quickly offered the job of editing one by one of the companies he had been particularly hard on. (He accepted and is said to have acquitted himself admirably.) I was amused to learn during a discussion with John Magnus Lindberg, head of the City Environment Group, one of whose tasks is to combat the pernicious effects of the automobile on the city, that he is a top executive in Volkswagen's distribution apparatus in Sweden. He was surprised when I asked the company's attitude on his outside activity. "As far as I know, they have no opinion," he replied. "They've never said anything, and I've never asked them."

Paradoxically, it may just be this tolerance of dissent that holds it down. It is easy to pity Sweden for its lack of, say, an occasional Dwight MacDonald, the effects of whose social criticism are decidedly healthy in the long run. On the subject of the *Partisan Review* survey of intellectual opinions in the United States (one wonders what Susan Sontag, who called America the "world's most conservative country," would say about conformist Sweden), I mentioned this lack to Lars-Olof Franzén, who seemed so happy about the impending doom in the United States, and asked where the counterparts of such people were in Sweden. At first, he couldn't think of any, but finally brought up the name of Jan Myrdal (the peppery son of Gunnar). Indeed, almost invariably when I posed this same question, I got the same answer. But Myrdal, though undeniably original and imaginative, is hardly a nonconformist. He is an orthodox Social Democrat and shares all the commonly accepted points of view. Under other circumstances he might have become a Paul Goodman, but in Sweden he serves the Establishment (a degree of tolerance that is all the more astonishing when one considers that in education-mad Sweden Myrdal holds no advanced degree).

In other words, a good deal of venom directed at the status quo never develops because the potential rebel is treated too well. Eric Hoffer has written of the intellectual with latent rebellious instincts: "There is a moment in the career of almost every fault-finding man of words when a deferential or conciliatory gesture from those in power may win him over to their side. At a certain stage, most men of words are ready to become timeservers and courtiers." Or, as Wallace Stevens says: "... the difficulty of rebellious thought/When the sky is blue...." Dieter Strand, the Social Democratic theoretician, explained the whereabouts of some of the potential critics: "After thirty years of social engineering, at least 50 percent of the bright young people have been swallowed up by the apparatus: they have respected positions; they are sitting on committees that go on for three to five years and produce volumes that you can hardly read."

Professor Gunnar Boalt, Sweden's leading sociologist and one of the most interesting Swedes I have met, bemoaned to me the difficulty of being a rebel. "The criticism is always accepted," he complained. "That's no fun. If I tried to get out of the Establishment, they would just reach out and pull me back in." He told me of a book he had written in 1965 criticizing certain educators. "It was a damned nasty book," he said, "but what do you think happened? The chairman of Uppsala University expressed great appreciation for the ideas, and the critics said it was excellent." He concluded gloomily: "I know of no country in the world where professors have such high and totally unjustified prestige."

Yes, I believe Sweden is boring—at least by the standards many non-Swedes would apply. If a good part of the boredom arises from the good common sense and spirit of harmony and cooperation in Swedish life, it is, of course, difficult to recommend that all these worthy elements be junked in favor of more variety. But it also seems that the careful attention paid to the efficient organization of the social machinery has had, to some extent, a depressing effect on the quality of life. In their zeal to get everything organized in proper working order, the social planners want to provide the average man with health care, educational possibilities, and the possibility of buying all the equipment for the good life (a car, a washing machine and a TV set), but they are not so eager that he have any fun, since that might disturb the workings of this magnificent machinery of life. But as marvelous as are the benefits provided by the Swedish state, one doth not live by social benefits alone. The subsidized medical care, for example, is in my opinion a hugely worthwhile advance, but after all, one can't very well go to the hospital every day; one occasionally longs for other types of amusement.

When medical or educational facilities fall short of the demand, there are certain people whose duty it is to worry about the fact, but apparently no one is in charge of worrying about the country's insufferable boredom. The public is not being forced into this pattern, of course, and in many ways the Swedes in general have eagerly participated in the construction of the boredom apparatus. But since the government is so careful to appoint committees and special officials to ponder all conceivable problems, one can hope that eventually the hitherto overlooked problem of the country's deadly calm will prove to be a *tankställare* (something to think about).

XIV

Fragments for a Conclusion

Some of my comments about Sweden in the preceding pages are on the critical side, but I hope the reader will not include me among the critics who regard the welfare state—if by that is meant the system of welfare benefits—as a first-class catastrophe and who blame it for having destroyed initiative, promoted dullness, and concentrated the Swedes' attention on coarsely materialistic values.

I definitely do not believe that, and even if I did, I would not necessarily feel that a sufficient reason to suggest that the social benefits system be abolished. Actually, I regard most formal elements of the Swedish system (*e.g.,* the social benefits, economic policies, measures to protect individual freedom, and the subsidies to the arts) as excellent social advances. Unfortunately, Sweden is characterized by a spirit of dullness, stiffness, and passivity that I do not find quite so admirable; in fact, I find it quite disagreeable.

Many observers have made the mistake of assuming that the tranquil Swedish character is a direct product of the system. The facts are quite the opposite. The tranquillity is not a result of this streamlined modern system (as anyone can verify by reading the comments of foreign travelers in the eighteenth or nineteenth century); it is one of the creative forces behind the system. Only by being calm, unemotional, and coldly rational could the Swedes have built their highly sensible system, avoided the rancorous conflicts that have torn so many countries apart, and achieved the harmony that has been so necessary an ingredient in the progress of the past half century or so. This calmness has also led to a certain lack of excitement that can be irritating to a visitor, but it is not a product of the system—it is a cause.

(There has been, of course, something of a circular movement at work. The basic, rather boring tranquillity characteristic of the Swede has helped promote the efficient organization of society, which has produced more harmony and tranquillity, which in turn has made Sweden even more calm and boring and susceptible to more efficiency moves—and so on. The question is whether the forces that keep this circle spinning are more powerful than outside forces that might break it down.)

Another common objection (or perhaps the same objection, differently worded) is that although the system has been marvelously effective in providing for the citizen's material welfare, it has failed to give him happiness. This is probably accurate, but one might as well say it has not made chickens lay square eggs. It is not certain that a government can make a man happy; it can perhaps give him the opportunity to create his own happiness. The Swedish government has certainly done this, in overwhelming measure. If the Swede has failed to take advantage of it, it is the fault of the individual, not the government.

But there is no evidence that Swedes in general are unhappy, even though they may have used their resources in building a style of life that many foreigners find not to their taste. In a Swedish public opinion poll in 1958 the overwhelming majority of respondents named Sweden as the country where people were happiest. It is conceivable, of course, that the Swedes, as Bernard Shaw once remarked of the English, "really do not seem to know when they are thoroughly miserable."

The common Swedish attitude toward the calmness and orderliness so characteristic of Sweden is not easy for foreigners to grasp. The British journalist Patrick O'Donovan writes of Sweden: "It chose dullness and with it security, efficiency and incorruptibility.... It is a place where *ennui* is accepted as a condition of public life...." In speaking to Sven Hultgren, head of SIFO, the Swedish Public Opinion Institute, I learned that SIFO has a loose working arrangement with a dozen or so similar bodies in other countries and that on occasion all the institutes ask the public the same question at about the same time. One such poll took place at the beginning of 1966, when the people were asked whether they thought the new year would be "better or worse" than 1965. In Sweden a smaller percentage of those polled were optimistic than in any of the other countries, and 64 percent were looking neither for better nor for worse times—the highest of any of the countries and 24 percentage points above the runner-up in this respect. Hultgren told me that in no similar multicountry poll had Sweden diverged so greatly from the others. When I asked him if he had an explanation, he said: "It's a sign perhaps that we are not so happy. We have no dreams. But we have security. We have no need of dreams."

The lack of dreams may not be the tragedy some people might think. Gunnar Boalt, the sociologist, spoke to me of the emphasis on planning so many areas of life and the assumption that this makes life boring. "I can't agree that Sweden is boring," he said. "We believe it is most unboring to plan. It is our most highly cultivated hobby. Everybody here loves to plan. It makes our life very exciting."

But Sweden is changing rapidly, so rapidly that I have been worried that if I didn't finish this book quickly, I would have nothing left to complain about. The younger generation no longer feels that a full life consists only of a clean, well-ordered neatness in which everyone owns a car, a TV set, and a summer cottage. Even on the surface a spirit of most un-Swedish liveliness has sprung up here and there. During 1966 and 1967 a handful of beer and wine private clubs (in which the "private" label can be legally maintained by barring anyone who declines to cough up the nominal membership charge and which are generally open from midnight to 4 A.M.) has been set up in cellars and other localities, and some of them offer a casualness and relaxing atmosphere that one would never have thought possible a few years ago. Moreover, the official liquor-dispensing rules have been eased a notch or two and the number of resorts allowed to stay open until 2 A.M. has been greatly expanded. The capital falls well short of the epithet "Swinging Stockholm" that some natives feel inclined to grant, but the trend, as yet still fragile, is unmistakable.

However, more important and more fundamental changes also appear to be in the offing. For one thing, Sweden's isolation from the rest of the world is becoming less pronounced. Among the influences at work is TV, where a special effort has been made to show the Swedes that there is a non-Swedish world. Nils-Erik Baehrendtz, TV chief, told me: "Swedes were formerly very isolated; they looked on foreigners as very peculiar. To be un-Swedish was considered to be a fault. I think TV has helped change this attitude."

Another powerful force has been the growing popularity of foreign travel; cheap charter flights often make it cheaper to go to Italy, say, than to stay in Sweden. Gunner Heckscher has writtten: "Forty years ago, it was exceptional to find anyone who had been abroad, while today it is nearly impossible to find anyone who hasn't been, especially among the younger generation." At present more than a million Swedes travel abroad each year (not counting those who travel only to other Scandinavian countries). Many of them travel in tight, all-Swedish groups (and very often to certain all-Swedish villages in Spain and Italy), and one may be stunned when intelligent, well-educated Swedes tell of sitting for three weeks on a beach a short bus trip's distance from the glories of Botticelli, Tintoretto, and Giotto without ever having the curiosity to go take a look. Anyone who has traveled with these groups (as I have) often receives the impression that the Swedes' principal interest is to confirm that the country they are visiting (whatever it is) has a lower living standard than Sweden. Nevertheless, some impression of the world's variety and color must inevitably seep in; this can only benefit society.

The increasing importance of foreign trade has also had an effect, as has the sharp change in its character. Before World War II Sweden's principal exports came from its natural resources—principally forest products and iron ore. Everyone knew about Swedish forest products and iron ore, and anyone who needed these commodities bought primarily on the basis of price. Little selling effort was necessary. But the country's sophistication and engineering skills have risen so rapidly that (even though exports of paper, pulp, and ore have expanded) Sweden's trump cards today are its autos, high-voltage transmission systems, pneumatic equipment, and other items that require the Swede to make a real contact with the foreign customer in order to explain the product. Keeping abreast of developments in foreign markets has become a vital necessity; this often means that businessmen supplement their reading of the parochial Swedish press with such foreign journals as *The Economist, Newsweek, L'Express,* and *Der Spiegel.* This close contact will become even closer when (as appears inevitable) Sweden becomes associated with the Common Market. This move will probably require abandonment of the remaining barriers to trade internationalism (such as the restrictions on cross-border capital movements), which will be all to the good.

Contact with foreigners has also increased through an influx of foreigners into Sweden. One of the advantages of the full employment policy is that it has created a labor shortage, which has been met to a great extent through imports of several hundred thousand foreign workers (principally from the other Scandinavian countries, but also from Greece, Turkey, Italy, and Yugoslavia), bringing strange habits and ways of thinking with them. To tell the truth, the Swedes, who often consider themselves too civilized to harbor racial feelings, have not reacted altogether positively to this trend. A 1966 public opinion poll showed only 26 percent of the people thought the immigration predominantly advantageous, and although this was higher than in a similar poll in 1957 (when the figure was 15 percent), it was still less than the 29 percent who thought it predominantly disadvantageous. In 1967 curbs were put on the immigration of foreigners in search of jobs, but the inflow will doubtless continue, though at a slow rate. These immigrants (who usually start by willingly accepting the most undesirable jobs in foundries and restaurants) will, if they stay on, perhaps enrich the life of Sweden, as immigrants of other times have done in America.

The Swedish awareness of other countries has obviously risen in recent years. Erik Hökby, head of Prisma Books, a paperback-publishing firm, told me: "Before about 1960 there was never much interest in world affairs. But then we published a book on East-West political developments. We never thought it would sell much, but it went into four or five editions and sold about 35,000 copies altogether. Next year we are publishing a book on strategy in nuclear war. We would never have dared do this a few years ago."

The avid Swedish interest in the world outside is most noticeable in the numerous demonstrations against the United States, South Africa, Portugal, Spain, and Greece (after the coup in 1967) and in favor of the Vietcong, Fidel Castro, American Black Power leaders, and South American guerrilla movements. Swedes generally feel all this is a healthy development because it represents a sharp change from only a decade ago. From this point of view, perhaps it is. It is certainly encouraging to see that Swedes are able to become enthusiastic about something, but one might wish there were something more substantial involved than the exuberance of youth (these causes are almost the exclusive property of teen-agers and thus must compete for attention with the twist, shake, and other amusements). All the movements are marked with roughly the same type of conformity as is apparent in other intellectual areas in Sweden. There is little interest in examining the real background of the issue among the enthusiasts, many of whom do not even take

advantage of the thin diet of foreign news supplied by the Swedish press and sometimes hardly know the locations of the countries they are demonstrating for or against. Virtually all the
books on world affairs written by Swedes or translated into
Swedish possess a heavy bias to the left. The accepted opinions
for and against the various issues are seemingly swallowed in
one gulp by the participants. A few days ago, an all-purpose
meeting protesting against "imperialism" in general was held,
it was deemed unnecessary by the organizers to explain in detail
all the many causes that were included, since it was only natural
that everyone would agree on which imperialisms must be opposed. It may appear amusing to witness a parade of pale-
cheeked blue-eyed Swedish youths parading angrily in promotion of Black Power, but this is typical of the spirit of unreality
in which this agitation takes place.

The movements seem somewhat less encouraging when one
realizes that the potential impact on events is almost nil, since
none of the causes supported or opposed so fanatically is in
Sweden or even has anything to do with Sweden. (Swedes generally tend to exaggerate the importance of their voice in world
affairs. I once was asked to accompany a group of American
journalists who had been invited to Sweden on a one-week tour
of the country's industrial establishment. For some reason, a
number of Swedes they spoke to asked what the U.S. reaction
had been to [Foreign Minister] Torsten Nilsson's latest pronouncement on Vietnam and were taken aback at the inevitable
reply: "Who is Torsten Nilsson?") Swedes—not even teen-agers
—do not demonstrate about anything in Sweden. This suggests
that the whole thing has no more importance than a kind of
game, although it is at least something that foreign affairs are
receiving some attention, even of this kind.

The brutal fact is that either most of Sweden's own problems
really have been solved or solutions to them are being worked
out by committees sifting through tons of statistical and factual
material—hardly a stimulus to demonstrations. The remaining
problems do not tend to be colorful. Recently a prize given to
the book most penetratingly examining a critical Swedish so-

cial problem went to a work on air pollution. A prominent member of parliament, who is constantly involved in family allowances, illness reimbursements, Labor Market Board activities, and other vital, but rather undramatic, domestic issues, told me he had tried to direct his daughter's interest to such matters, but she impatiently replied, "Oh, Father, how can you ask me to bother with such trivia when I am concerned with the really important problems: Vietnam! *Apartheid!* Cuba!"

The excitement generated by domestic political issues may be somewhat increased by the defeat of the Social Democrats in the parliamentary elections in the fall of 1968—a defeat which some political analysts expect. In the 1966 municipal elections the Social Democrats suffered the worst setback in more than thirty years (their share of the total vote was 42.3 percent, compared with 50.2 percent in 1962). Since then the party has been moving perceptibly, though slowly, to the left, in response to an increasingly vocal left-wing movement (the Communists raised their share of the vote to 6.4 percent from 3.8 percent). Although the left-wingers are quite loud, they each still have only one vote, and many observers believe that the average Swede, who has been growing increasingly bourgeois over the years, will find the new revolutionary spirit perhaps sporadically entertaining but not especially appealing.

Whatever happens, the political trend seems certain to bring some change in the placid Swedish scene. The Social Democrats moved ever so slightly to the left following the 1966 elections. For example, a $100,000,000 state-owned development bank was established. At this writing, its method of functioning is not quite clear, but it seems certain to be used as a means of increasing the government's influence in the management of businesses, which in the past has always been scrupulously avoided. There are also increasing cries for nationalization of industry and other radical moves. If this trend continues, it could break up the harmonious relationship between industry and the government; this would mean more arguments, more conflicts, and more excitement.

If the three opposition parties (Liberal, Conservative, and Center, formerly Farmers'—not including the Communists) should be able to unite, they might take over the government. No large-scale changes could be expected (the system of welfare benefits would definitely not be disturbed), but there might be a slightly different spirit, perhaps slightly more encouragement of individual enterprise, though by no means a move to total laissez-faire capitalism.

In either case the alterations won't be much, but there will most unavoidably be changes.

One coming event which will, I believe, have an enormous impact on society is the liquidation of rent controls and creation of a free housing market. It is impossible to exaggerate the pervasive effects of the present situation, which almost completely eliminates the possibility of choosing the location of one's home. I think people have become so accustomed to this restrictive system (which does not even have the loopholes that exist in, say, France), that the full possibilities of controlling one's own destiny are not appreciated nearly so much as they could be. This development will be slow in coming, but there is still a hope that it will materialize over the next few years, and if so, its net effect will be extremely healthy.

To some extent the very development of the Swedish system carries the seeds of its destruction. Two of the most potentially explosive elements are the state efforts to stimulate the arts and the vast expansion of educational opportunities. Both artists and intellectuals have always been notoriously subversive, and even in the tranquil Swedish atmosphere an increase in their strength cannot help being followed by more originality and more intellectual curiosity. I believe that a considerable change for the better in the country's intellectual climate is unavoidable and that a more skeptical, questioning attitude must develop. (The more technical intricacies of the educational system lie outside the range of this book, but it is worth noting that current efforts are now pointing toward substantially more variation in subject choice than has up to now been possible.) The creation of a large and increasingly belligerent class of intellectuals is shown by the huge growth of SACO, the intellectuals' union. Intellectuals have always been the object of enormous respect in Sweden. But in the SACO strike of 1966, 20,000 teachers (who represented not only the normally docile intellectuals but also the even more docile civil servants) contentedly took a four-week vacation until they were given what they considered a fair shake. Deriding all ideas of solidarity with the workers that were urged on them, they replied, in effect, that the workers could go to hell and demanded salaries befitting their position. This increasing unrest of increasing numbers of intellectuals will doubtless result eventually in more active intellectual discussions.

There are crosscurrents, of course. I have had the impression that the younger generations are even more anxious to live up to the traditional middle-class ideals, which include a fair amount of stuffed-shirt stiffness, than the older generation.

But my opinion is that in the long run the tendencies working for more variety and more movement will win out. If there is a great striving toward the middle class, it can be hoped that the middle class may become less ironbound in its outlook. (It is interesting to note that the faster-growing white-collar unions are considerably less placid in their relations with the establishment than LO, the virtually static industrial union.)

It may take a long time, but it is very likely that the famous Swedish rationality will break up and that some of the harmony will disappear. By that time, of course, all the basic elements in the system will be in place, and it is not probable that it will be abandoned or even appreciably modified. However, it can be expected that society will be marked by considerably more conflict than is now the case, but life in Sweden should also have become richer, more varied, and more stimulating.

Index